Women C

Frauenki

Eglise de femmes

Yearbook of the European Society of Women in Theological Research

Jahrbuch der Europäischen Gesellschaft für die theologische Forschung von Frauen

Annuaire de l'Association Européenne des femmes pour la recherche théologique

Volume 3

Advisory Board:

Women Churches
Networking and Reflection in the European Context
Frauenkirchen
Vernetzung und reflexion im europäischen Kontext
Eglise de femmes
Réseaux et réflections dans le contexte européen

Editors:
Angela Berlis
Julie Hopkins
Hedwig Meyer-Wilmes
Caroline Vander Stichele

Pharos

Kok Pharos Publishing House - Kampen
Matthias-Grünewald Verlag - Mainz

CIP-GEGEVENS KONINKLIJKE BIBLIOTHEEK, DEN HAAG

Yearbook of the European Society of Women
in Theological Research, 3

© 1995, Kok Pharos Publishing House - Kampen/the Netherlands
© 1995, Matthias-Grünewald Verlag, Mainz/Germany
ISBN Kok Pharos 90 390 0213 4
ISBN Grünewald 3-7867-1877-6
Cover design by Margret Omlin-Küchler/adapted by Dik Hendriks
Typesetting Veronika Schlöder

INHALT - CONTENTS - TABLE DES MATIÈRES

Editorial

Wenn eine europäische Gesellschaft ein Jahrbuch zum Thema 'Frauenkirche' herausgibt, kann man erwarten, daß Profil, Inhalte, Diskussionen, Praxis und Visionen dieser Kirche von Frauen in und jenseits patriarchaler Kirchen zum Ausdruck kommt, aber auch Probleme, Konflikte und Grenzen. Wir hoffen, daß uns beides gelungen ist. Das Konzept Frauenkirche war zu Beginn unserer Diskussionen in Europa so etwas wie eine nordamerikanische 'Importware', die in die jeweiligen nationalen Kontexte übersetzt wurde. So beginnt denn dieser Band mit einem Artikel von Elisabeth Schüssler Fiorenza, in dem die Vordenkerin dieser Vision ihr Konzept von Frauenkirche im Patriarchat vor dem Hintergrund der Machtunterschiede zwischen Frauen ausbuchstabiert. Der Versuch Frauenkirche in der Spannung von 'innen' und 'außen' zu leben und zu denken, ist ein Stichwort das sich in vielen Beiträgen wiederfindet (vgl. Jones und Hampson). Der Beitrag von Liesbeth Huijts zeigt, wie sich Frauenkirche in den Niederlanden eher thematisch als strukturell konsolidiert, der Beitrag von Michaela Moser weist auf die Schwierigkeiten einer europäischen Vernetzung. Maria Kassel führt uns vor Augen, welche Auswirkungen eine tiefenpsychologische Kritik christlicher Gottesvorstellungen für die Glaubenspraxis von Frauen haben kann. Es dürfte kein Zufall sein, daß diese zur Zeit in der deutschen Theologie am härtesten unter Kritik stehende theologische Richtung bei vielen Frauen auf fruchtbaren Boden fällt. Geht sie doch davon aus, daß Selbsterkenntnis der Weg zur Gotteserkenntnis sein kann, von dem nicht nur die Bibel, sondern auch unsere Träume, Intuitionen und persönlichen Krisen erzählen.

In Frauengottesdiensten werden verschiedene Charakteristika von Frauenkirche beispielhaft sichtbar. Regula Schmid's Beitrag, im Kontext der Züricher Frauenkirche entstanden, weist uns auf alte und neue Lieder für 'den Herrn'.

Bevor Schüssler Fiorenza und Radford Ruether ihr Konzept von Frauenkirche vorgelegt haben, stand für viele christliche Frauen die Frage zentral, ob sie in der Kirche bleiben oder ihr den Rücken kehren sollen. Daphne Hampson, die erste Präsidentin der Europäischen Gesellschaft für theologische Forschung von Frauen, stellt diese Frage erneut, um zu zeigen, daß die akademische Lehre und Forschung doch noch einen Raum für feministisch gesinnte (postchristliche) Theologinnen bietet. Daß Frauenkirche sich nicht nur aus einem Selbstverständnis von Gegenmacht, sondern auch aus dem der

Teilhabe speist, zeigen uns die 1993 erstmals in der anglikanischen Kirche von England ordinierten Frauen. Penny Jones bewertet in ihrem Beitrag diesen 'historischen' Schritt und erzählt uns von ihren Erfahrungen als "gepriesterte" Frau.

Die Länderberichte, dieses Mal aus Polen (Elzbieta Adamiak) und den Niederlanden (Anne Marie Korte) machen deutlich, in welch' widersprüchlichen Verhältnissen Frauen in Europa Theologie betreiben. Anne Marie Korte berichtet über Ausmaß, Fülle und Qualität von Frauenforschung und Lehre an den theologischen Fakultäten der Niederlande, die immer noch nicht dazu geführt hat, daß man hier einen regulären Lehrstuhl für theologische Frauenforschung eingerichtet hat. Elzbieta Adamiak zeigt die Schwierigkeiten polnischer Theologinnen auf, angesichts einer fehlenden gesellschaftlichen Frauenbewegung und einer kirchlichen Ignoranz gegenüber Laien überhaupt zu existieren.

Die Spurensuche nach Frauentraditionen führt uns dieses Mal zu der italienischen Prophetin und Predigerin Domenica da Paradiso (Adriana Valerio) und den Waldensern in Piémont. Dagny Kaul zeigt, wie im Austausch zwischen Frauen im Amt und feministischen Theologinnen im zeitgenössischen Norwegen Frauentraditionen entstehen, die aus beiden Quellen - den Erfahrungen von Amtsträgerinnen einerseits und den Erkenntnissen der feministischen Theologie anderseits - schöpfen. Die jüdische Bibelwissenschaftlerin Athalya Brenner gibt uns in einer Art Werkstattbericht Aufschluß über die erkenntniskritischen Probleme, die bei einer solchen Suche nach Frauentraditionen entstehen.

Der Büchermarkt bietet eine Bibliographie zum Thema dieses Jahrbuches, eine Übersicht über Neuerscheinungen und Doktorarbeiten im Bereich der theologischen Frauenforschung seit 1993 sowie einige Rezensionen.

Die kritische Hymne an die Frauenkirche von der Deutsch-Niederländerin Irmgard Busch hat uns Herausgeberinnen inspiriert, unser 'Gesicht' zu zeigen. Als in den Niederlanden 'ansässige Fremde' geben wir im Epilog Auskunft darüber, in welchem Kontext dieses Buch entstanden ist.

Wir danken *Veronika Schlöder* für ihre fachliche Kompetenz und ihre Akribie bei der Fertigstellung dieses Buches.

Nijmegen/Kleve im Februar 1995, *Angela Berlis, Hedwig Meyer-Wilmes, Julie Hopkins, Caroline Vander Stichele.*

Elisabeth Schüssler Fiorenza

Patriarchale Herrschaft spaltet / Feministische Verschiedenheit macht stark: Ethik und Politik der Befreiung[1]

Heldinnen[2]

Außergewöhnlich
ja, abnormal
zieht ihr eure langen
Röcke
quer durch das neunzehnte
Jahrhundert.
Euer Geist
brennt lange nach eurem
Tod
nicht wie der Hafen-
Leuchtturm
sondern wie ein Scheiter-
haufen von Treibholz
am Strand.

Euch blieb erspart
Analphabetentum,
Tod durch Lungen-
entzündung,
ausfallende Zähne,
der Näherin schwache
Augen,
der Spinnerin mühevolles

Atmen
wegen einer Konstellation
von Umständen
bald bekannt als
Klassenprivileg.....

Ihr könnt SklavInnen
erben
aber habt nicht die Macht
sie zu befreien.
Eure Haut ist hell.
Ihr habt gelernt, daß Licht
kam
zu dem Dunklen Kontinent
mit weißer Macht,
daß die Indianer
in Verkommenheit leben
und in okkulten
bestialischen Riten.
Eure Mutter trug Korsette
um ihren Geist zu
erwürgen...

Ihr habt viele Predigten
gehört
und habt eure eigenen
Interpretationen
verschlossen im Herzen
getragen:
Du bist eine Frau
stark und gesund
auf Grund einer Reihe von
Umständen
bald bekannt
als Klassenprivileg...

Euer Geist brennt
nicht wie das Leuchtfeuer
im Hafen
sondern wie ein Feuer
wilderen Ursprungs.
Ihr beginnt den Mund
aufzumachen
und ein großer Windstoß
von Freiheit
stürmt herein mit euren

---

[1] Ich schulde Lieve Troch und Hedwig Meyer-Wilmes großen Dank. Sie haben mich nicht nur zur Arbeit an diesem Thema ermuntert, sondern auch darauf bestanden, daß ich mich theoretisch mit der allgemeinen feministischen Theoriediskussion auseinandersetze. Die oft technische Sprache meines Beitrags ist von diesem Theorie-Engagement bestimmt. Zugleich möchte ich mich herzlich für das Interesse und den Enthusiasmus bedanken, mit dem die Frauenbewegung in den holländischen Kirchen mich und meine Arbeit unterstützt und bereichert hat.
[2] Dies ist meine Übersetzung von A. Rich, *A Wild Patience Has Taken Me This Far*, Poems 1978 - 1981, New York 1981, 33-36.

Worten.
Doch immer noch sprecht ihr
in der gebrochenen Sprache
einer teilweisen Vision.

Ihr zieht eure langen Röcke
abweichend
quer durch das neunzehnte Jahrhundert.
Ihr registriert Ungerechtigkeit
aber scheitert sie zu berichtigen.

Wie kann ich verfehlen
eure Klarheit und Wut zu
lieben?
Wie kann ich
euch geben, was euch gebührt
Mut von eurem Mut nehmen
euer Erbe ehren
genau wie es ist
und zugleich erkennen
daß es nicht genügt?

Postmoderne feministische Theorien haben ins Bewußtsein gerufen, daß die Weise, wie wir unsere Texte situieren und unsere rhetorischen Strategien auswählen, Machtfragen aufwirft, die deutlich gemacht werden müssen. Die meisten von uns, die an feministischen Diskursen oder Kongressen teil-nehmen können, sind mit den Worten von Gayatri Chakravorty Spivak "unendlich privilegierte" Frauen.[3] Da auch FeministInnen in das Geflecht von Über- und Unterordnung verstrickt sind, müssen feministische Diskurse diejenigen institutionellen Strukturen und akademisch- oder kirchlich-patriarchalen Orte theoretisch sichtbar machen, von denen aus wir sprechen.

Der Ort, von dem aus ich spreche und wo ich meine kritische Intervention beginne, ist nordamerikanische feministische Theologie.[4] Um diesen Ort zu markieren, habe ich meinen theoretischen Reflexionen ein Gedicht von Adrienne Rich vorangestellt, das die widersprüchlichen Positionen und das Erbe der amerikanischen Frauenbewegung des neunzehnten Jahrhunderts zur Sprache bringt. Ich werde meine Überlegungen mit einem Auszug aus einer Ansprache abschließen, die die afrikanische Amerikanerin Julia Cooper im Jahre 1893 auf einem Weltkongreß von Frauen in Chicago gehalten hat.

---

[3] Sarah Harayman (Hg.) / Gayatra Chakravorty Spivak, *The Post-Colonial Critic. Interviews, Stategies*, Dialogues, New York 1990, 42ff.

[4] Hier beziehe ich mich auf 'womanistische' und 'mujerista' Theologie. Afrikanisch-amerikanische Feministinnen haben den Begriff "womanist" von Alice Walker übernommen, vgl. auch Katie G. Cannon, *Black Womanist Ethics*, Atlanta 1988 und die Podiumsdiskussion "Christian Ethics and Theology in Womanist Perspective", *JFSR* 5/2, 1989, 83-112. Meines Wissens ist der Ausdruck "mujerista" erstmals von Ada Maria Isasi-Diaz verwendet (vgl. ihren Artikel "The Bible and Mujerista Theology"); sowie in Susan Brooks Thistlewhaite & Mary Potter Engel (Hg.), *Lift Every Voice. Constructing Christian Theologies from the Underside*, San Francisco 1990, 261-269.

Dadurch, daß ich meinen Text auf diese Weise markiere, versuche ich die Diskussion einer feministischen Ethik und Politik der Befreiung ausdrücklich in den Diskursen der nordamerikanischen Frauenbewegung zu verorten. Damit möchte ich meine LeserInnen einladen, selbst zu beurteilen, ob und inwiefern meine theoretischen Reflexionen zu feministischen Konversationen in anderen geopolitischen Situationen beitragen können. Obwohl ich vom Kontext der U.S.amerikanischen Frauenbewegung in Theologie und Kirche aus spreche, spreche ich doch nicht als 'Einheimische' sondern als eine zugezogene Ausländerin. Der Begriff 'ansässige Ausländerin' situiert mich als jemand, die zugleich 'drinnen und draußen' ist: In den USA 'gehöre ich dazu' aufgrund meiner langen Ansässigkeit und meiner beruflichen Position als Professorin. Doch bleibe ich Ausländerin aufgrund meines deutschen Akzents, meiner Erfahrung und meiner Geschichte. Wenn ich Deutschland besuche, werde ich als 'einheimisch' betrachtet auf Grund meiner Staatsangehörigkeit, Kultur und Sprache. Doch werde ich auch zugleich als 'nicht dazu gehörige Fremde' eingestuft, wenn ich als Deutsch-Amerikanerin oder als Vertreterin amerikanisch-feministischer Theologie bezeichnet werde. Aus ähnlichen, doch auf ganz anderen Erfahrungen beruhenden Gründen, hat die Soziologin Patricia Hill Collins argumentiert, daß schwarze Bürgerinnen, besonders womanistische Intellektuelle, eine solche "doppelte" Insider / Outsider Position einnehmen.[5]

Ich schlage daher vor, daß die Metapher der 'ansässigen Ausländerin' oder 'einheimischen Fremden' ein geeignetes Bild für eine feministische Bewegung und Politik der Befreiung im Kontext westlicher Gesellschaften und Kirchen darstellt. Wenn die "Weiße Dame"[6] als Vermittlerin von Zivilisation und gleichsam als weiblicher 'Klebstoff' zum Zusammenhalt westlich-patriarchaler Herrschaft gedient hat, dann müssen weiße Frauen, die recht frische 'Einwanderinnen' in theologische Wissenschaft und kirchliches Amt sind, auf der Hut sein, Alibifunktionen für westliche patriarchale Zivilisation zu übernehmen. Wir müssen uns weigern, Wissen zu produzieren oder zu verbreiten, das intellektuelle oder religiöse Strukturen legitimiert, die Frauen herabwürdigen, unterwerfen oder einschränken. Um solch eine Praxis der Disloyalität gegenüber patriarchaler Autorität zu praktizieren, müssen

[5] Patricia Hill Collins, "Learning From the Outsider Within. The Sociological Significance of Black Feminist Thought", in: *Social Problems* 33/1986, 14-32.
[6] H. V. Carby, "On the Threshold of Woman's Era. Lynching, Empire and Sexuality", in: H. L. Gates jr. (Hg.), *Race, Writing, and Difference*, Chicago 1986, 301-328.

feministische Theorie und Theologie an ihrem 'ausländischen' Charakter festhalten, indem sie sich als eine 'Reflexion zweiter Ordnung' von Befreiung verstehen, die sich zugleich diesen Kämpfen gegenüber verantworten muß.

Akademische Frauen- und besonders Geschlechter(Gender-)forschung sucht oft ihre Position als 'ansässige Ausländerin' dadurch zu überwinden, daß sie sich dem akademischen System anpaßt. Natürlich ist es notwendig, daß akademische FeministInnen ihre Diskurse in Hinsicht auf die wissenschaftlichen Maßstäbe der Universität formulieren. Doch muß eine solche Überlebensstrategie als das gesehen werden, was sie ist: Eine Kollaboration mit androzentrisch-akademischen Diskursen, die die Existenz von Frauen mit Schweigen übergehen oder Frauen als 'die Anderen' marginalisieren. Ebenso sind ordinierte Frauen oft gezwungen, gewisse kirchliche Diskurse fortzusetzen, um ihr Amt ausüben zu können. Doch muß eine solche Wahl zur Kollaboration mit dem herrschenden Diskurs immer ethisch gerechtfertigt und als strategische taktische Untergrabung von patriarchalen Wissens- und Herrschaftssystemen legitimiert werden. Andernfalls laufen feministisch-theologische Diskurse sowie Frauen- und Geschlechterstudien Gefahr, einfach das Wissen über die Frau zu reproduzieren, das dem patriarchalen Denkschema, das Frauen marginalisiert und mundtot macht, verhaftet bleibt.

Uns in der Position der 'eingewanderten Fremden' zugleich als 'drinnen-draußen' zu verstehen statt uns in den Grenzbereichen feministischer *sex-gender* Konstruktionen als 'Andere' anzusiedeln, verlangt ein Ethos und eine Ethik patriarchaler Entschleierung, gemeinsamen politischen Kampfes und einer multikulturellen Befreiungsvision. Ein solches Ethos drückt nicht nur aus, wer wir sind, sondern konstituiert [auch], wer wir sind. Es macht eine permanente Kritik unserer eigenen Projekte und ihrer möglichen ideologischen Verflechtung, Kooptation und Begrenzung durch die historisch-institutionellen Strukturen, in denen wir denken und handeln, erforderlich.

Feministische Befreiungsstrategien als in der Spannung zwischen Zentrum und Grenze angesiedelt zu artikulieren, bedeutet jedoch nicht, starre oppositionelle Positionen zu befürworten. Vielmehr erfordert dies ein situationsgerechtes Abwägen und eine strategische Auswahl, die den sich ständig ändernden Beweggründen für feministische Kämpfe gegen patriarchale systematische Unterdrückung gerecht werden kann. Eine solche Konzentration auf die Theorie und Praxis des Frauenkampfes für die Veränderung patriarchaler Herrschaftsverhältnisse konstituiert sowohl ein tatsächliches als auch ein normatives Prinzip für eine feministische Befreiungsethik.

Im letzten Jahrhundert erfuhr eine Sklavin mit dem Namen Isabella ihre eigene Befreiung als Teil der SklavInnenemanzipationsbewegung und wurde dadurch verändert. Sie markierte ihre Befreiungserfahrungen religiös dadurch, daß sie einen neuen Namen wählte: Sojourner Truth.[7] Obwohl die Beziehung und die Wechselwirkung zwischen provisiorischem Aufenthalt (sojourn) und Wahrheit (truth) auf verschiedene Weise verstanden, ausgelegt und aufeinander bezogen werden kann, artikuliert die dynamische Spannung zwischen *sojourn and truth* nach meiner Meinung eine Durchhaltevision für die Praxis einer Ethik des Kampfes um Veränderung. Wenn in den Worten von Nelle Morton "die Reise das Zuhause" ist,[8] dann ist es wichtig, 'Auftankstationen' für Solidarität, Ermächtigung und Freundschaft im feministischen Befreiungskampf zu schaffen.

Patriarchat als *sex-gender* - Dualismus

Von Anfang an haben feministische Diskurse versucht, Freiräume für Frauen nicht am Rande, sondern im Zentrum von Akademie und Kirche zu schaffen. Deshalb hat feministische Theorie androzentrische Dualismen und asymmetrische binäre Konstruktionen von Geschlechtsdifferenz analysiert und kritisiert. Trotzdem haben die feministischen Diskurse es nicht vermieden, dualistische Klassifikationen zu wiederholen und diese dann als exklusive Alternativen darzustellen: entweder reformistisch oder radikal, sozialistisch oder liberal, privat oder öffentlich, auf Gleichberechtigung oder Befreiung hin orien. 3 4olitisch, essentialistisch oder konstruktivistisch, europäisch oder amerikanisch, weiß oder schwarz, Frauenperspektiven der sogenannten ersten oder dritten Welt.

Die Religionsethikerin Carol Robb hat überzeugend argumentiert, daß die Unterschiede in den theoretischen Ansätzen feministischer Ethik durch voneinander abweichende Analysen von Frauenunterdrückung und ihrer Wurzeln bedingt sind.[9] Anstatt die verschiedenen, inzwischen wohlbekannten und vielbemühten Typologien feministisch-theoretischer Ansätze zu wiederholen, möchte ich hier jedoch auf den Begriff des Patriarchats

---

[7] Vgl. B. J. Loewenberg and R. Bogin (Hg.), *Black Women in Nineteenth-Century American Life*, University Park 1976, 234-242.

[8] Vgl. Nelle Morton, *The Journey Is Home*, Boston 1985.

[9] Carol S. Robb, "A Framework for Feminist Ethics", in: B. Hilkert Andolsen/Ch.E. Gudorf/M.D. Pellauer (Hg.), *Women's Consciousness, Women's Conscience. A Reader in Feminist Ethics*, Minneapolis 1985, 211-234.

zurückkommen[10], einen Begriff, der in meinem Text immer wieder aufgetaucht ist, dessen kritische Diskussion ich aber bisher verschoben habe. Während einige feministische TheoretikerInnen Patriarchat als ein unhistorisches, universalistisches und totalistisches Konzept ablehnen, verwenden andere es als theoretischen Schlüsselbegriff, um das Entstehen und Fortbestehen sexueller, sozialer, politischer und ideologischer Männerherrschaft über Frauen zu benennen. In feministischer Theorie wird daher der Begriff des Patriarchats nicht länger auf die Macht des Hausvaters über die Großfamilie beschränkt, wie das noch weithin in den Sozialwissenschaften der Fall ist. Vielmehr wird der Begriff dazu benutzt, diejenigen sozialen Herrschaftsstrukturen und Ideologien zu benennen, die es dem Mann erlaubt haben, die Frau im Laufe der Geschichte zu bevormunden und zu beherrschen.

Wenn der Begriff Patriarchat im Sinne männlich-weiblicher Geschlechterdifferenz verstanden wird, wird Geschlechterdifferenz zur primären Form von Herrschaft und Unterdrückung. Der Unterschied zwischen männlich und weiblich wird zum grundlegenden und wesentlichen Unterschied von Menschsein. Eine solch essentialistische Auffassung der Geschlechterdifferenz kann eine konstruktivistische Wendung nehmen, wenn angenommen wird, daß die binäre Geschlechterdifferenz nicht biologisch determiniert oder göttlich ordiniert, sondern sozial geschaffen ist. Solch ideologische Konstruktionen der Geschlechterdifferenz unterstützen patriarchale Herrschaft und lassen sie als naturgegeben und selbstverständlich erscheinen, und zwar nicht nur für Männer, sondern auch für Frauen. Obwohl die Mehrzahl der FeministInnen eine Form konstruktivistischsozialer Geschlechteranalyse vertritt, neigen neuerdings andere wieder zu einem biologischen Determinismus oder einem philosophischen Essentialismus von Weiblichkeit, manche auch zu beidem.[11]

Während FeministInnen im allgemeinen darin übereinstimmen, daß das herrschende soziokulturelle Geschlechtersystem entmystifiziert werden muß,

---

[10] Zur Diskussion und Definition der Begriffe vgl. Maggie Humm, *The Dictionary of Feminist Theory*, Columbus 1990, 159-161; Gerda Lerner, *The Creation of Patriarchy,* New York 1986, 231-243. Im Unterschied zu Lerner bin ich nicht an den Ursprüngen patriarchaler Herrschaft interessiert, sondern an ihrer Ausarbeitung als heuristische historische Kategorie.
[11] Zur Problematisierung und Diskussion des essentialistischen/konstruktivistischen Gegensatzes vgl. Diana Fuss, *Essentially Speaking. Feminism, Nature & Difference*, New York 1989.

gehen ihre Meinungen darin auseinander, wie ein positiver Standpunkt im Befreiungskampf bestimmt werden kann, wenn 'Weiblichkeit/Frau' problematisch sind. Doch muß feministische Theorie nach einem solchen alternativen theoretischen Ort suchen, da nur eine kritisch-theoretischer Standpunkt, der sich von dem herrschenden Geschlechtersystem unterscheidet, die Entmystifizierung und Entlarvung sozial kultureller Herrschaftsideologie möglich macht. Die Aussicht, einen solchen theoretischen Ort zu finden, hängt jedoch meines Erachtens von der Existenz einer sozialen Bewegung ab, die sich für die Aufhebung patriarchaler Herrschaftsverhältnisse einsetzt. Umgekehrt ermächtigt die theoretische Artikulation eines solchen feministischen Ortes wiederum die feministische Bewegung als eine soziale Befreiungsbewegung.

Die TheorikerInnen der 'neuen', 'ganz anderen' Weiblichkeit suchen einen solchen weiblichen Ort nicht nur auf epistemologischer, sondern auch auf sozialer Ebene theoretisch zu benennen, indem sie den Begriff der Weiblichkeit aus dem herrschenden Geschlechtersystem herauszulösen, neu zu verorten und zu werten suchen. Die italienische Feministin Adriana Cavarero formuliert einen solchen theoretischen Standort:

> ... mit wesentlicher und ursächlicher Differenz meine ich, daß das ins Leben gerufene Sein in Differenz für Frauen nicht zur Diskussion steht; denn für jede, die weiblich geboren ist, ist dies immer schon so und nicht anders. Sie ist in ihrem Wesen verwurzelt nicht als etwas Überflüssiges oder etwas Zusätzliches, sondern als das, was sie notwendigerweise ist: Weiblich.[12]

Im Kontext der USA haben sich drei strategische Grundpositionen entwickelt, die Weiblichkeit als alternativen theoretischen Ort artikulieren: Die erste Strategie besteht in der feministischen Aneignung und kritischen Neuformulierung der Jung'schen Psychoanalyse, die den verdrängten weiblichen Archetypus[13] rehabilitiert. Die zweite Position, von Mary Daly

---

[12] Adriana Cavarero, "L'elaborzione filosofica della differenza sessuale", in: Maria Christina Marcuzzo und Ana Rossi-Dora (Hg.), *La ricerca delle donne. Studi femministi in Italia,* Turin 1987, 173-87 p. 180. Siehe auch ihren Beitrag "Die Perspektive der Geschlechterdifferenz", in: Ute Gerhard (et al.), *Differenz und Gleichheit. Menschenrechte haben (k)ein Geschlecht,* Frankfurt 1990, 95-111.

[13] Für die USA siehe insbesondere die Bücher von Anne Ulanov, in Deutschland die Arbeit von Christa Mulack und die Diskussion ihrer Arbeit durch Cornelia Giese, *Gleichheit und Differenz. Vom dualistischen Denken zur polaren Weltsicht,* München 1990.

äußerst brilliant formuliert, wählt eine ontologisch-linguistische Strategie zur Artikulierung eines solchen Andersseins. Es ist ein Prozeß des Werdens, hervorgerufen durch die wilde, sich selbst verwirklichende Frau, die den Sprung von der Phallokratie in die Freiheit vollzogen hat, in die Andere-Welt des Seins. Diese Strategie wird durch metamorphosierende Frauen ver-wirklicht: Durch Das Weib und Die Ursprüngliche Hexe, durch die archaische elementale, sich metapatriarchalisch bewegende Frau. Sie ist diejenige, die eine neue Spezies darstellt, eine ursprüngliche Rasse.[14]

Die dritte Strategie zur Aufwertung und Rehabilitierung der Frau und des Weiblichen spielt in letzter Zeit eine große Rolle in den feministischen akademischen Diskussionen. Die Theorie des Mütterlich-Weiblichen ist Import einer Bewegung, die in den USA gemeinhin als *French Feminism* bezeichnet wird, sich aber nur auf die Werke von Kristeva, Cixous und Irigaray bezieht.[15] Obwohl amerikanische Arbeiten über das 'Mütterliche' sich im allgemeinen auf den sozialgeschichtlichen Aspekt von Mutterschaft als Institution konzentriert haben, werden in jüngeren interdisziplinären Studien über mütterliches Denken[16] oft "prae-ödipale Schrankenlosigkeit, Verbundenheit, Pluralität, Fruchtbarkeit, Zärtlichkeit und Sorgen um ... im Namen des Andersseins weiblicher Identität gepriesen."[17]

---

[14] Vgl. Mary Daly, *GynÖkologie*, Eine Meta-Ethik des radikalen Feminismus, München 1981. Zur kritischen Auseinandersetzung mit dem Werk Mary Dalys siehe Hester Eisenstein, *Contemporary Feminist Thought*, Boston 1983, insbesondere S. 107-115; Ruth Großmaß, "Von der Verführungskraft der Bilder: Mary Daly's Elemental-Femi-nistische Philosophie", in: R. Großmaß / C. Schmerl (Hg.), *Feministischer Kompaß, patriarchales Gepäck. Kritik konservativer Anteile in neueren feministischen Theorien*, Frankfurt 1989, 56-116.

[15] Zur kritischen Diskussion vgl. Stanton Domna, "Language and Revolution. The Franco-American Dis-Connection", in: H.Eisenstein und A. Jardine (Hg.), *The Future of Difference*, Boston 1980, 73-87; Gayatri Chakravorty Spivak, "French Feminism in an International Frame", in: *In Other Worlds. Essays in Cultural Politics*, New York 1987, 134-153; Alexandra Busch, "Der metaphorische Schleier des ewig Weiblichen - Zu Luce Irigaray's Ethik der sexuellen Differenz", in: *Feministischer Kompaß*, (op.cit.), 117-171.

[16] Sara Ruddick, "Maternal Thinking", in: *Feminist Studies* 6, 1980, 342-67; zur kritischen Diskussion vgl. Anne Carr / Elisabeth Schüssler Fiorenza (Hg.), *Motherhood. Experience, Institution, Theology*, Concilium 206, Edinburgh 1989; Ursula Pasero und Ursula Pfäfflin (Hg.), *Neue Mütterlichkeit. Ortsbestimmungen*, Gütersloh 1986.

[17] Donna C. Stanton, "Difference on Trial. A Critique of the Maternal Metaphor in Cixous, Irigaray and Kristeva", in: Nancy K. Miller (Hg.), *The Poetics of Gender*, New York 1986, 176.

Feministische WissenschaftlerInnen versuchen zwar hervorzuheben, daß die Theorie des Mütterlich-Weiblichen die angebliche Objektivität von logo- und phallozentrischen Prinzipien, Repräsentationen und Wissen untergräbt und damit bestehende Formen von Schreiben und Wissen in einer Weise, die bisher undenkbar war, zu untergraben sucht. Doch hat die amerikanische Rezeption der sogenannten französisch-feministischen Theorie und ihre Betonung des Weiblichen als Metapher und Konstrukt die Tendenz, kulturelle Weiblichkeit fort- und festzuschreiben. Diese Gefahr besteht besonders in der populären Rezeption von Weiblichkeit durch religiöse FeministInnen: Fließendes, Weichheit, Pluralität, Meer, Natur, Friedfertigkeit, das Nährende, Körper, Leben, Mutter-Göttin werden als Gegensatz zu Festigkeit, Härte, Starrheit, Agressivität, Vernunft, Kontrolle, Tod, Vater-Gott verstanden. Folglich ist die Theorie des MütterlichWeiblichen in Gefahr, die kulturellreligiösen Zuschreibungen von Weiblichkeit und Mütterlichkeit, die uns aus päpstlichen Verlautbarungen so vertraut sind, in postmoderner Sprache derart zu reproduzieren, daß diese jetzt zur feministischen Norm werden.

In den achziger Jahren -so wird behauptet- hat sich feministische Theorie über die liberale Kritik am Sexismus von Wissen und die strukturelle Kritik an patriarchalen Theorien hinausbewegt hin zu einer Kritik des Phallozentrismus, der universale Modelle bereitstellt, um von beiden Geschlechtern in männlicher Begrifflichkeit zu sprechen. Der autonome Feminismus hat sich angeblich wegbewegt von einer Theorie, deren Analyseobjekte Sexismus und Frauen sind, hin zu einer kritischen Untersuchung von Theorie, die ihren maskulinen Charakter zu verschleiern sucht. Ein offenes Anerkennen der 'Männlichkeit des Wissens', so wird argumentiert, ist notwendig, um einen Raum innerhalb des 'universal Gültigen' für Frauen als Frauen freizulegen, einen Ort, wo weibliche Differenz artikuliert werden kann.

Durch die Untersuchung der Sprache von Weiblichkeit und Autonomie hat feministische Theorie die Möglichkeit des Dialogs zwischen denjenigen Wissensformen, die jetzt als männlich bestimmt akzeptiert werden, sowie der 'fremden' oder 'anderen' Stimme von Frauen eröffnet.[18]

---

[18] E. A. Grosz, "The In(ter)vention of Feminist Knowledges", in: Barbara Caine/E. A. Grosz/ Marie de Lepervanche (Hg.), *Crossing Boundaries. Feminisms and the Critique of Knowledges.* Sydney 1988, 97-103.

Jedoch verschweigt -ja verdrängt sogar- eine solche periodizierende Darstellung der Wiederentdeckung des Weiblichen, daß das weltweite Lautwerden vieler unterschiedlicher feministischer Stimmen und die damit verbundene Dekonstruktion eines einheitlichen essentialistischen Verständnisses der Frau den wichtigsten Durchbruch feministischer Theorie in den achziger Jahren darstellt. Daher ist es sehr beunruhigend, daß weiße feministische Theorie und Theologie in den USA von der europäisch-amerikanischen Artikulation von sexueller Differenz und Aufwertung des Weiblichen gerade in dem Augenblick fasziniert sind, in dem wichtige theoretische Werke von afrikanisch-amerikanischen Frauen erschienen sind, die nicht nur den Primat von geschlechtlicher Unterdrückung in Frage stellen, sondern auch unterschiedlich auslegen.[19]

Patriarchat als Herrschaftssystem
Um sich einer Neubestimmung des Zentrums feministischer Diskurse anzunähern, argumentiere ich, muß feministische Theologie und Theorie die Privilegierung des binären Geschlechterdualismus als ihren theoretischen Denkrahmen aufgeben, in dem 'die sexuelle Differenz den Horizont' unseres Denkens bestimmt (Irigaray). Statt dessen habe ich versucht, den Begriff des Patriarchats als primäre analytische Kategorie feministischer Theorie so zu rekonzeptualisieren, daß er die Verzahnung und Wechselbeziehung der verschiedenen, miteinander in Konflikt stehenden Formen von Frauenunterdrückung erfassen kann. Anstatt eine dualistische Herrschaftstruktur von Mann-Frau zu postulieren, muß das Patriarchat als ein pyramidales, politisch-kulturelles System von Herrschaft und Unterordnung theoretisch erfaßt werden - als ein Herrschaftssystem, das durch Geschlecht, Rasse, Klasse, religiöse und kulturelle Zugehörigkeit und andere historische

---

[19] Vgl.z.B. Bell Hooks, *Feminist Theory. From Margin to Center*, Boston 1984; ad., *Talking Back. Thinking Feminist/Thinking Black*, Boston 1989; ad., *Yearning. Race, Gender and Cultural Politics*, Boston 1990; Paula Giddings, *When and Where I Enter. The Impact of Black Women on Race and Sex in America*, New York 1984; Cheryl A. Wall (Hg.), *Changing Our Own Words. Essays on Critism, Theory and Writing by Black Women*, New Brunswick 1989; Henri Louis Gates (Hg.), *Reading Black. Reading Feminist*, New York 1990; Patricia Hill Collins, Black *Feminist Thought. Knowledge, Consciousness on the Politics of Empowerment*, Boston 1991; Joanne M. Braxton / Andree Nicola McLaughlin (Hg.), *Wild Women in the Whirlwind. Afro-American Culture and the Contemporary Literary Renaissance*, New Brunswick 1990.

Herrschaftsformulierungen, strukturiert wird.[20]

Europäische und amerikanische feministische Theorien und Theologien, die den westlichen Herrschaftsdiskurs über sexuelle Differenz verabsolutieren und universalisieren, verschleiern nicht nur die komplexe Verzahnung patriarchaler Herrschaftsformen, die die individuelle Erfahrung von Frauen und die Beziehungen zwischen Frauen prägt. Sie verschleiern auch die Beteiligung weißer privilegierter Frauen und christlicher Religion an patriarchaler Unterdrückung, insofern beide als zivilisierende Kanäle sowohl für patriarchales Wissen und kulturelle Werte gedient haben.

Die politische, philosophische und religiöse Rhetorik von Unterdrückung und 'naturgegebenen Differenzen' hat dazu gedient, die 'Anderen' des privilegierten reichen europäischen Mannes von demokratischer Selbstbestimmung, voller Bürgerschaft und individuellen Rechten auszuschließen. Der westliche 'Mann der Vernunft' beansprucht Universalität und Wahrheit für sich selbst. Er ist nicht nur Mann, sondern auch weiß. Er ist europäisch, gebildet, begütert und privilegiert. Dieser weiße, begüterte, gebildete westliche Mann hat nicht nur die privilegierte weiße Frau als seine 'Andere' definiert, sondern auch Menschen anderer Rassen, Klassen und Kulturen. Eine solche Zivilisation und philosophische Bestimmung all dieser 'Anderen' als minderwertig im Namen westlicher moderner Demokratie diente dem Zweck ihrer Unterordung und Ausbeutung.[21] Es ist der westliche, privilegierte, gebildete Mann, der Wissen und Wissenschaft betrieben und darauf bestanden hat, daß nur seine Interpretation der Welt wahr und richtig ist. Wissen selbst ist damit nicht nur geschlechtlich, sondern auch rassistisch, eurozentrisch, und klassenbestimmt. Deshalb müssen feministische Diskurse erkennbar machen, daß die universalistische, androzentrische Wissenschaftsrhetorik westlich-männlicher Eliten nicht nur einfach die Dominanz des männlichen Geschlechtes fortschreibt, sondern den 'Weißen Vater' oder den 'Boss-Man' -wie ein afrikanisch-amerikanischer Ausdruck ihn nennt-, als universales Subjekt legitimiert hat und immer noch legitimiert.

---

[20] Sylvia Walby, *Patriarchy at Work. Patriarchal and Capitalist Relations in Employment*, Minneapolis 1986, 5-69. Die Autorin versteht Patriarchat als ein komplexes System von aufeinander bezogenen sozialen Strukturen. Die verschiedenen Gruppen patriarchaler Beziehungen verlagern sich im Laufe der Zeit und verursachen zu unterschiedlichen Zeiten und in unterschiedlichen Kulturen jeweils andere Konstellationen.

[21] Zusätzlich zu der Arbeit von Chakravoty Spivak vgl. Trin T. Minh-ha, *Woman, Native, Other. Writing Postcoloniality and Feminism*, Bloomington 1989.

Kurzum, es ist gerade die Koppelung des Ausschlusses von demokratischen Bürgerrechten privilegierter westlicher Frauen mit dem aller anderen 'Unpersonen' (Gustavo Gutierrez) als auch die ideologische Legitimierung von geschlechtlichen, Rassen-, Klassen- und kulturellen Differenzen als naturgegeben oder gottgewollt, die feministisch-theoretisch bedacht werden muß. Dies wird übersehen, wenn einige FeministInnen einen angeblichen Gegensatz zwischen dem Feminismus der sechziger und siebziger Jahre, der sich angeblich nur gegen den Sexismus und für die Gleichberechtigung von Frauen eingesetzt hat, und dem der achziger Jahre konstruieren, der angeblich erst für die Autonomie und Selbstbestimmung von Frauen gekämpft hat.[22] Denn eine derartige dualistische Periodisierung feministisch intellektueller Geschichte der letzten dreißig Jahre mißversteht zwei entscheidende Punkte.

Erstens: Emanzipatorische Bewegungen -die Frauenbefreiungsbewegung eingeschlossen- kämpfen nicht für Gleichberechtigung, um männlich und privilegierten Männern gleich zu werden, sondern sie kämpfen für die Rechte, die Verantwortung und die Privilegien gleichberechtigter StaatsbürgerInnenschaft, die ihnen als legitim zustehen, ihnen aber vom demokratisch-kapitalistischen Patriarchat verweigert werden. Emanzipatorische Bewegungen sind diskursive Gemeinschaften, die sich auf demokratische Rechte und Werte gründen, Ausgrenzungen in Frage stellen und Ansprüche auf Autorität und Würde für rechtlose Menschen geltend machen. In den vergangenen Jahrzehnten ist die feministische Frauenbefreiungsbewegung in Gesellschaft und Religion eines der lebendigsten Beispiele solcher emanzipatorischer Gegenbewegungen gewesen. Sie hat sich als ein öffentliches Forum für die kritische Analyse patriarchaler Unterdrückung und die kritische Artikulation von Fraueninteressen und Hoffnungen konstituiert. Insofern sich aber feministische Bewegungen als eine einheitliche oppositionelle Front dargestellt und eine universalisierende Kritik des Sexismus vom Standpunkt der Frau artikuliert haben, sind sie immer in Gefahr gewesen, feministische Gegenöffentlichkeit als hegemonisches Gebiet privilegierter weißer, westlicher Frauen zu konstituieren.

Zweitens: Oppositionelle Diskurse wie feministische Theorie und Theologie

---

[22] Elisabeth Gross, "Conclusion: What is Feminist Theory?", in: Carol Pateman und Elisabeth Gross (Hg.), *Feminist Challenges. Social and Political Theory*, Boston 1986, 195.

sind nicht unabhängig von den herrschenden Diskursen der patriarchalen Gesellschaften, Kirchen und Institutionen, in denen sie leben. Im Gegenteil, sie sind unentrinnbar in deren Herrschaftsdiskurse verstrickt, insofern sie durch diese bedingt sind. Die feministisch neubelebte Theorie und Theologie von Weiblichkeit ist daher verquickt mit der patriarchalen Herrschaftsideologie, die biologische Geschlechtsdifferenz 'naturalisiert', als ob Geschlechtsunterschiede für alle Frauen in allen Situationen dieselben wären. Hand in Hand mit den herrschenden patriarchalen Ideologien von Geschlechterdifferenz schärfen oppositionelle Weiblichkeitsdiskurse ein, daß Geschlecht und Rasse 'natürliche' Kategorien sind, da sie Geschlechts- und Rassendifferenz als 'real' und 'alltäglich' erscheinen lassen. Dies wird dadurch erreicht, daß 'biologischen Unterschieden' tiefe symbolische Bedeutung für unser Leben zugeschrieben wird, anstatt zu versuchen, solche Unterschiede als soziopolitische und religiöse Konstrukte zu 'entnaturalisieren' und zu entmystifizieren. Anstatt die Eigenschaften der weißen privilegierten Frau als natürliche und wesentliche Geschlechtsdifferenz zu universalisieren, muß eine kritische feministische Befreiungsinterpretation versuchen, ein diskursives Forum zu schaffen, in dem Frauen sich als politische Handlungssubjekte bestimmen können, ohne gezwungen zu sein, patriarchal-strukturell bedingte Spaltungen und Vorurteile unter Frauen zu verdrängen. Durch Dialog, Streitgespräch und Überlegung können theologische Diskurse dazu beitragen, vereinheitlichte, patriarchale Identitätsformationen in kreative Verschiedenheit umzuwandeln und entsprechende politische Strategien für eine vielstimmige und vielschichtige feministische Bewegung zu erarbeiten.

Drittens: Statt das Patriarchat als eine allumfassende Totalität aufzufassen, der FeministInnen nur durch den Sprung ins 'Jenseits' oder die Flucht in eine befreite Gemeinschaft entkommen können, müssen wir im Herzen des demokratischen Patriarchats einen 'anderen' alternativen theoretischen Ort artikulieren, von wo aus wir sogenannte anthropologische Differenzen als soziopolitisch-religiöse Herrschaftsstrukturen benennen können.

Frauen - *ekklēsia*

Um einen solchen kritisch-alternativen Ort politisch-theologisch zu benennen, habe ich den Bildbegriff Frauen-*ekklēsia* eingeführt. John McGowan's Untersuchung verweist auf die Möglichkeit eines solchen alternativen Ortes, wenn er von der 'schwierigen, ja sogar antithetischen' Beziehung der Demokratie zum Kapitalismus spricht und betont, daß nur die Berufung auf solche politischen und ethischen Prinzipien, die einer Gesellschaft innewohnen, Pluralismus und Differenz sichern kann. Demokratische Prinzipien wie Freiheit und Gleichberechtigung sind in patriarchal-demokratischen Gesellschaften und Religionen nicht als starre Grundbegriffe, sondern als sinnvermittelnde Handlungsbegriffe zu begreifen.

Wenn feministische Theorie und Theologie eine demokratische Gesellschaft oder Kirche als 'soziales Ganzes' verstehen würde, das in quasi-autonome Bereiche ausdifferenziert ist und Demokratie als soziale Norm hat,[23] könnten sie einen politischen Ort konzipieren, von dem aus sie Differenz positiv theoretisch fassen könnten. Sie könnten dann die Frauen-*ekklēsia* als einen theoretischen Ort begreifen, von dem aus sie politische-kulturelle Veränderung bedenken und sich für einen demokratischen Pluralismus einsetzen könnten. Ein solcher theoretischer Rahmen wäre fähig, das Herrschaftskonstrukt von der Frau als der Anderen, das feministische Theorie von Weiblichkeit und Mütterlichkeit fortschreibt, durch das radikal-demokratische Konstrukt der Frauen-*ekklēsia* zu ersetzen, das zugleich unerfüllte Vision und historische Wirklichkeit ist. Frauen-*ekklēsia* ist jetzt bereits eine Realität in Gesellschaft und Kirche, aber noch nicht voll verwirklicht, bereits real, aber noch im Prozeß der Verwirklichung begriffen. Historisch und politisch ist das Bild der Frauen-*ekklēsia*, verstanden als demokratischer Kongreß oder Parlament der Frauen, ein Oxymoron, d.h. eine Kombination von sich widersprechenden Begriffen, das ein feministisch-politisches 'Anderes' artikulieren will. Die Übersetzung von 'ekklēsia gynaikōn' mit Frauenkirche, verstanden als Alternativbegriff zu patriarchaler Kirche, sucht christliche Gemeinde und Theologie als wichtige Orte feministischer Kämpfe für die Veränderung des westlichen Patriarchats zu benennen.

Wenn feministisches Theoretisieren und Theologisieren in der Praxis und Vision der Frauen-*ekklēsia* angesiedelt wird, ist es möglich, die sogenannte natürliche sexuelle Differenz ähnlich wie rassisch, ethnologisch und klassenbedingte Unterschiede als sozio-politisches, religiöskulturell ideologisches Konstrukt zur Legitimation von patriarchaler Demokratie zu begreifen. Frauen leben in Gesellschaften, die nicht einfach pluralistisch sind. Vielmehr sind Gesellschaften in Schichten geteilt, unterteilt in soziale Gruppierungen mit ungleichem Status, ungleicher Macht und ungleichem Zugang zu den

---

[23] McGowan, *Postmodernism*, 220-280.

Resourcen. Solche Achsen der Ungleichheit haben sich entlang der patriarchalen Grenzen von Klasse, Geschlecht, Rasse, ethnischer Zugehörigkeit und Alter entwickelt.[24] Daher muß feministische Theorie auf der Hut sein, diese patriarchalen Standesunterschiede und Spaltungen unter Frauen nicht als positive feministische Verschiedenheit und Pluralität fortzuschreiben. Vielmehr muß eine kritisch-feministische Befreiungstheorie und -praxis patriarchale Statusbestimmungen wie Rasse, Geschlecht, Klasse oder Heterosexualität 'entnaturalisieren' und relativieren. Sie kann dies tun, wenn sie begreift, daß sexuelle Differenz zusammengeschweißt ist mit einer Vielfalt von anderen biologischen, sozialen, kulturellen und religiösen Unterschieden in Frauen selbst und zwischen Frauen.

Daher ist es möglich, Frauen-*ekklēsia* als einen theoretischen Ort zu schaffen, an dem der Sinn von Frauen als soziopolitischer Kategorie und als Kollektivität praktisch und theoretisch gedacht werden kann. Von einem solchen theoretischen Ort aus kann feministische Theologie soziale Annahmen über Geschlecht, Sexualität, oder Weiblichkeit 'entnaturalisieren' und politisieren. Eine solche soziopolitische Dekonstruktion der Begriffe Frau und Weiblichkeit braucht Geschlechtsunterschiede weder zu verdrängen noch zu bestreiten. Vielmehr geht es darum, diese nicht in einen essentialistischen, dualistischen Denkrahmen einzuspannen, um sie dann mit ontologisch-symbolischer Bedeutung auszustatten und ihre historisch-kulturell bedingten vergeschlechtlichten Bedeutungen zu universalisieren.[25]

Die *ekklēsia* der Frauen darf auch nicht unter Bezugnahme auf das allen Frauen als Frauen Gemeinsame definiert werden. Feministisch-politische Analysen haben belegt, daß die Annahme einer gerechten politischen Ordnung, die in feministischen Texten auftauchen, sich in den von Plato und Aristoteles gezogenen Grenzen bewegen. Platos Vorstellung von einem politisch geschaffenen Gemeinwesen, das eine heterogene Bevölkerung in einer hierarchisch organisierten Meritokratie zusammenbringen soll, spiegelt sich in der liberal-feministischen Rhetorik von negativ bestimmter Freiheit,

---

[24] Nancy Fraser, *Unruly Practices. Power, Discourse and Gender in Contemporary Social Theory*, Minneapolis 1989, 165.

[25] Rita Felski, *Beyond Feminist Aesthetics. Feminist Literature and Social Change*, Cambridge 1989, 170. Genau diese Kritik an einer oppositionellen vergeschlechtlichten Identität bestätigt gleichzeitig deren vorrangige Existenz - nicht als eine ontologische gegebene, sondern als tatsächlich existierende diskursive Form, die eine Kette unterschiedlicher und widersprüchlicher politischer und kultureller Aktivitäten nach sich gezogen hat.

formaler rechtlicher Gleichheit und politischer Teilnahme. Aristoteles' Verwechslung von Gleichheit und Gleichförmigkeit als Vorbedingung politischer Mitgliedschaft in einer exklusiv verstandenen *polis* hallt in Kritik und Traum des feministischen Seperatismus nach.[26]

Die Frauen-*ekklēsia*, verstanden als feministisch-politische Versammlung, muß daher die exklusiven Alternativen klassischer Philosophie vermeiden. Entweder formale Gleichheit, die patriarchale Spaltungen von Frauen in Rasse, Klasse, Sexualität, Religion oder Ethnozentrismus nicht kritisch befragt, sondern fortschreibt; oder feministische Gleichheit, die Frauenräume oder feministische Orte dadurch schafft, daß sie theoretische und praktische Unterschiede zwischen Frauen überspringt.

Kurzum, die Frauen-*ekklēsia* kann sich weder im Sinne von formaler Gleichheit konstituieren, die fortbestehende patriarchale Spaltungen nicht antastet; genausowenig aber kann sie sich als Gleichheit im Sinne von Gleichsein verstehen, die Homogenität unter Frauen voraussetzt. Vielmehr muß ihre Praxis und Theorie eine feministische Öffentlichkeit schaffen, die Gleichheit und BürgerInnenschaft von Frauen anstrebt. Sie kann dies dadurch tun, daß sie patriarchale Spaltungen theoretisch benennt, mutig konfrontiert und praktisch bekämpft, aber nicht dadurch, daß sich sich als befreite, schwesterliche Gemeinschaft ausgibt. Vielmehr muß sie die theoretischen und praktischen Unterschiede zwischen Frauen als demokratisch-diskursive Handlungsmöglichkeiten feministisch ausloten.

Daher muß die Frauen-*ekklēsia* auf der Hut sein, ihre Beziehungen in familiäre, privatisierte Bildsprache zu kleiden. Während in den siebziger Jahren 'Schwesterlichkeit' die bevorzugte feministische Metapher war, um Gemeinsamkeit und Solidarität unter Frauen auszudrücken, ist es in den achziger Jahren die Weiblichkeit und das Mutter-Tochter-Band gewesen. Insofern jedoch das feministische Verständnis von Schwesterlichkeit und Mütterlichkeit auf dem gemeinsamen Opferstatus und der darauf bestehenden kollektiven Macht von Frauen ruht, kann es weder die Machtunterschiede zwischen Frauen offenlegen noch die individuellen Stärken und Talente hervorragender Frauen anerkennen.

Die Rhetorik der nicht-miteinander-konkurrierenden Strukturlosigkeit und

---

[26] M. E. Hawkesworth, *Beyond Oppression. Feminist Theory and Political Strategy*, New York 1990, 156.

Gruppenkollektivität erlaubt es Frauen, die wenig Selbstvertrauen und Macht haben, ihre Minderwertigkeitsgefühle an anderen Frauen auszulassen, hervorragende Frauen zu erniedrigen und traditionell weibliche, indirekte, manipulierende Macht auszuüben. Sie tabuisiert den kritischen Dialog und führt zum 'Ausgebranntsein' leitender Frauen, das durch die Verdrängung von Ärger und dem Mangel an Anerkennung und Respekt verursacht wird. Eine solche feministische Rhetorik ruft Schuldgefühle hervor und führt zur Aufrechnung von Unterdrückungserfahrungen. Sie pflegt eine Art von weißem feministischen Konfessionalismus, der Kollektivschuld bekennt, aber keine praktischen Schritte auf verantwortliche Solidarität und praktische Veränderung hin macht. Wenn die Metapher der Schwesterlichkeit durch die der Frauenzuneigung oder Frauenfreundschaft[27] ersetzt und Freundschaft im aristotelischen Sinne als 'anderes Selbst' definiert wird, besteht ebenfalls die Gefahr, daß nicht nur privatisierende Schwesterlichkeit fortgeschrieben, sondern auch die aristotelische Identifikation von Gleichheit und Selbigkeit festgeschrieben wird. Zwar gibt Frauenfreundschaft einer politischen Vision Tiefe und Geist, doch kann sie nicht konstitutiv für die Schaffung von Frauen*ekklēsia* als politische Bewegung und theoretisches Forum sein.

Feministische Theoretikerinnen, die Machtunterschiede zwischen Frauen anerkennen, haben im vergangenen Jahrzehnt die Mutter-TochterBeziehung problematisiert und neu bewertet. Doch bleibt das Konstrukt der 'symbolischen Mutter' dem Horizont sexueller Unterschiede verhaftet.[28] Obwohl diese Metapher Ungleichheiten zwischen Frauen anerkennt, die Kommunikation zwischen Frauen verschiedener Generationen fördert und Austausch von Wissen und Sehnsüchten über Unterschiede hinweg ermöglicht, schreibt sie doch die totalisierende Theorie universaler Geschlechts-

---

[27] Janice Raymond, *Frauenfreundschaft. Philosophie der Zuneigung*, München 1987; Mary E. Hunt, *Fierce Tenderness. A Feminist Theology of Friendship,* New York 1991. Diese Autorinnen bemühen sich, über den aristotelischen Freundschaftsbegriff hinauszugehen und dennoch die Frauen-Kirche in der Begrifflichkeit von Freundschaft zu erklären.

[28] Theresa de Lauretis, "The Essence of the Triangle", (*op. cit.*), 25, unter Berücksichtigung des italienischen Begriffs affidamento als soziale Praxis des Anvertrauens und Bewertens zwischen älteren und jüngeren Frauen. Dies ist ein sehr bedeutendes Konzept insofern, als jüngere Feministinnen dazu neigen, ihre akademischen oder religiösen 'Väter' zu schätzen, aber ihre Eigenheit und Unabhängigkeit von ihren feministischen 'Müttern' aufgrund institutionellen Drucks hervorzuheben. Dieser Begriff muß daher neu definiert werden, und zwar eher im institutionell-politischen Sinn als im essentialistischen Sinn von Geschlechtsdifferenz.

differenzen, die von weißen FeministInnen entwickelt wurde, unkritisch fort. Statt in der psycholanalytischen Theorie von sexueller Differenz, die Männlichkeit als Ablösung von der Mutter und Weiblichkeit in Kontinuität mit dieser 'ersten Verbindung' versteht, befangen zu bleiben, muß Frauen-*ekklēsia* nach einem Interpretationsrahmen suchen, der das dualistische und totalisierende *sex-gender*-System nicht einfachhin fortschreibt oder negiert, sondern es aushöhlen kann.

In ihrem Buch "Die Fesseln der Liebe"[29] versucht Jessica Benjamin zu klären, warum wir trotz der bewußten Verpflichtung zu Gleichheit und Freiheit Beziehungen von Dominanz und Unterordnung akzeptieren und leben. Nachdem sie die komplexe Verflechtung familiär-geschlechtlicher und sozial-politischer Herrschaft demonstriert hat, die einen solchen psychologischen Prozeß von Mittäterschaft auslöst, bietet sie die intersubjektive Theorie anstelle der Konstruktion eines weiblichen Gegenbegriffs zu phallisch-symbolischem Begehren als feministischpsychologischen Interpretationsrahmen an.

Die intersubjektive Theorie siedelt Geschlechtsidentität in der Beziehung zwischen dem Selbst und den Anderen im Spannungsfeld zwischen Gleichsein und Differenz an. Sie konstruiert diese Beziehung nicht als lineare Bewegung zwischen Einssein und Getrenntsein, sondern als ein flexibles Erkennen, das die spannungsvolle und paradoxe Balance zwischen beiden aufrechterhalten kann. So kann sich eine Person abwechselnd als "Ich - eine Frau"; "Ich - ein geschlechtsloses Subjekt"; "Ich - wie ein Mann oder: wie eine Frau" erleben. Eine Person, die diese Flexibilität bewahrt, kann alle Teile ihrer eigenen Persönlichkeit und der anderer akzeptieren.[30]

Dieser intersubjektive Rahmen wird am besten mit der Metapher des 'offenen gebundenen Raumes' nach Benjamin symbolisiert. Diese Kategorie kann meines Erachtens nicht nur auf Individuen angewendet werden, sondern verweist auf einen Ort, wo die feministische Andersheit der Frauen-*ekklēsia* als offenes rhetorisches Forum vorgestellt werden kann, der eingebunden ist in die Frauenkämpfe gegen die vielfältigen Formen von Unterdrückung. Die Frauen-*ekklēsia*, nicht als Schwesternschaft oder Weiblichkeit beschrieben, sondern als 'offener gebundener Raum' kann feministische Gemeinschaft und

---

[29] Jessica Benjamin, *Die Fesseln der Liebe*, Frankfurt/Main 1993.
[30] Benjamin, *Die Fesseln der Liebe*, 112.

historische Kontinuität zur Sprache bringen, ohne die existierenden Erfahrungs- und Machtunterschiede zwischen Frauen und die zwischen Männern und Frauen zu verleugnen. Statt einer uniformen, diskursiven Oppositionsgemeinschaft ist Frauen-*ekklēsia* am besten konzipiert als eine Koalition sich überschneidender feministischer Teilgemeinden und quasi-unabhängiger Bereiche, die alle ein gemeinsames Interesse an der Veränderung patriarchaler Herrschaft haben. Als feministisch offener Raum ist die *ekklēsia* oder das Parlament der Frauen nicht als ein einheitlicher monolithischer Block, sondern als ein heterogenes, vielsprachiges Forum von miteinander konkurrierenden Diskursen zu sehen.

Ethik und Politik der Solidarität in der Frauen-*ekklēsia*
Als Schnittpunkt einer Reihe von öffentlichen, feministischen Diskursen und als ein Ort umkämpfter soziopolitischer Widersprüche, feministischer Alternativen und bisher unrealisierter Möglichkeiten verlangt die Frauen-*ekklēsia* nach einer rhetorischen und nicht nach einer positivistischen wissenschaftlichen Konzeptualisierung feministischer Theorie und Theologie.[31] Um *ekklēsia* als diskursives, öffentliches und demokratisches Forum zu konstituieren, das Frauen als eine politisch-historische Kategorie bestimmen kann, müssen feministischtheologische Diskurse unterschiedliche rhetorische Strategien gleichzeitig einsetzen und sich zugleich zwischen ihnen hin und her bewegen, anstatt solche Strategien als starre gegensätzliche Positionen zu betrachten, die einander ausschließen. Als solche wichtige feministischtheologische Strategien schlage ich vor: Die Rhetorik der Befreiung, die Rhetorik der Differenzen und nicht nur der Differenz, die Rhetorik der Solidarität und die Rhetorik der Vision.

Feministisch theoretische Diskurse lassen sich daher am besten im Sinne der klassischen beratenden Rhetorik verstehen. Eine solche Rhetorik sucht demokratische Versammlungen zu überzeugen und Argumente abzuwägen, um Entscheidungen zum Wohle der *ekklēsia* zu treffen. Feministische Theologie und Strategie muß zum Beispiel vermitteln zwischen Argumenten für das ewig Weibliche oder einmütiger Schwesterlichkeit und Argumenten für eine historischpolitische Partikularität von Frauen, die Klasse, Rasse, Geschlecht, ethnische Zugehörigkeit und sexuelle Vorliebe zugleich in Betracht ziehen. Ein solches Miteinanderzu-Rate-Gehen der Frauen-*ekklēsia*

---

[31] Vgl. mein Buch *But She Said. Feminist Practices of Biblical Interpretation*, Boston 1992.

im Kontext diverser Kämpfe und politischer Koalitionen, kann unterschiedliche diskursive feministische Stimmen, die sich in einer Vielfalt intellektueller Denkvorstellungen und konkurrierender Interessengruppen äußern, positiv anerkennen.

Wenn unterschiedliche feministische Öffentlichkeiten ihre Analysen, Voraussetzungen und Strategien verschieden formulieren, wird es notwendig, solch konkurrierende feministische Wirklichkeitsdefinitionen und alternative Konstruktionen von Symbolwelten sorgfältig abzuwägen und zu diskutieren. Solche konkurrierende feministische Analysen von patriarchaler Realität und divergierende Artikulationen von feministischen Zielen und Utopien sind nicht einfach entweder richtig oder falsch. Sie dürfen nicht als doktrinäre Positionen verstanden, sondern müssen als strategische Handlungsentwürfe beurteilt werden. Als eine Form solcher rhetorischer Interventionen verlangt feministische Theologie nach öffentlicher Diskussion und Abwägung, wenn sie nicht in dogmatisches Sektierertum ausarten soll. Wenn es nicht nur *eine* feministische Strategie und *eine* wahre Position, sondern eine Vielfalt feministischer Strategien und Diskurse gibt, muß feministische Theologie und Praxis in und durch verantwortliche Streitgespräche und pragmatische Lösungen verkörpert werden.

Die Frauen-*ekklēsia* kann einen solchen vielsprachigen feministischen Diskurs bereitstellen, in den individuelle Frauen ihre eigene Geschichte im Gespräch mit der Geschichte zeitgenössischer, historischer oder biblischer Frauen einbringen können. Solche Diskurse müssen diejenigen Frauen sichtbar und hörbar machen, die bisher auch in feministischen Diskursen nicht genügend vorkommen. Indem sie auf die theoretische und praktische Hörbarkeit von farbigen, lesbischen, alten, armen, behinderten oder fremden Frauen bestehen, können feministische Theorie und Theologie deutlich machen, daß 'Frauen' kein einheitliches weibliches Wesen haben, sondern eine historisch gewachsene kulturelle und religiöse Vielfalt repräsentieren - nicht nur als Gruppen, sondern auch als Individuen. So haben z.B. viele amerikanische Frauen nicht nur afrikanische, sondern auch uramerikanische, europäische und asiatische Vorfahren. Schließlich müssen die feministischen Diskurse der Frauen *ekklēsia* auch darauf achten, daß sie nicht eine bestimmte Gruppe von Frauen, wie z.B. Lesben, als monolithische und undifferenzierte Größe frei von gegensätzlichen Interessen, Werten und

Konflikten darstellen.[32]

Kurz, eine solche Konzeptualisierung von Frauen-*ekklēsia* als demokratisch-feministisches Forum für praktische Beratung und verantwortliche Wahl braucht nicht die Debatten über unterschiedliche theoretische Ansätze und Strategien zu verdrängen, sondern kann solche Diskussionen hervorrufen und pflegen. Anstatt theoretisch-praktische Unterschiede als spaltend für die Frauenbefreiungsbewegung unter den Tisch zu kehren, müssen wir eine Streitkultur pflegen, die aufzeigen kann, wie diese feministischen Positionen und Argumente mit herrschenden Diskursen verflochten sind oder mit konkurrierenden Bedürfnissen von Teilgruppen der Frauenbefreiungsbewegung zusammenhängen. Durch ständiges Auslösen von freundlicher Kritik, Diskussion und Konfrontation kann die Frauen-*ekklēsia* nach besser geeigneten Strategien und überzeugenderen Visionen suchen, um systemischpatriarchale Spaltung zu vermeiden und eine bessere feministische Wirklichkeit zu schaffen. Indem sie umstrittene Konzepte und Voraussetzungen klären und beurteilen, wollen feministische Befreiungsdiskurse einen langen Prozeß ethischer Reflexion und praktischer Solidarität in verschiedenen, oft miteinander konkurrierenden Befreiungskämpfen fördern.

Die Entwicklung einer Ethik und Politik der Solidarität ist deshalb wichtig für die dialogische und strategische Praxis der Frauen-*ekklēsia*, weil ihre verschiedenen Teilgruppen sich nicht nur durch Rasse, Klasse, Kultur oder Religion voneinander, sondern auch durch institutionelle Positionen, berufliche Bildung und konfessionelle Überzeugung[33] unterscheiden und sich auf eine große Spannbreite von theoretischen Ansätzen berufen können. Doch selbst wenn eine solche feministischrhetorische Praxis dazu verlockt, dürfen theoretische und strategische Differenzen nicht in einen lähmenden Pluralismus ausarten, der sogar die reaktionärste Politik als feministisch ausgeben kann. Eine Ethik der Solidarität muß besonders diejenigen patriarchalen Herrschaftszusammenhänge, die in ihre eigenen Diskurse und Strategien eingeschrieben sind, klar benennen. Sie muß feministische Beurteilungs- und Bewertungskriterien formulieren, die die Theorien und Strategien derjenigen FeministInnen bevorzugen, die aus der Erfahrung von multiplikativen patriarchalen Unterdrückungsstrukturen heraus sprechen.

---

[32] E. Frances White, "Africa on My Mind. Gender, Counter Discourse and African-American Nationalism", in: *JWH* 2/1, 1990, 87.
[33] Felski, *Beyond Feminist Aesthetics*. 171.

Wenn es nicht nur eine einzige richtige feministische Position, sondern eine Vielfalt von feministisch diskursiven Handlungsmöglichkeiten gibt, kann eine feministische Ethik und Politik der Solidarität nicht in unkritischer Zustimmung bestehen. Vielmehr muß sie in verantwortlicher Debatte und praktischem Urteil realisiert werden. Sie sollte sich in dialogischen Erwägungen ethisch-politischer Handlungsmöglichkeiten und dem Versuch bewähren, nicht nur zu entscheiden, was als nächstes zu tun ist, sondern auch, was in einer bestimmten Situation und für eine bestimmte Gruppe von Frauen am besten ist.

Eine feministische Ethik und Politik der Solidarität setzt daher die demokratische Handlungsvollmacht und Selbstbestimmung von Frauen als conditio sine qua non voraus. Frauen haben das Recht und die Macht, ihre eigene Realität zu interpretieren und ihre eigenen Ziele zu bestimmen. Doch darf eine Gruppe von Frauen nicht vorgeben, für alle Frauen zu sprechen. Miteinander im Konflikt stehend Interessen von Frauen müssen in öffentlicher Diskussion ausgesprochen und bewertet werden, damit Strategien von Solidarität zwischen Frauen geschmiedet werden können. Die Frauen-*ekklēsia* muß zugleich ihre eigene diskursive Praxis kritisch hinterfragen, um so die Selbstbestimmung individueller Frauen und feministischer Teilgruppen zu gewährleisten. Welche Stimmen dürfen reden? Welche Stimmen werden nie laut oder gehört? Wer darf reden, welche Geschichten sind noch zu erzählen und welche Vorschläge noch zu machen? Einander widersprechende Interessen als gültig anzuerkennen, kann für weiße westliche FeministInnen heißen, Macht abzugeben. Kurz, die Frauen-*ekklēsia* muß Modelle dafür schaffen, wie Menschen in komplexen Situationen und Machtverhältnissen zusammenarbeiten können, ohne sich gegenseitig auszubeuten.

Positiv sucht eine feministische Ethik und Politik der Solidarität ein vielgestaltiges Befreiungsbewußtsein zu entwickeln, das die multiplikative Verästelung patriarchaler Herrschaft sowohl in der herrschenden Gesellschaft als auch in Befreiungsbewegungen selbst ausloten und in Frage stellen kann. Sie besteht darauf, daß Frauen, die unter mehrfachen Unterdrückungsstrukturen leiden, nicht nur Opfer sind, sondern auch Strategien zu täglichem Widerstand entwickelt haben. Gleichzeitig hat sie die Verherrlichung der geopferten 'Anderen' und die romantische Verklärung farbiger oder armer Frauen in Frage zu stellen - eine Romantisierung, die so typisch ist für westliche privilegierte Frauen.

Als radikal demokratische *ekklēsia* können Frauen verschiedener Gruppierungen, wenn sie wollen, miteinander als Individuen zusammenarbeiten ohne immer als Repräsentantinnen ihrer Rasse, Klasse, Kultur oder Religion sprechen zu müssen. Eine Ethik und Politik der Solidarität sucht daher Respekt und 'Befreundung' zwischen Frauen zu fördern, aber legt dazu nicht die 'natürliche' Solidarität von Weiblichkeit oder die feministische Freundschaft der Schwesterlichkeit zugrunde. Wenn für feministische Identitätsfindung in der Frauen-*ekklēsia* letztlich nicht Geschlecht und Biologie, sondern historische Erfahrungen und Kämpfe gegen patriarchale Herrschaft konstitutiv sind, muß eine Ethik und Politik der Solidarität darauf achten, wie wir unsere Geschichten erzählen und wie wir Frauengeschichte schreiben. Ich habe diesen Beitrag mit einem Gedicht von Adrienne Rich begonnen, das die Kämpfe unserer Vormütter und Vorschwestern im 19. Jahrhundert beschreibt. Doch selbst dieses Gedicht einer bekannten amerikanischen Feministin erzählt die Geschichte des feministischen Frauenkampfes als die Geschichte von weißen, amerikanischen, privilegierten Frauen. Die amerikanischen UreinwohnerInnen, die afrikanischen SklavInnen und die weißen Immigrantinnen aus der europäischen Unterschicht kommen nur als Opfer vor. Selbst in feministischer Geschichtsrekonstruktion sind somit Frauen, die als Frauen und als AfrikanerInnen, EinwanderInnen, Arme, oder Eingeborene für gleiche Rechte gekämpft haben, weithin abwesend. In dieses geschichtliche Schweigen hinein müssen die Visionen und Kämpfe von marginalisierten oder totgeschwiegenen Frauen gesprochen werden, wenn der Feminismus weißer, privilegierter Frauen sich über seine dualistische 'Geschlechtsgefangenschaft' und Mittäterschaft hinausbewegen soll. Ich möchte daher mit einer Rede der afrikanisch-amerikanischen Feministin Anna Julia Cooper schließen, die eine solche inklusive Vision ausdrückt und uns in den offenen gebundenen Raum der Frauen-*ekklēsia* hineinführen kann.

Nun ich denke, falls ich die Stimmung meiner Anhängerschaft herauskristallisieren und diesem Kongreß als Botschaft überbringen könnte, so wäre dies etwa folgendes: Laßt die Ansprüche der Frauen im Konkreten ebenso umfassend sein wie im Abstrakten. Wir stehen auf dem Standpunkt der Solidarität mit der Menschheit, der Einheit des Lebens und der Unnatürlichkeit und Ungerechtigkeit aller besonderen Bevorzugung, ganz gleich ob aufgrund des Geschlechts, der Rasse, der Nationalität oder der Geburt. Wenn auch nur ein Glied einer Kette zerbrochen wird, so wird die ganze Kette durchbrochen. Eine Brücke ist nicht stärker als ihr schwächstes Glied und eine Sache nicht wertvoller als ihr schwächstes Element..... Wir fordern keinen engen Torweg für uns selbst, unsere Rasse, unser Geschlecht oder unsere Glaubensgemeinschaft, sondern eine breite Hauptstraße für die Menschheit. Die farbige Frau fühlt, daß die Sache der Frauen eine und universal ist, und solange nicht das Bild Gottes, ganz gleich ob aus Elfenbein oder aus Ebenholz, heilig und unzerstörbar ist; solange nicht

Rasse, Farbe, Geschlecht und Geburt als Zufall und nicht als Wesen des Lebens gesehen werden; solange nicht der universale Anspruch der Menschheit auf Leben, Freiheit und Streben nach Glück allen unveräußerlich zusteht; solange ist die Lehre der Frauen nicht gelehrt und die Sache der Frauen nicht gewonnen - nicht die der weißen, der schwarzen oder der roten Frau... Das Zustandekommen ihrer 'Rechte' wird den endgültigen Triumph von Recht über Gewalt, die Überlegenheit der moralischen Vernunftkräfte und der Gerechtigkeit und der Liebe in der Regierung aller Nationen dieser Erde bedeuten.[34]

---

[34] Bert Lowenberg, Ruth Bogin (Hg.), *Black Women in Nineteenth-Century American Life. Their Words, Their Thoughts, Their Feelings*, University Park 1976, 330ff.

Summary

Fiorenza criticises the tendency in European-American feminist theory and theology to universalize gender difference. In her opinion, this masks the complex interstructuring of patriarchal dominations inscribed in the lives of individual women. She argues that we need to clear a discursive space where women as a political collectivity can define ourselves without needing to suppress the patriarchal structural divisions between us. For Fiorenza the *ekklēsia* of women is such an open rhetorical space bounded by its struggle against multiform oppression. Here, different strategies can be developed and the conflicting interests of women can be articulated and adjudicated within an ethic of solidarity.

Sommaire

Dans les théories et théologies féministes d'Europe et d'Amérique du Nord, Schüssler Fiorenza critique la tendance à universaliser la différence des "genres" (masc./fém.). Selon son opinion, cette universalisation en arrive à masquer les structures interdépendantes et complexes des dominations patriarchiques inscrites dans la vie personnelle des femmes, ainsi que dans les relations de domination et de subordination que existent entre les femmes elles-mêmes.

Elle soutient qu'il est nécéssaire de dégager un espace discursif dans lequel les femmes, en tant que collectivité politique, puissent se définir elles-mêmes sans avoir besoin de supprimer les divisions structurelles patriarcales qui existent entre elles.

Pour Schüssler Fiorenza, "*Ekklēsia* des femmes" est un de ces espaces rhétoriques ouvert, dans lequel se retrouvent les luttes contre les formes multiples d'oppression. Là, des stratégies différentes peuvent se mettre en place, et les interêts conflictuels des femmes peuvent être définis et répartis, dans une éthique de solidarité.

Elisabeth Schüssler Fiorenza ist Professorin für Neues Testament an der Harvard Divinity School in Cambridge (USA). Neben vielen Buchpublikationen wie "Zu ihrem Gedächtnis", "Brot statt Steine" und "Mirjam's Child and Sophia's Prophet" ist sie eine der inspirierendsten Initiatorinnen und Mitarbeiterinnen der internationalen Frauenkirchebewegung.

Maria Kassel

Image de Dieu - Identité des femmes - Eglise de femmes

Introduction

Une Eglise de femmes - quelle que soit la façon dont elle se conçoive: en tant qu'Eglise au sein des Eglises ou en tant qu'entité cherchant à s'émanciper par rapport aux Eglises patriarcales, - devra en tous cas s'interroger sur l'influence directe et indirecte de l'image chrétienne de Dieu. Car dans une religion théiste telle que le christianisme, c'est-à-dire une religion où le principal symbole religieux est l'image d'un Dieu personnifié, cette représentation divine détermine non seulement les enseignements théologiques, mais aussi dans une large mesure la conception de l'être humain. Et cette conception à son tour se manifeste dans les pratiques religieuses telles que le culte; elle intervient également au niveau des rôles qu'hommes et femmes sont amenés à assumer dans leur vie quotidienne. De même, l'identité et le sentiment d'identité de ceux dont la foi est centrée sur l'image de Dieu obéit à l'idée de ce que l'on est ou est censé/censée être. Si donc une Eglise de femmes réfléchit aux symboles religieux significatifs pour la conscience féminine, elle sera forcément amenée à remettre en question l'image traditionnelle de Dieu du christianisme.

C'est pourquoi je voudrais dans ce texte étudier la corrélation entre l'image chrétienne de Dieu et la conception de l'être humain qui en résulte, en mettant l'accent sur la formation de l'identité féminine et sur l'influence exercée par cette image divine au niveau de la situation ecclésiale des femmes. Ce faisant, je me réfère à ma propre expérience dans le cadre du christianisme catholique-romain; mais on verra sans doute que les énoncés fondamentaux concernant la représentation divine et ses implications anthropologiques s'appliquent également à d'autres confessions chrétiennes.

L'approche herméneutique et méthodique que j'ai choisie pour aborder ce thème relève de la psychanalyse féministe: la perspective féministe s'intéresse à la réalité et aux effets inconscients, pour ainsi dire souterrains, des symboles religieux. Je m'efforcerai d'éclaircir certains facteurs inconscients en analysant le rapport qu'il y a entre l'image divine et la formation de l'identité féminine.

Mon étude s'articulera autour de six thèses dérivant l'une de l'autre; celles-ci seront justifiées et commentées au fur et à mesure. *in proportia as*

Thèse 1: Selon la conception chrétienne fondamentale, Dieu est masculin et il est père

Cette thèse correspond à une idée (révélation) généralement admise et souvent critiquée par la théologie féministe. Mais c'est seulement en observant la manière dont cette idée se concrétise dans les énoncés théologiques que l'on peut mesurer la portée de cette affirmation. Quelques citations permettront d'illustrer ce phénomène.

Au sein de la théologie, c'est de la psychologie religieuse que l'on est en droit d'espérer une présentation et une analyse critique de l'image chrétienne de Dieu. Chez le père de la psychologie religieuse en Europe, A. Vergote, on trouve les phrases suivantes:

> *Dans la ... tradition judéo-chrétienne, le ... nom de Père est l'insigne suprême d'un Dieu qui s'est révélé dans sa majesté et sa radicale transcendance, d'un Dieu qui conteste inlassablement les anthropomorphismes religieux et les idolâtries. (155)*

> *... à son propre niveau déjà, l'image du père présente davantage que la figure simplement symétrique et inverse de la mère. (192)*

> *... au-delà de ses applications au réel humain, ce schéma (= de Dieu le père, M.K.) vise une réalité plus fondamentale, une loi de l'être humain et du monde, peut-être même un Père absolu qui fonde toute paternité humaine. (186)* [1]

Trois aspects caractérisent ce que Vergote nous dit à propos de la paternité divine:

a) "Majesté et radicale transcendance"; ceci établit une distance par rapport à l'être humain et implique l'éloignement, la supériorité et la domination.

b) Comparée à l'image paternelle de Dieu, la "figure de la mère" - pas

---

[1] Antoine Vergote, *Psychologie Religieuse*, Bruxelles 1966.
Les quelques citations choisies sont représentatives de la teneur de ce livre qui se prétend le résultat d'études empiriques.

son image - lui est inverse, c'est-à-dire qu'elle est secondaire; ici, le mot "symétrique" signifie que la mère est dérivée de l'image du père, qu'elle est élaborée à partir de l'image du père et va lui faire pendant.

c) Le "Père" est non seulement prédicat de Dieu, mais aussi "une loi de l'être humain et du monde". Par conséquent, la nature paternelle-masculine de Dieu détermine également la nature de l'être humain et du monde (entier?). Peut-on, sur le plan religieux, trouver une justification plus complète du patriarcat? Chez Vergote, le concept de la paternité de Dieu procède d'une psychologie qui est, d'une certaine façon, tordue: ce n'est pas par analogie et différenciation que ce concept est dérivé de la paternité humaine empirique; au contraire, la paternité divine est envisagée comme un fait primordial, donc comme un postulat théologique que Vergote qualifie de "révélation", et c'est la paternité empirique qui en est dérivée. Dans une telle perspective psychologico-religieuse, l'analyse critique de l'image paternelle de Dieu est impossible.

Si l'interprétation de Vergote date déjà d'un quart de siècle, la principale signification de la paternité divine est toujours d'actualité dans la théologie. En 1981, la revue internationale "Concilium" a publié un numéro consacré au thème: "Dieu le père?". Dans l'introduction, le fondateur de la théologie politique, J.B. Metz, écrit: "'Dieu le père?' C'est une question cruciale pour le dogme chrétien".[2]

Le point d'interrogation derrière le titre trahit chez les théologiens masculins un certain flottement en ce qui concerne le prédicat "Père" associé à Dieu. Pourtant la théologie psychologique et la théologie politique, deux courants qui en d'autres domaines sont plutôt opposés, font preuve d'une remarquable concordance de vues quand il s'agit de reconnaître l'importance majeure de l'énoncé chrétien: Dieu est père. Du coup, la critique féministe de l'image divine paternelle représente une critique fondamentale de la tradition et du dogme ecclésial.

A une époque plus récente, H. Wöller a défini ce que l'image divine paternelle signifie du point de vue féministe:

Au cours des vingt dernières années, un nombre croissant de femmes s'est rebellé contre le fait que l'on s'adresse à Dieu en l'appelant "Père". Le concept d'un Dieu paternel ne leur permet pas d'y associer une figure à laquelle elles puissent faire confiance, qu'elles puissent

---

[2]   Concilium D 17 (1981) 3, 173.

aimer, mais évoque au contraire le despotisme et la violence. Cette contestation des femmes a suscité et suscite encore maintes frayeurs et beaucoup d'incompréhension. C'est comme si les femmes venaient ébranler les fondements mêmes de la foi chrétienne.[3]

Le rejet de la représentation divine chrétienne évoqué par H. Wöller est dû au fait que cette représentation est à la fois globale, étriquée et limitative. En gros, cette image divine se présente comme suit: Dieu est conçu comme une personne de sexe masculin et sa nature se manifeste dans la paternité: paternité par rapport à Jésus-Christ d'une part, par rapport aux êtres humains d'autre part, les êtres humains étant dans une très large mesure assimilés à des "fils".[4] Dans le christianisme, la parole de Dieu est androcentrée, car elle est axée sur des perspectives et des valeurs masculines, et elle est patriarcale, car centrée sur une image paternelle qui implique toujours domination et éloignement du monde. Dans les systèmes qui résultent de cette représentation divine, les femmes et les valeurs liées à la vie féminine n'ont en fait aucune place; elles peuvent au mieux y être tolérées. Cette situation, qui prévaut depuis longtemps dans les structures ecclésiales aussi bien que dans les structures psychiques, repose sans aucun doute sur des causes profondes.

Thèse 2: L'image chrétienne de Dieu est une réduction théologique et anthropologique

Une religion monothéiste se caractérise par une représentation de Dieu restrictive, qui exclut les images multiples et diversifiées du divin. Dans le christianisme, le "Toi seul es saint, Toi seul es le Seigneur, Toi seul es le Très Haut"[5] s'applique aussi à l'image de Dieu. Du point de vue théologique, le Dieu masculin est une réduction, car la réalité indicible de Dieu est assimilée à *une seule* image (cet aspect sera approfondi dans la thèse 3); du point de vue anthropologique, c'est une réduction car cette image sert à opprimer l'*un* des deux sexes, les femmes, à l'amoindrir dans sa dignité humaine et l'aliéner dans son identité, et ce au profit de l'élévation de l'autre sexe, les hommes.

Dans les deux sens il s'agit du processus de la projection. Ce Dieu

---

[3] Hildegunde Wöller, *Vom Vater verwundet*, Stuttgart 1991, 7.
[4] Cf. Paul, p. ex. Galatéens 3,26; 4,1-7; Romains 8,14-17 e.a.
[5] Cf. le Gloria de la messe catholique.

totalement annexé par les hommes nous montre que ceux-ci omettent de développer par eux-mêmes leur propre force intérieure; ils refusent le travail psychique nécessaire pour aller sublimer dans le divin leur potentiel humain non-réalisé et échapper ainsi à la critique concernant leur refus de se développer par eux-mêmes. Dès qu'il est transposé dans Dieu, c'est-à-dire projeté en lui, ce manque masculin est interprété comme un pouvoir sur..., puisqu'il est de caractère divin; et puisqu'il est masculin, les hommes considèrent qu'ils sont invités à participer à ce pouvoir. Ce processus inconscient est parfaitement illustré par l'aphorisme de M. Daly: "Si Dieu est masculin, le masculin est Dieu".[6]

Cette projection consolide une immaturité psychique de l'homme; l'incomplétude masculine étant une non-valeur, elle est reportée sur la femme; là, elle est ridiculisée, punie, on essaie même de l'exterminer au nom du pouvoir masculin-divin sur...

La comparaison avec des religions nées dans le même espace géographique que le christianisme mais qui étaient axées sur une image *féminine* de Dieu fait apparaître que ce substrat inconscient est propre aux représentations divines exclusivement masculines. Dans les figurations des déesses de l'Orient antique en effet, le sexe masculin est toujours inclue: soit sous forme de divinités masculines autonomes, soit par une symbolique masculine qui est associée à la déesse, comme celle du fils-amant de la déesse qui meurt et est ressuscité par elle.[7] Dans les représentations divines masculines des religions monothéistes en revanche, l'élément féminin a été totalement éliminé.

Certes, en ce qui concerne l'Eglise catholique, on ne peut nier que Marie, "la déesse secrète dans le christianisme"[8], supplée/suppléait en quelque sorte à l'élément féminin absent de la représentation divine, surtout dans la religiosité populaire. Néanmoins, je ne crois pas que Marie puisse nous sauver du caractère unilatéralement masculin de l'image divine chrétienne, car l'ecclésiologie et la mariologie ont toujours catégoriquement rejeté la divinité de Marie.

Certaines tendances de la théologie féministe[9] espèrent trouver une issue

---

[6] Mary Daly, *Jenseits von Gottvater, Sohn & Co.*, München 1980, 33.

[7] Comme p. ex. dans le mythe sumérien d'Inanna et dans la religion babylonienne d'Ishtar, ainsi que dans le mythe égyptien d'Isis.

[8] D'après le titre d'un livre de Christa Mulack, *Maria. Die geheime Göttin im Christentum*, Stuttgart 1985.

[9] Cf. p. ex. Catharina J.M. Halkes, *Suchen, was verloren ging* (GTB 487), Gütersloh 1985,

grâce à la troisième personne de la Trinité, le Saint Esprit; dans la Bible hébraïque en effet, le mot "Esprit" est du point de vue linguistique une entité féminine: "ruah" dans le sens d'Esprit féminin, de force créatrice et vitale. Et dans la Trinité, l'Esprit n'incarne pas un principe masculin dominateur, mais bien la relation d'amour entre le Père et le Fils qui, de toute éternité, engendre l'Esprit. Cependant, il ne faut pas perdre de vue que l'Esprit (féminin/masculin) est l'amour personnifié de deux entités divines *masculines*. C'est de l'amour Père-Fils qu'il s'agit ici, pas d'une relation entre ou avec des femmes; l'Esprit non plus n'incarne ni la mère, ni la fille, ni la partenaire. Vouloir dépasser la réduction de l'image divine masculine à l'aide des symboles traditionnels de "Marie" et de "l'Esprit féminin/masculin" risque donc d'être illusoire.

Thèse 3: Il existe une interaction entre l'image de Dieu et le niveau psychique de la communauté religieuse, ici l'Eglise

Dans la thèse 2, nous avons déjà évoqué la corrélation entre le niveau de conscience des hommes et l'image de Dieu. Cette corrélation existe aussi dans un sens plus large et même fondamental. Comme tout discours sur Dieu procède de la conscience humaine, il peut seulement dire de Dieu ce que la conscience humaine, finie et limitée, est en mesure de comprendre. Il ne s'agit donc jamais de Dieu en soi, puisqu'IL/ELLE est une entité illimitée. La conception humaine de Dieu et le discours qui s'y rattache doivent se contenter de comparaisons, d'images, de représentations issues de la réalité finie pour aborder l'infinitude de la réalité divine. Même l'*expérience* directe de Dieu doit se servir de ces images à la fois ressemblantes et dissemblables pour s'exprimer. Du coup, penser, sentir et parler de Dieu se fait toujours par le biais d'images; et il peut, non, il faut qu'il y ait beaucoup d'images de Dieu pour éviter de LE/LA identifier à *une seule* image.

De ce fait, les représentations divines reflètent toujours aussi le niveau de conscience et le système de valeurs de la communauté religieuse qui se réfère à ces images. Si dans le christianisme Dieu est essentiellement représenté par des images masculines et principalement présenté comme étant le Père, cela

---

notamment: "Unsere Mutter, der Heilige Geist", 159 sqq.; *Das Antlitz der Erde erneuern* (GTB 499), Gütersloh 1990: à divers endroits. Elisabeth Moltmann-Wendel, *Das Land wo Milch und Honig fließt* (GTB 486), Gütersloh 1985, chapitre: "Gott, unsere Mutter", 97 sqq. et ailleurs.

signifie que la conscience de la communauté religieuse y est régie par les phantasmes et les valeurs de la vie masculine. Les Eglises et les sociétés fondées sur une conscience patriarcale sont incapables d'avoir d'autres représentations de Dieu que celles du type masculin-paternel.

Or, si le niveau de conscience détermine les représentations divines, ces représentations influencent à leur tour le niveau de conscience. Le sexe représenté dans l'image de Dieu devient le modèle de la condition humaine et participe finalement de la souveraineté et de la puissance de Dieu. C'est ainsi que, dans le christianisme, l'homme peut faire remonter **son** identité humaine à Dieu, un processus qui s'opère même lorsque les hommes ne le font pas consciemment; car dans les Eglises et les sociétés marquées par le christianisme, la corrélation entre le sexe masculin et l'image de Dieu est depuis longtemps une réalité profondément enracinée et agissante au niveau de l'inconscient.

Ceci permet notamment d'expliquer une psychologie "tordue" comme celle de Vergote[10]: l'image divine paternelle est devenue si évidente que son origine psychique a été oubliée; elle produit désormais un effet (rétroactif) universel puisque la paternité s'est élargie jusqu'à devenir une "loi de l'être humain et du monde". Quoique ce processus s'opère au niveau inconscient, il influence profondément la conscience: il fait partie intégrante de la théologie et constitue une prémisse de l'action ecclésiale.

Thèse 4: Les représentations divines sont étroitement liées à l'identité humaine

Dans le christianisme, ce lien est le fondement même du dogme, en vertu duquel l'être humain fut créé à l'image de Dieu; son origine biblique se trouve dans la Genèse 1, 27:

> *Ainsi Dieu créa l'homme ('adam) à son image;*
> *il le créa à l'image de Dieu.*
> *Il créa un homme et une femme.*

Cette ressemblance à l'image de Dieu est ici expressément stipulée pour les deux sexes. Malgré cela, la réalité de la vie des femmes n'a jamais été

---

[10] Cf. note 1.

représentée dans l'image divine et du coup, la dignité de la femme n'a pas été garantie. Bien au contraire: jusqu'à une époque assez récente, on a toujours nié que la femme fût directement à l'image de Dieu; en commençant par Paul: 1 Corinthiens 11, 7, selon lequel l'homme est l'image et la gloire de Dieu (eikón kaì dóxa theou), la femme la gloire de l'homme (dóxa andròs); et dans V.3, cet ordre hiérarchique divin-masculin est justifié comme suit: Jésus est le seigneur de l'homme, l'homme le seigneur de la femme et Dieu le seigneur du Christ. A partir de cet ordre hiérarchique, l'Epître aux Ephésiens post-paulinienne (5, 22-24) formule à l'égard des femmes l'exigence qu'elles se soumettent aux hommes. Avec ce texte, qui accompagnait l'ancien rite nuptial catholique, d'innombrables générations de femmes ont été condamnées à la soumission vis-à-vis de l'homme et du Dieu conçu comme étant masculin. Dans les déclarations ecclésiastiques et théologiques, on trouve des milliers d'exemples pour attester ce fait: quand l'image de Dieu est exclusivement masculine, l'homme est divinisé et la femme dévalorisée sur le plan humain. Prenons un exemple dont les effets se sont fait sentir pendant longtemps. Thomas d'Aquin (XIIIe siècle), dont les écrits ont encore fait autorité jusqu'au milieu de ce siècle dans la théologie catholique-romaine, dit ceci:

> *L'image de Dieu se trouve dans l'homme, mais pas dans la femme. Car l'homme est l'origine et le but de la femme, tout comme Dieu est l'origine et le but de toute la création.*[11]

On ne s'étonnera guère de ce que les Droits de l'Homme qui, d'une certaine manière, consacrent cette ressemblance à l'image de Dieu sous une forme laïque, aient encore été refusés aux femmes sous la Révolution française (1789). Même dans la "Déclaration universelle des droits de l'homme" des Nations-Unies de 1948, les êtres humains sont invités à la "fraternité" au lieu de "l'amour du prochain" (article 1).

Pratiquement jusqu'à l'époque contemporaine, la femme ne pouvait prétendre à cette ressemblance à l'image Dieu que si elle se conformait à l'image que les hommes se font des femmes. Or, comme la symbolique de la représentation divine chrétienne a toujours exclu les aspects féminins, le christianisme a empêché la formation d'une authentique identité féminine. Les phantasmes masculins sur l'identité de la femme ont oscillé entre deux pôles: Eve, celle

---

[11]   *Summa theologiae* I,93,4 ad 1.

qui invite au péché et Marie, la femme pure privée de sexualité. Même chez un théologien psychanalyste comme Eugen Drewermann[12], on retrouve cette image dédoublée de la femme. Par le biais de la représentation divine chrétienne, les femmes ont été privées de leur propre identité psychique et n'ont pas eu la possibilité de devenir le sujet de leur vie et de leur foi.

La discrimination et les injustices dont les femmes font l'objet dans les Eglises, notamment leur exclusion du sacerdoce dans l'Eglise catholique-romaine - récemment réaffirmée et entérinée (!) par le Pape -[13] reposent sur des motifs beaucoup plus profonds qu'on ne le pense en général, même dans le mouvement féministe. Tant que le niveau de conscience des hommes sera inconsciemment légitimé par une seule et unique image divine - l'image masculine - et tant que le niveau de conscience des femmes sera limité par cette même image, les modifications du statut ecclésial des sexes ne seront guère plus que des retouches de façade. A eux seuls, les processus d'émancipation ne suffiront pas à supprimer la valorisation inégale des sexes et à libérer les femmes. Il faut des changements psychiques profonds et à long terme. A mon avis, les projets visant à créer une Eglise de femmes devraient absolument en tenir compte. Les structures d'une Eglise de femmes doivent elles aussi être enracinées dans un substrat psychique inconscient. Les femmes élevées dans la foi chrétienne, ainsi que celles qui ont déjà travaillé dans l'Eglise, doivent envisager cela comme un processus de longue durée; car l'enracinement dans une symbolique et des structures religieuses appropriées aux femmes implique un déracinement: l'abandon de l'ancienne image de Dieu qui a sécurisé les femmes aussi.

Mais espérer le soutien des Eglises masculines sera, probablement longtemps encore, illusoire. Car les hommes n'ont pas envie d'opérer un changement aussi radical en eux-mêmes, surtout s'il s'agit d'une remise en question de la représentation divine qui stabilise leur niveau de conscience masculin. D'après mon expérience, ceci ne s'applique d'ailleurs pas seulement aux hommes de l'Eglise catholique, mais aussi à ceux des Eglises réformées. Dans des groupes de travail, j'ai souvent constaté que ces derniers rejetaient les approches psychanalytiques et féministes de façon bien plus

---

[12] Cf. mon approche critique de la théologie psychanalytique de Drewermann, in: *rhs* (cours de religions dans les écoles supérieures) 33 (1990) 1, 48-57, et in: *Lutherische Monatshefte* 32 (1993) 5, 7-9.

[13] Cf. l'encyclique "Ordinatio Sacerdotalis", 1994.

fanatique que le clergé catholique. La Déesse archaïque de l'Antiquité invoquée par les femmes qui estiment pouvoir y trouver une image divine plus appropriée semble ici susciter l'anathème le plus virulent.

Thèse 5: Pour le Dieu masculin et les Eglises chrétiennes, la Déesse représente une instance critique

Dans la quête d'une identité féminine authentique, la référence à la Déesse revêt une grande importance. Du point de vue psychanalytique, la réflexion à son sujet ne vise pas à réactualiser un culte de la Déesse, mais à retrouver les origines non-patriarcales de la condition féminine et à symboliser en termes religieux les valeurs de l'existence féminine. C'est seulement lorsqu'on se place *à l'extérieur* de la tradition chrétienne que l'on commence à mesurer à quel point la réalité humaine et l'être sont morcelés et déformés dans une image de Dieu exclusivement masculine.

Les représentations des déesses de l'Orient antique par contre reflètent une unité et une totalité universelles qui s'expriment dans de *nombreuses* images de la divinité - ce que le christianisme a erronément assimilé au polythéisme. Je pense notamment à Inanna la sumérienne, Ishtar la babylonienne, Anat la syrienne, Isis l'égyptienne. Sous des noms et des visages multiples, la Déesse incarne la réalité *unique*: celle des femmes et des hommes, de l'histoire, de la nature et du cosmos, du monde matériel et de la vie psychique, autant d'aspects qui forment un tout homogène. Dans le rituel symbolique de la mort et de la renaissance, ou résurrection, le flux vital de ce tout est maintenu en marche, renouvelé et développé.

Certes, dans le christianisme aussi, l'unité et la totalité de toute la création est présentée comme étant l'oeuvre de Dieu qui s'en porte garant, mais dans les symboles, les rites et la pratique de la foi, ils ne sont guère présents puisque la moitié de l'humanité est exclue de l'image divine qui est au centre de la symbolique religieuse.

Le mythe de la Déesse comporte en outre des valeurs ayant trait à la non-violence, notamment l'idée d'une souffrance dénuée de violence, qui sont étrangères à l'image chrétienne de Dieu. Le mythe sumérien de la déesse Inanna, avec sa douloureuse descente aux Enfers et sa résurrection[14], est

---

[14] Le mythe date de la première moitié du IIe millénaire av. J.-C.; une traduction anglaise figure dans: D. Wolkstein / S.N. Kramer, *Inanna - Queen of Heaven and Earth*, New York

particulièrement intéressant: c'est de son plein gré que la déesse fait ce chemin pour aller mourir. Elle le fait au nom de tout ce qui vit; mais sa mort est sans violence, à l'inverse de la crucifixion de Jésus. Inanna meurt d'une mort naturelle. Et dans ce mythe, les concepts de renaissance et de résurrection sont interchangeables; avec le symbole de la naissance associé à cette représentation divine, la religion de la Déesse rend justice à la force créatrice féminine. Du point de vue de l'histoire des religions, l'évolution ultérieure des éléments fondamentaux de ce mythe fait apparaître que, avec l'émergence du patriarcat, le caractère destructif et la violence vont prendre de plus en plus de place dans ces traditions.[15]

Aujourd'hui, le souvenir de la Déesse peut - au-delà de sa fonction critique - aider les femmes à redécouvrir des forces ensevelies, sur le plan historique et personnel; en associant ces forces aux valeurs symbolisées par la Déesse, elles pourront progressivement trouver une identité authentique qui ne soit pas déterminée par l'imaginaire masculin.

Thèse 6: La transformation de l'Eglise et la création d'une Eglise de femmes sont impensables sans modification de l'image de Dieu

Etant donné que les représentations divines sont toujours en corrélation avec la réalité sociale et que l'image masculine de Dieu continue à conforter le sexe masculin, même dans les sociétés laïques qui ont volontairement écarté la référence à Dieu, il faut engager l'action au niveau socio-politique, aussi et surtout dans les Eglises. Et comme la supériorité du sexe masculin constitue un pouvoir établi de longue date, la libération du sexe soumis, les femmes, doit se faire par des moyens politiques. Cela exige une action commune de toutes les femmes, une action que les détenteurs du pouvoir devraient percevoir comme une pression venant de la base. Les institutions ecclésiastiques doivent enfin comprendre que ces actions ne vont pas à l'encontre du christianisme, qu'elles sont souvent provoqués par le refus de changement de ces mêmes institutions et de leurs représentants officiels.

Les femmes devraient apprendre à pratiquer une sorte d'insubordination civile vis-à-vis des Eglises. L'Eglise catholique-romaine fournit une preuve

1983, 51-73.
[15] Cf. Maria Kassel, "Tod und Auferstehung", in: *Feministische Theologie*, Stuttgart 1988, 191-226.

tout à fait actuelle de ce que les femmes, notamment les associations féminines, ne s'inclinent plus devant le refus catégorique opposé par le Pape à leur désir de participer aux ministères ecclésiaux; au contraire, dans leurs groupes de travail elles continuent à discuter énergiquement du sacerdoce des femmes; grâce à elles, ce thème est toujours à l'ordre du jour du débat ecclésiastique. Par ailleurs, la théologie féministe peut s'engager activement sur un autre plan, qui est étroitement lié au sujet de cette étude, et ce au sein de toutes les Eglises: elle doit poursuivre ses réflexions sur le thème de la Déesse, même s'il est ignoré par la théologie et l'Eglise des hommes, même s'il est ridiculisé, diffamé par ignorance[16] ou stigmatisé comme blasphématoire et impie par des chrétiens et chrétiennes de tendance fondamentaliste[17]. La grande diversité des réactions négatives montre en effet que la critique de l'image masculine de Dieu suscitée par le concept de la Déesse ébranle les fondements mêmes de l'identité chrétienne, aussi bien chez les hommes que chez les femmes. Continuer à s'engager publiquement pour la révision de l'image unilatérale de Dieu du christianisme exige donc une bonne dose de courage civique. Il va de soi que cette démarche sera plus efficace si elle est accomplie par tout un groupe de personnes. D'après moi, c'est à ce niveau qu'une Eglise de femmes aura à jouer un rôle. Face aux attitudes de résignation et de découragement, elle pourra relancer le mouvement en faisant preuve d'initiative et d'audace. La question de savoir quelle sera la forme structurelle d'une telle Eglise de femmes ne me semble pas si importante; je peux imaginer différentes structures coexistantes, mais à l'heure actuelle, je ne suis pas encore capable d'en décrire les formes concrètes. Ce qui me semble important, c'est qu'une Eglise de femmes - dans laquelle j'inclus les mouvements féminins officiels, les diverses associations ainsi que les groupes plus marginaux - doit affirmer son dynamisme et sa présence dans le domaine public, au sein et à l'extérieur des Eglises. Et surtout, elle ne doit pas renoncer, même en cas de revers ou d'une réaction à grande échelle; elle doit toujours garder à l'esprit la force authentique des

---

[16] Cf.p.ex."Stellungnahme der Feministischen Theologie", élaboré par le Prüfungssausschuß der Evangelisch-Theologischen Fakultät der Universität Tübingen, Stuttgart 1990, 17 sq. (G. Schneider-Flume), 22 sqq. (P. Beyerhaus); ou la procédure disciplinaire intentée par la Evangelische Landeskirche de Würtemberg contre Jutta Voss; voir *Schlangenbrut* n° 42, août 1993, 40 sqq. et n° 44, février 1994, 38.

[17] Cf. p.ex. le pamphlet de "Christen für Wahrheit", 74415 Gschwend, juillet 1994, contre Herta Leistner et Renate Jost.

femmes et chercher d'autres voies.

Certes, ceci n'est pas facile car l'action politique risque de virer au pragmatisme et de perdre son fondement religieux-spirituel. C'est pourquoi, tout autant que l'action politique au niveau ecclésial - et même plus dans l'optique psychanalytique - il est important que les symboles religieux masculins soient privés de leur pouvoir inconscient par le biais d'une profonde transformation psychique, car ce sont eux qui continuent à légitimer et à maintenir les structures patriarcales. Mais on ne peut changer des symboles sur simple résolution, encore moins l'image de Dieu. Les nouveaux symboles doivent procéder de nouvelles expériences et se développer progressivement. Cependant, pour s'engager dans des expériences religieuses qui ne sont pas approuvées par l'Eglise, des expériences qui peuvent aussi modifier l'image de Dieu, il faut avoir la volonté de se transformer soi-même jusque dans les profondeurs de son âme. Cette transformation personnelle intérieure est d'ailleurs beaucoup plus difficile à réaliser que les changements extérieurs que les femmes ont déjà introduit dans les pratiques ecclésiales et religieuses, surtout au niveau de la base; je songe notamment au domaine liturgique qui, dans les offices réguliers des paroisses, continue à ignorer les femmes sur le plan linguistique et à parler de Dieu comme d'un homme; à ma connaissance, ceci s'applique à toutes les confessions.

Les offices religieux sont aussi le lieu privilégié où la symbolique de l'image divine agit le plus directement. C'est pour cette raison que les offices dans lesquels les femmes pratiquent une symbolique appropriée à la féminité - p.ex. des danses, des gestes différents etc. - sont très importants. De manière pour ainsi dire subversive, ils introduisent dans la tradition chrétienne une nouvelle symbolique qui tient compte des femmes. Mais d'après moi, une Eglise de femmes devra dans ce domaine aborder bien des questions. D'abord, pourquoi ces nouvelles pratiques et formulations liturgiques, si répandues dans les groupes féminins, ont-elles si peu d'écho dans les offices normaux. Certes, l'interdit proclamé par les institutions ecclésiastiques y est pour beaucoup. Mais est-ce seulement cela? Dans quelle mesure nous, les femmes, continuons-nous à tolérer que l'oeuvre de Dieu soit encore et toujours louée et annoncée par le biais de métaphores exprimant la souveraineté et la puissance?

On peut observer un peu partout que les métaphores viriles employées pour des sujets religieux et ecclésiastiques sont profondément enracinées dans l'esprit des hommes d'Eglise, et donc très difficiles à éradiquer. Un exemple:

le 22.9.1993, le président de la Conférence épiscopale de l'Eglise catholique
en Allemagne fit un discours télévisé à propos du nombre impressionnant de
personnes qui quittent l'Eglise (1992: 200.000 personnes en Allemagne, un
nombre très élevé pour l'Eglise catholique-romaine). Il déclara ceci:

Nous devons nous préparer à devenir une communauté plus petite. Mais si, dans ce
processus, nous parvenons à former une petite troupe combative, c'est très bien.[18]

J'avoue que je n'ai pas écrit la lettre de protestation qu'aurait mérité cette
réquisition dans une "troupe (ecclésiale) combative"; pas par paresse, mais
parce que, déjà dans le passé, les critiques que j'avais adressées par écrit à
cet évêque ont eu des résultats négatifs. Ce genre de discours nous montre
bien que les femmes ne doivent pas trop espérer désamorcer les images
masculines (de Dieu) inconscientes chez les hommes d'Eglise.

L'idée d'une Eglise de femmes suscite en revanche beaucoup d'espoir,
même si ses manifestations vis-à-vis des Eglises existantes devraient encore
longtemps rester modestes. Ce qui me vient tout d'abord à l'esprit, c'est une
vision: dans un office du dimanche tout à fait normal, un groupe de femmes -
une petite Eglise de femmes? - se réunit pour prononcer à voix haute la fin
du "Notre Père" ("Car c'est à toi qu'appartiennent le règne, la puissance et
la gloire...") en ces mots: "Car tu es l'amour, la force et la beauté..."; ou
alors une autre variante: "Car tu es la joie et la force et la grâce - de toute
éternité. Amen".

Je sais que c'est à peine faisable. Et pourtant, je peux me l'imaginer, car
j'ai fait avec les femmes des expériences particulièrement intenses dans mon
travail psychanalytique sur la modification des images religieuses destructri-
ces de l'identité. Ce que les femmes vivent dans ces moments-là est toujours
un passage douloureux aboutissant à une expérience de libération, car il s'agit
de défaire les images patriarcales qui ont forgé l'identité des femmes pendant
leur croissance. Dans ce travail de transformation des symboles religieux, je
vois jaillir des sources où les femmes peuvent aller puiser des forces, où leur
propre expérience vient alimenter l'imagination créatrice de symboles.
Une telle expérience avait par exemple résulté d'un travail créatif [19] sur

---

[18]   Noté directement après avoir été entendu.
[19]   Au sujet de mes travaux psychanalytiques sur les symboles religieux, surtout bibliques, cf.
Maria Kassel, *Sei, die du werden sollst*, Freiburg-Basel-Wien 1993, partie 5; id. *Das Auge*
im Bauch. Erfahrungen mit tiefenpsychischer Spiritualität, Olten (5e édition) 1994; id.

la symbolique de la croix et de la résurrection. Une femme y avait personnellement vécu le fait d'être attachée sur la croix. Ensemble, les femmes du groupe ont retravaillé cette expérience féminine caractéristique dans un drame symbolique.[20] Toutes les participantes étaient profondément émues, car nous avions vécu de l'intérieur - pas seulement par le langage - cet aspect inhérent au symbole de la croix et à l'image de Dieu sous-jacente qui vise à opprimer les femmes; ensuite, dans un travail symbolique commun, nous avions eu une intuition de comment dépasser ce symbole religieux destructeur en élaborant des symboles libérateurs. Le dîner qui suivit se déroula dans un silence absolu d'une intensité religieuse. Nous l'avons vécu comme un culte et cela nous a profondément liées; la fête joyeuse qui suivit en faisait également partie. Le douloureux processus de délivrance relatif à cette croix qui, d'une certaine manière, a imprimé sa marque dans la chair de nos vies - l'exemple évoqué ici représente le début d'un processus de transformation intérieure - équivalait en même temps à un retour; retour à un lieu où les femmes peuvent faire leur propre expérience religieuse, une expérience authentique qui n'est pas aliénée par les conceptions masculines de Dieu.

Je pense que c'est ce type d'expériences qui pourrait venir alimenter la spiritualité d'une Eglise de femmes; et lorsque cette spiritualité se sera épanouie et aura pris de l'ampleur, elle pourra peut-être contribuer à une transformation générale de l'image masculine-patriarcale de Dieu.

Traum, Symbol, Religion. Tiefenpsychologie und feministische Analyse, Freiburg i. Br. 1991, notamment 1,7; id. "Religiöse Metamorphosen. Biographische Szenen und ihre religionspädagogische Deutung", in: R. Lachmann / H.F. Rupp (Hg.), *Lebensweg und religiöse Erziehung. Religionspädagogik als Autobiographie*, Weinheim 1989, tome 2, 145 sqq.

[20]   Cf. ibid.

Zusammenfassung

Gottesbilder spiegeln den Bewußtseinszustand und die geltenden Werte einer Glaubensgemeinschaft. In sechs Thesen arbeitet Maria Kassel aus tiefenpsychologisch-feministischer Sicht die Wechselwirkung zwischen den männlich geprägten christlichen Gottesbild und der Identitätsbildung von Frauen heraus. Durch emanzipatorische Prozesse allein ist die tiefsitzende Ungleichbewertung der Geschlechter nicht zu beheben. Einer Umgestaltung der Kirche wird nur dann Erfolg beschieden sein, insofern die Lebenswirklichkeit von Frauen als positive religiöse Symbolisierung in das christliche Gottesbild Aufnahme finden wird.

Summary

Metaphors of God reflect the consciousness and the values of religion and church. In six theses the author gives an explanation about the relationship between male christian metaphors of God and the identity of women. Only through a process of emancipation and participation will patriarchal structures not be transformed. A change within the (roman-catholic) church will just succeed if the reality of women's lives can be symbolized and integrated in a christian metaphor of God.

Maria Kassel, geb. 1931. Studium der Theologie und Germanistik. Bis 1992 Lehre und Forschung an der Katholisch-Theologischen Fakultät der Universität Münster/ Deutschland. Arbeitsschwerpunkte: Tiefenpsychologisch-feministische Theologie und Spiritualität; Untersuchung des Verhältnisses von Traum, Symbol und Religion; Vergleich von Aussage und Wirkung des männlichen Gottesbildes im Christentum mit weiblichen Gottesbildern in altorientalischen Religionen.

Regula Schmid

"Singt dem Herrn ein neues Lied...".
Liturgie in der Frauenkirche

Ich möchte im folgenden Artikel der Frage nachgehen, in welchem Verhältnis Frauengottesdienste und Frauenkirche zueinander stehen. Dabei vertrete ich die These, daß in Frauengottesdiensten viele Charakteristika von Frauenkirche exemplarisch sichtbar werden, und möchte dies aufzeigen.

Ich werde zuerst der Frage nachgehen, welche Funktionen ein Gottesdienst erfüllt. Danach skizziere ich kurz die Geschichte der Zürcher Frauenkirche. Anschließend versuche ich, die oben erwähnte These anhand von drei Themenkreisen zu überprüfen. Die Ergebnisse verdeutliche und erweitere ich danach am Beispiel zweier Liederbücher, einem traditionellen und einem Frauenliederbuch, und schließe mit einem kurzen Rückblick.

Bevor ich beginne, möchte ich kurz meinen eigenen Standort angeben. Ich habe im Zweitstudium Theologie studiert (v.a. in Zürich) und im Rahmen meiner Abschlußarbeit die Zürcher Frauenkirche 1985-1990 untersucht. Seit 1. Januar 1994 bin ich Pfarrerin in einem Zürcher Stadtquartier. Ich betrachte mich als Teil der Zürcher Frauenkirche und bin Mitglied der 'Oekumenischen Frauenbewegung'.

Die Funktionen des Gottesdienstes
Der Gottesdienst spielt nicht nur in der Frauenkirche, sondern auch in den gewöhnlichen Kirchgemeinden ein zentrale Rolle. Nach innen hat er die Funktion, die Mitglieder an einem zentralen Ort zu einem immer gleichen Zeitpunkt zu sammeln, nach außen repräsentiert er die Gemeinde.

Diese zwei Funktionen sind in der Frauenkirche in besonderem Maß von Bedeutung. Frauenkirche ist ja nicht Territorialgemeinde, sondern Interessengemeinde. Das heißt, sie ist nicht durch politische Grenzen, sondern durch gemeinsame Interessen definiert. So ist sie noch vitaler auf ein organisiertes Zusammenkommen angewiesen als herkömmliche Gemeinden.

Im Gottesdienst werden Erfahrungen erinnert und dargestellt, reflektiert und auf zukünftig mögliche Erfahrungen hin geweitet. Aber auch in der Feier selbst werden neue Erfahrungen gemacht, die Kraft und Gemeinschaft in Gegenwart und Zukunft ermöglichen. Einerseits ist also der Gottesdienst der Brennpunkt der Gemeinde, der Ort, wo die Strahlen aus der Vergangenheit gebündelt werden, eine konkrete Gestalt annehmen und ihrerseits wieder in die Zukunft strahlen. Andererseits ist jeder Gottesdienst eine öffentliche Handlung. Dadurch nun, daß die Frauengottesdienste ein anderes Modell von symbolischer Darstellung von Wirklichkeit, Reflexion und Zukunftsvision neben das Bestehende setzen, provozieren sie auch öffentliche Zustimmung und Ablehnung.

Die Geschichte der Zürcher Frauenkirche

Wenn ich im folgenden die Geschichte der Frauenkirche nachzeichne, muß ich zuerst fragen, was dieses Wort genau bezeichnet. Ursprünglich stammt der Begriff 'Frauenkirche' aus den USA. Vor allem in der katholischen Kirche nehmen sich Frauen seit den 70-er Jahren bewußt religiös und kirchlich als Subjekte wahr.

Inzwischen wird dieser Begriff auch in der Schweiz gebraucht, wenn auch nicht allgemein anerkannt. Carmen Jud, eine Schweizer Theologin, schreibt dazu:

> *In der Schweiz ist der Anfang dieser Selbstverständlichkeit datierbar. 'Wir Frauen sind Kirche, worauf warten wir noch.' Diese Aufforderung von Marga Bürig [eine der Mütter der feministischen Theologie, Anm.d.V.] am Schweizer Frauenkirchenfest vom 24.Oktober 1987 traf irgenwie in ein gemachtes Nest und war genau das, was noch fehlte.[1]*

Frauen sind also nicht 'das andere', die Adressatinnen der Kirche - sie sind selbst Kirche, und zwar mit ihren Erfahrungen, ihren Körpern, ihren Worten und Liedern. Das ist der erste Skandal, der in den Feiern der Gottesdienste elementar sichtbar wird: Aus bisher mitgemeinten Objekten werden gestaltende Subjekte.

Wie aber entstand dieses Frauenkirchenbewußtsein in der Schweiz? Schon seit Mitte dieses Jahrhunderts spielten die kirchlichen Bildungshäuser in der Schweiz eine wichtige Rolle. Sie ermöglichten Begegnungen zwischen Frauen der Kirche und der Frauenbewegung(en) und boten Raum zur

---

[1] Carmen Jud, *Die religiöse Praxis der Frauenbewegung oder feministische Theologie nimmt Gestalt an*, 3 (Broschüre).

religiösen und politischen Bewußtseinsbildung.

Ein zweiter Bezugspunkt bildete daneben die 'Disputation 84'. Verschiedene Gründe, zuletzt das Zwinglijubiläum von 1984, ließen beim Kirchenrat und einer Gruppe von ProtestantInnen im Kanton Zürich die Idee entstehen, in einer Art LaiInnenparlament eine Standortbestimmung der Reformierten Landeskirche vorzunehmen. 'Ecclesia reformata semper reformanda' - auf welche Weise dieser Grundsatz der Reformation in der Frauenkirche neu Wirklichkeit werden würde, hätte wohl zu Beginn der Disputation niemand auch nur geahnt. Eine Kommission erarbeitete vorgängig acht Themenpapiere - aber die Perspektive der Frauen war nicht vorgesehen. Als Reaktion darauf entstanden im ganzen Kanton Frauengruppen, die ihre eigenen Vorstellung erarbeiteten und einbrachten.

An der Eröffnungsveranstaltung im Mai 1984 wurden vier Gottesdienste gefeiert. Einer davon, von einer Frauengruppe gestaltet, unterschied sich deutlich von den anderen. Bereits hier wurden neue Elemente sichtbar, die auch in späteren Frauengottesdiensten wiederkehren:
Es ist eine Gruppe, die ihn durchführt, die eigene Erfahrung wird angesprochen und reflektiert, neue Lieder mit ungewohnten Bildern werden gesungen. So ist es - ich werde dies noch genauer ausführen - sicher kein Zufall, daß sich Frauenkirche zuerst in einem Gottesdienst bemerkbar macht.

Einzelne Gruppen suchten auch nach außerkirchlichen liturgischen Formen, und im Dezember 1984 feierte erstmals eine Gruppe die Wintersonnenwende, woraus sich die bald regelmäßig stattfindenden Jahreszeitenfeste entwickelten. Diese sind keine Gottesdienste, sondern Feiern des Jahreszyklus'.

Am 14.Januar 1989 konstituierte sich die 'Oekumenische Frauenbewegung Zürich' als Verein. Verschiedene feministisch-religiöse Frauengruppen schlossen sich zusammen. Zur Zeit sind es etwa 300 Mitglieder in über zehn sogenannten Projektgruppen, die der Bewegung angehören.

Eine dieser Projektgruppen ist für die seit 1985 regelmäßig stattfindenden Frauengottesdienste zuständig. Sie bereitet sie nicht selbst vor, sondern organisiert Gruppen, die die Gestaltung eines Abends übernehmen. Interessanterweise wurden gerade diese Gottesdienste zum Politikum. An ihnen wird offensichtlich exemplarisch sichtbar, wie Frauenkirche eingefahrene Strukturen und Denkweisen in Frage stellt. Im Frühling 1989 wurde den Frauen das Gastrecht im Fraumünster entzogen. Damit verlieren sie die Kirche, in der sie fünf Jahre lang Gottesdienste feierten, und die wie keine andere in Zürich eine 'weibliche' Tradition verkörperte: Dort stand das

seinerzeit von Zwingli aufgehobene Frauenkloster.
Kirchenpflege und Pfarrer warfen den Frauen vor, sie betrieben eine (zu) feministische Theologie (und/oder heidnische Bräuche), jüdische und katholische Frauen feierten ohne vorherige Information der kirchlichen Behörden mit, die Gottesdienste seien zu weit verbreitet...
Frauengottesdienste stellen etwas in Frage, weil sie sich daneben stellen. Etwas Selbverständliches wird fragwürdig, nicht weil es in Frage gestellt wird, sondern weil neben das 'eine wahre Selbverständliche' ein zweites, anderes Selbverständliches gestellt wird. Jede Macht basiert u.a. darauf, daß sie sich als einzig mögliche darstellt. Frauenkirche macht in ihren Gottesdiensten aber eine andere Möglichkeit sichtbar. Und so stehen plötzlich Fragen im Raum, die vorher kaum möglich waren:
Wer bestimmt, welche Theologie betrieben werden darf?
Wer bestimmt, welche Tradition christlich ist?
Wer bestimmt, wer zu Gottesdiensten willkommen ist?
Wem 'gehören' die Kirchen?
So wird die Liturgie unversehens zu *dem* sichtbaren Ausdruck verschiedenster Charakteristika von Frauenkirche. Es wird exemplarisch sichtbar, worum es geht, wo gestritten wird - und zwar nicht nur in Worten, sondern in liturgisch gestalteten Formen.

Drei Charakteristika von Frauenkirche
Ich möchte im folgenden drei Themenkreise konkreter beleuchten, die m.E. das versinnbildlichen, was Frauenkirche ist, und was in der Liturgie exemplarischen Ausdruck findet:

Eine Gemeinschaft von Gleichgestellten
Bereits in der Phase der Vorbereitung eines Gottesdienstes wird deutlich, daß dieser von unterschiedlichsten Erfahrungen lebt. Nicht eine Einzelperson ist verantwortlich für die Gestaltung, sondern eine Gruppe. Diese wiederum hat ihr Amt nicht auf Dauer, sondern auf Zeit. So bestimmt die Situation die Position. Manchmal arbeitet eine Theologin mit, manchmal nicht. Auf der Basis eines Grundkonsenses, z.B. der Art der Lieder, dem feministischen Sprachgebrauch oder der Einbeziehung sinnlich wahrnehmbarer Zeichen, sind die Gruppen in der Gestaltung ihres Gottesdienstes weitgehend frei. Infolgedessen sieht ein Gottesdienst einer katholischen Frauengruppe ganz anders aus als der der Theologinnen einer theologischen Fakultät.
Eine Gruppe gestaltet die Liturgie, nicht eine einzelne Person - das heißt

auch, daß es nie nur *eine* Frage gibt, auf die nun die Vorbereitenden eine
Antwort zu geben wüßten. Es sind oft nicht Texte und Lieder aus einem Guß,
sondern in Form gebrachte Auseinandersetzungen zwischen verschiedenen
Frauen. Manchmal sehr disparat, manchmal in lebendigem Dialog - immer
aber kritisch gegenüber allem, das Anlaß geben könnte zu meinen, es gebe
nur *eine* Wahrheit. Oberstes Ziel ist nicht größtmögliche Einheit, sondern
größtmögliche Ehrlichkeit. Zur Gleichberechtigung aller gehört auch das
'offene Mikrophon'. Es folgt auf die Beiträge der vorbereitenden Frauen, und
gibt allen Anwesenden die Möglichkeit, eigene Gedanken zu formulieren und
mitzuteilen. Meist wird es rege benutzt, so daß das Thema nochmals in ganz
neuem Licht gesehen werden kann.

Erneuerte Tradition - zur Tradition gewordenes Neues
Jede Bewegung, die nach neuen Wegen sucht, muß sich über ihr Verhältnis
zum 'Alten' klarwerden. Wenn die bisherige Tradition nicht fraglos
übernommen werden kann, muß sie deswegen ganz über Bord geworfen
werden, können einzelne Elemente übernommen oder abgeändert werden,
kann die Struktur, aber nicht der Inhalt beibehalten werden? Die Basisge-
meinden Lateinamerikas z.B. feiern in ihren Gottesdiensten ganz selbstverständlich die katholische Liturgie und passen sie einfach der konkreten
Situation an. Für Frauen der Frauenkirche dagegen sind die üblichen
Gottesdienste sowohl der reformierten wie auch der römisch-katholischen
Kirche fragwürdig geworden. Das reformierte Gottesdienstformular läßt zwar
theoretisch viel Freiheit für eigene Formen. Dennoch sind die meisten Feiern
äußerst wortkonzentriert, ohne jedes sinnliche Zeichen und ohne Gemeindebe-
teiligung (außer bei den Liedern und dem 'Unser Vater'). Die katholische
Liturgie hat zwar viel mehr an konkret symbolischen Zeichen bewahrt, aber
viele Formeln können Frauen nicht mehr nachsprechen ("Herr, ich bin nicht
würdig, daß du eingehst unter mein Dach...") und die Sprache der Lieder ist,
wie auch im reformierten Kirchengesangbuch, durch und durch patriarchal.
Auch die Konzentration auf den Priester ähnelt dem reformierten Einmann-
betrieb: Dennoch heißen Frauengottesdienste 'Gottesdienste', nicht 'Meditation', 'Feier' oder ähnliches. Darin drückt sich aus, daß kein totaler Bruch
mit dem Bisherigen, sondern eine eigene Art von Kontinuität angestrebt wird.
Deshalb, denke ich, provozieren diese Gottesdienste auch immer wieder Auseinandersetzungen. Sie machen auf vergessene, totgeschwiegene Traditionen
der eigenen Geschichte aufmerksam. Sie zeigen als 'unmöglich' Bezeichnetes

konkret und selbstverständlich und sie lachen über Todernstes, 'ewig und einzig Wahres'. So erschweren sie, ihrerseits wieder totgeschwiegen zu werden. Sie stellen dem Gewohnten das Neue zur Seite und ermöglichen Querverbindungen.

So steht jeder Gottesdienst im Zeichen der Spannung zwischen Experiment und Tradition. Die Liturgie entwickelt sich jeweils vom Thema ausgehend, doch werden nicht einfach alle traditionellen Elemente abgelehnt. Sie sind nicht schlecht, weil sie 'alt' sind, sondern weil sie Frauen ausschließen, vereinnahmen oder vergessen. Gebet, Segen, Bibelbesinnung und anderes hat seinen Platz - aber nun in einem neuen Kontext.

Diese Traditionen erfahren in den Frauengottesdiensten eine Transformation auf zwei Ebenen: Erstens werden die Elemente im Interesse der Gleichberechtigung aller und im Interesse der nachvollziehbaren Erfahrung verwendet. Zweitens erhalten die Elemente oft andere Formen. So kann ein Gebet als Gedicht erscheinen, eine Gabe zum Nachhause-nehmen als Segen, das Hinstellen einer Kerze als Fürbitte. Oft wird auch Traditionelles mit Neuem verbunden.

Grundsätzlich kann wohl gesagt werden, daß Elemente, seien sie traditionell oder neu, im Hinblick auf ihre Funktion überprüft werden.

In der Zürcher Frauenkirche hat sich inzwischen eine Liturgie herauskristallisiert. Zwar feiert jede Gruppe in ihrer eigenen Form, dennoch läßt sich eine Art Grundmuster erkennen:
Musik
Begrüßung (Vorstellung des Themas, der Gruppe, der Intention)
Lied
Text (Bibeltext, Meditation)
Mittelteil (Gedanken der Frauen und Lied/Musik im Wechsel)
Offenes Mikrophon
Gebet/Fürbitte
Mitteilungen/Schlüsselübergabe (zur Türe der Kirche, in der der nächste Gottesdienst gefeiert wird)
Segen
Musik/Lied

Auch diese neue Liturgie wird immer wieder an der oben beschriebenen 'Funktionalität' der Elemente gemessen werden müssen, will sie nicht selbst wieder unhinterfragt traditionell werden. Das heißt, sie hat ihre Legitimation nicht dadurch, daß frau es 'einfach so' macht. Sie ist aus dem Experiment und dem genauen Hinhören entstanden, und kann nur insofern bestehen, als sie dem Inhalt dient, der vermittelt werden soll.

Viele der Elemente, die die Gottesdienste prägen, sind so gesehen nicht neu in dem Sinn, daß sie vorher noch nie ausprobiert worden wären. Neu ist aber ihr Kontext und ihre Funktion als Gegenmodell zur traditionellen Liturgie.

So stehen am Anfang meist die eigenen Erfahrungen. Sie treten in ein Gespräch mit dem Thema, das eine biblische Geschichte oder nur ein Vers daraus sein kann, ein anderer Text oder allgemein ein Thema, das die Gruppe beschäftigt ('Bäume', 'Jahreszeiten - Lebenszeiten', 'Hildegard von Bingen' etc.).

Oft sind die Gottesdienste auch auf die Jahreszeiten abgestimmt. Im allgemeinen wird Mundart gesprochen, und die Sprache und die Lieder zeigen, daß für die Frauen in diesem Bereich feministische Kriterien selbstverständlich sind.

Meist sind die Stühle kreisförmig angeordnet, Blumen, Brot und Wein, Erde, Kerzen etc. symbolisieren das Thema und zugleich das Zentrum. Weitere Elemente sind Tanz, Imagination und öffentliche Klage.

Frauen berufen sich klar auf christliche Traditionen - fragen aber gleichzeitig hartnäckig danach, was denn diese christliche Traditionen bedeuten und ob die Grenzziehungen zwischen christlich und nichtchristlich, lebensfreundlich und lebensfeindlich wirklich am rechten Ort geschehen seien. Der Rahmen, in dem dieser Prozeß der Auseinandersetzung und Aneignung geschieht, sind die Frauentraditionen innerhalb und außerhalb des Christentums. Auch christliche Liturgien werden also auf ihre Funktion hin befragt: Wem dienen sie, welches religiöse und auch politische Bewußtsein kommt zum Ausdruck? Außerchristliche Traditionen sind nicht von vornherein auf der Gegnerseite, und christliche nicht per se akzeptiert. Das Gleiche gilt auch für die Auseinandersetzung mit der Bibel. Sie hat nicht unhinterfragbare Autorität, sondern ihre Wichtigkeit bemißt sich an den Lebenserfahrungen von Frauen. Ihr zur Seite werden verschiedene, auch außerchristliche Frauentraditionen gestellt, ebenso moderne Gedichte und Bilder.

Sinnlichkeit und Erfahrung
Die Kirche ist eine Gemeinschaft von Menschen, die zusammenkommen, die sichtbar sind als Körper.

Sie sind anwesend als soziale Körper, mit den Erfahrungen, die in dieser Gesellschaft Frauenkörper machen: Gewalt, Benachteiligung, Macht, Bloßstellung...

Zugleich sind sie anwesend als individuelle Körper, fähig zur Bewegung, zu Lust, Berührung und Wahrnehmung, zum Riechen und Hören, Singen, Lachen und Weinen.

Frauengottesdienste versuchen, diesen Körper in seiner Gesamtheit wahrzunehmen und anzusprechen. Dabei spielt der je eigene Lebenshintergrund jeder Frau eine entscheidende Rolle. Katholikinnen haben meistens einen selbverständlicheren Zugang zu sinnlichen Zeichen als reformierte Frauen und Frauen aus einem nicht kirchlich geprägten Umfeld. Als erstes wird der Körper bereits beim Eintreten angesprochen: Mittelpunkt ist nicht Kanzel oder Altar, sondern das Zentrum des Kreises, den die Stühle bilden. Sinnliche Anwesenheit, in dem sich die Frauen wahrnehmen können, und das symbolische Zeichen der unsichtbaren Mitte.

Die Lieder werden oft mehrmals gesungen, so daß daraus eine Art von Musik entsteht, bei der nicht mehr die Worte im Zentrum stehen, sondern ein Mitschwingen, ein sich Einstimmen auf den gemeinsamen Rhythmus und die Melodie.

Auch Tanz und Pantomime drücken die Körperlichkeit des Glaubens aus.

Dazu kommen symbolische Handlungen. So wird die Fürbitte zum Thema 'Wohnen' folgendermaßen gestaltet: In der Mitte steht eine Mauer von Backsteinen; jede Fürbitterin nimmt einen Stein und legt ihn auf den Boden. Beim Thema 'Salbung in Bethanien' spielt der Duft eine wichtige Rolle: Die Frauen salben einander mit einer wohlriechenden Salbe. Oft können die TeilnehmerInnen am Schluß ein Zeichen mit nach Hause nehmen, z.B. Blumen, Brot oder ein Lied; immer aber ist es etwas, das schon während der Feier wichtig war. Wenn das Ziel eines Gottesdienstes Befreiung, Gleichheit, Angenommensein ist, dann gehört der Körper jeder einzelnen zentral dazu. Und wieder muß sich jeder Gottesdienst darauf befragen lassen, wieweit die einzelnen Elemente dazu beitragen.

Lieder

Die Lieder haben in den Gottesdiensten einen wichtigen Anteil an der Liturgie. Sie sind ein Teil dessen, was nicht jedes Mal neu formuliert wird, und deshalb noch stärker den Hintergrund jeder Liturgie sichtbar macht.

Die Lieder versuchen Unsagbares sagbar zu machen. Es werden Bilder gebraucht für Inhalte des Glaubens wie Jesus Christus, Gott, die Gemeinde.

Einerseits wollen sie eine erfahrbare Realität benennen, andererseits drücken sie auch Ideale aus, sichtbar in Forderungen an den Glauben und das Tun. So verdeutlichen die Lieder dreierlei: Erfahrung, Deutung und Idealziel. Die Oekumenische Frauenbewegung hat seit 1991 ein eigenes Liederbuch. Darin sind Lieder gesammelt, die sich im Laufe der Jahre als brauchbar und akzeptabel für die Frauengottesdienste erwiesen haben. Um einige Thesen zu verdeutlichen, die ich im vorherigen Abschnitt ausgeführt habe, vergleiche ich im folgenden die Texte zweier Liederbücher:

Das 'Oekumenische Frauenliederbuch'[2] und das 'Gesangbuch der Evange-lisch-Reformierten Kirchen der Deutschsprachigen Schweiz'[3], das zum großen Teil die gleichen Lieder enthält wie sein katholisches Pendant. Da dieses Kirchengesangbuch das mit Abstand am meisten gebrauchte Lieder-buch ist, scheint es mir legitim, es als Konsens des traditionellen Gottesdien-stes zu betrachten.

Gottesbilder

Im Kirchengesangbuch (KGB) ist das Grundverhältnis zwischen Gott und Mensch Distanz, eine klare Hierarchie von oben und unten, stark und schwach, gebend und nehmend. Je mehr der Mensch seine Kleinheit sieht, sich klein macht, desto größer wird Gott. Das kann sich im Vertrauensbild von Hirte und Schaf, im Herrschaftsbild von Herr und Knecht, im Bild der hellen Sonne, die in die dunkle Welt hineinscheint, oder auch im patri-archalen Familienbild von Vater und Sohn/Kind ausdrücken. Eine reale Distanz zwischen Menschen wird also zum Vor-Bild für die Beziehung zwischen Mensch und Gott gemacht. Ohne Gott kann der Mensch nichts tun, außer Böses. Er ist von Gott absolut abhängig, kann nur sein Sündersein bekennen und auf Gnade hoffen.

Verschiedene Erfahrungen wie z.B. die Abwesenheit Gottes angesichts des Leidens oder die weltweite Ungerechtigkeit kommen überhaupt nicht vor.

Auch im Frauenliederbuch (FLB) ist oft von Gott die Rede, der handelt. Doch handelt er, indem er den Menschen nahe kommt. Er tritt ein in eine Beziehung, und stiftet die Menschen zum Handeln an. Nicht er an sich ist

---

[2] Lilo Schmidt / Susanne Kramer Friedrich (Hg.), *Oekumenisches Frauenliederbuch*, Zürich 1990.

[3] Schweizerischer Evangelischer Kirchenbund (Hg.), *Gesangbuch der evangelisch-reformierten Kirchen der deutschsprachigen Schweiz*, Art. Institut Orell Füssli (u.a.), Zürich 1952.

wichtig, sondern seine Wirkung im Menschen. Gott ist 'in mir', er durchströmt alles, er wird zum Weg. Als Gottesbild werden meist Begriffe und Bilder gebraucht, die keinen direkten Vergleich mit Menschen ermöglichen: 'Sonne', 'Licht', 'Stern', 'Anfang', 'Kraft'. Diese Abstrakta machen m.E. deutlich, daß sie *für* etwas stehen, während bei Worten wie 'Herr' oder 'König' die Identifikation mit real existierenden Menschen und Machtverhältnissen nahe liegt.

Das Jesus-/Christusbild

Im KGB wird oft 'Gott' und 'Jesus' identisch gebraucht. Jesus ist der sichtbare Gott. Vom Vater ans Kreuz geliefert, sühnt er die Schuld der Menschen mit seinem Blut. Er tut das, was Menschen nicht können. Von Jesus ist in den meisten Liedern die Rede, sogar an die Psalmlieder werden meist am Schluß eine oder zwei christologische Strophen angehängt. Er ist der 'Kriegsmann', der 'Held', der 'Sieger', das 'Gotteslamm'. Er herrscht zusammen mit dem Vater auf dem Thron und wird das Endgericht leiten. So ist sein Tod nur die Durchgangsstation zum Triumph.

Das FLB redet recht wenig von Jesus. Er ist 'Mensch', 'Bruder', 'Licht'. Auf der einen Seite historisches Vorbild für den guten, menschlichen Weg, wird er doch auf der anderen Seite auch als immer noch wirkend verstanden. Er ist in jedem Menschen, gibt Frieden. Er wird nirgends als Erlöser von Sünden dargestellt, sondern eher als der, der Gutes bewirkt, der zum Aufstand anstiftet. Während im KGB Tod und Auferstehung breit und dogmatisch, im Sinne der Übernahme traditioneller Worte, ausgeführt werden, sind die wenigen entsprechenden Lieder im FLB entweder übernommene traditionelle Verse oder Bibelzitate.

Das Bild des heiligen Geistes

Im KGB kommt der heilige Geist fast nur in den Pfingstliedern vor. Er ist abhängig von Gott, sein Werkzeug oder Gott selbst. Das Bild von ihm ist aber anders als andere Gottesbeschreibungen. Er ist ein Geist der Liebe, der Freude, er tröstet, ist Quelle der Weisheit. Aber auch er steht in großer Distanz zu den Menschen, steht innerhalb und im Dienst der schon beschriebenen Theologie und Christologie.

Im FLB spielt der heilige Geist eine ganz entscheidende Rolle. Er wird weiblich verstanden und genannt, oft wird auch das hebräische Wort 'Ruach' benutzt. Sie hat eine eigene Dynamik, ist Hoffnungsfunke, gibt Mut, ist das konstruktive Gegenteil zu Macht und Gewalt. Sie wird relativ selten mit Gott und nie mit Jesus in Verbindung gebracht.

Das Bild und die Aufgabe der Gemeinde
Gemeinde ist im KGB 'Brüderschar', 'Sünder', 'Jünger', 'Heer' und 'Eigentum'. Der Mensch kann Gottes Größe loben, sich unterwerfen, seine Schuld bekennen. Er soll streiten und seinem armen Bruder helfen. In einem gewissen Gegensatz dazu stehen einige Loblieder und verschiedene Psalmen, in denen der Mensch einen hohen Stellenwert hat. Doch im allgemeinen wird die Welt, in der ja die Gemeinde lebt, als düsteres Tal beschrieben. Sie ist der Ort der Sünde, des Kampfes, und viele Lieder sind geprägt von einer starken Sehnsucht nach einem Himmel, dem Reich Gottes, das nach diesem Leben folgt. Die Welt - ein Jammertal. Unsere Heimat - der Himmel. Die Auferstehung kommt erst nach dem leiblichen Tod, wo der Herrscher über alle Sünder richtet.

Im FLB handelt kein Lied von dem, was nach dem Tod kommt. Aufgabe der Menschen ist es, hier diese Welt zu gestalten. Viele Bilder fordern auf, es Gott gleichzutun: Licht zu werden, Frieden zu stiften etc. Gemeinde sind nicht die, die etwas Bestimmtes glauben, das sich definieren ließe, sondern die, die sich auf den Weg gemacht haben, um dieses Gottesreich in sich und in der Welt Wirklichkeit werden zu lassen.

Die Welt, die Natur wird grundsätzlich positiv gesehen, in einem zwar vielfach durch Lieblosigkeit gestörten, aber nicht zerstörten und vertrauensvollen Verhältnis zu Gott. Gott ist der, der das Gute in den Menschen unterstützt, anstiftet und bewirkt. Gerade weil nicht grundsätzlich alles, was sie tun, sündig ist, sind sie zu verantwortlichem Handeln aufgerufen. Dies zeigt sich auch umfangmäßig in den Liedern. Die Möglichkeiten sind vielfältig: Schweigen, Hören, die Schöpfung lieben, zu sich kommen, gemeinsam träumen, Frieden schaffen etc.

Sprache
Die Sprache des KGB's ist durch und durch männlich geprägt. Es gibt nur drei Lieder, in denen Gott mit einer Mutter verglichen oder zumindest in Verbindung gebracht wird. Sonst gibt es nur 'Brüder', 'Knechte', 'Könige', 'Herren', 'Sünder', 'Väter'.

Es gibt keine anderen Autoritäten als die männliche Trinität, und von diesen vor allem die ersten zwei Personen. Nichtchristlicher Glaube taucht nur im Hinblick auf dessen Bekehrbarkeit auf. Von Andersgläubigen zu lernen, fällt gänzlich außer Betracht. Da die meisten Lieder aus vergangenen Jahrhunderten stammen, schafft die Sprache eine große Distanz. Viele Formulierungen sind zu einer Kunstsprache geworden, die mit der heutigen Alltagssprache nichts mehr zu tun hat und zu der es im KGB keine korrektive Ergänzung gibt.

Im FLB fällt zunächst auf, daß viele Wörter und Vorstellungsweisen verschwinden. 'Sünde' und 'Buße' sind ersetzt durch die Ermutigung zum Guten. Das wahre Leben und die Auferstehung sind nur wichtig, wenn sie bereits in diesem Leben beginnen. Alle hierarchischen, militaristischen Bilder fallen ersatzlos weg. Traditionen beider Konfessionen haben ihren Platz, aber auch außerchristliche Traditionen. So finden sich u.a. ein Sufilied und eines des Liedermachers W.Biermann. Feinde oder Gegner, die frau bekämpfen müßte, kommen nicht vor. Wohl aber werden Angst, Lieblosigkeit und Unfreiheit als zerstörerisch und lebensfeindlich benannt, und sie sollen auch überwunden werden.

Aussagen aus der Hebräischen Bibel und jüdisch-israelische Lieder haben ihren eigenen Stellenwert, sie müssen nicht durch eine Christologie legitimiert oder ergänzt werden.

Zwei Lieder handeln explizit nur von Frauen.

So verdeutlichen auch die verwendeten Lieder, aus anderer Perspektive als die Liturgie, einige der zentralen Charakteristika von Frauenkirche.

An diesem Punkt möchte ich meine Überlegungen zu einem Ende und gleichzeitig zum Anfang zurück bringen.

Schlußwort

Aufgabe jeder Liturgie ist es, den Alltag mit Hilfe von Traditionen zu beleuchten und gleichzeitig neuen Traditionen Gestalt zu geben. Das Leben in seiner Vielfalt erhält so die Form, wie sie im Moment von der vorbereitenden Frauengruppe gefunden wird.

Gleichzeitig aber verdeutlicht die Liturgie auch all die grundsätzlichen Spannungen und Aufbrüche, die Frauen erleben, wenn sie sich ihrer Frauenrolle bewußt werden. Vergangenheit, Gegenwart und Zukunft, Momentanes und Konstantes, Individuelles und Gesamtgesellschaftliches, Erlebnis und Reflexion finden so in der Liturgie ihren gültigen Ausdruck. Darum konzentriert die Liturgie unseren Blick auf Wesentliches und gibt ihn danach wieder frei für Neues.

Summary

Many exemplary characteristics of the women's Church can be found in liturgies of women. The author discusses this thesis on the basis of three themes which can be found to take up an equally central place in women's liturgies and the women's Church: the women's Church as a community of equals, the way in which tradition is dealt with and the importance of sensuality and experience. The songs that are sung during a service also serve as a mirror of the way in which we experience the Church. Therefore Regula Schmid compares a traditional book of hymns from the Reformed Church of Switzerland with a book of women's songs.

Sommaire

On retrouve beaucoup de charactéristiques de Femmes/Eglise par excellence dans les services liturgiques des femmes. L'auteure argumente cette thèse sur base de trois thèmes occupant une place centrale, aussi bien dans les services liturgiques des femmes que dans Femmes/Eglise. Premièrement: Femmes/Eglise en tant que communauté d'égaux; deuxièmement: la façon d'interpréter et de faire usage de la tradition; et enfin: L'importance des sens et de l'expérience.

Les hymnes qui sont chantés au cours des services sont également un bon miroir des sensés de la manière dont nous expérimentons l'Eglise. C'est pourquoi Regula Schmid dresse une comparaison entre un livre d'hymnes traditionnels de l'Eglise Réformée de Suisse et un recueil de chansons de femmes.

Regula Schmid studierte nach ihrer Ausbildung zur Primarlehrerin Theologie. Sie ist seit dem 1. Januar 1994 Pfarrerin in einer reformierten Gemeinde in Zürich/Schweiz. Im Rahmen ihrer Abschlußarbeit hat sie die Zürcher Frauenkirche 1985-1990 untersucht, wo sie auch seit einigen Jahren Mitglied ist.

Penny Jones

The Implications of Women's Ordination to the Priesthood in the Church of England

An Historical Note

Following the ordination of women to the diaconate in the Church of England in 1988, debate continued around the proposals for women to be priested. The General Synod of July 1988 gave its 'general approval' to two measures, the first of which would enable women to be priested provided certain 'safe-guards' were observed and the second of which concerned the financial package to be provided for those clergy who chose to resign over the issue. These measures were then referred to the Church of England dioceses for further consideration at local level.

Following voting procedures in all the local synods, the legislation was presented once more in its final form to the General Synod on November 11, 1992, when it received the necessary two thirds majority in all three houses of the Synod, Bishops, Clergy and Laity. However opposition was swiftly rallied and measures drawn up to attempt to preserve the unity of the Church of England by making the greatest possible effort to accommodate the views of opponents. In particular the bishops produced a document known as the Act of Synod, to which the General Synod gave its consent in November 1993, to which was added in 1994 a Code of Practice to which the House of Bishops gave its assent also.

These documents made provision for a diocesan bishop to restrict the ministry of women as priests within their diocese. They also allowed for Parochial Church Councils to forbid women either to preside at or celebrate Holy Communion or pronounce Absolution in the Parish, and for benefice. Under the measures it also became possible for a Parochial Church Council to request alternative episcopal oversight should they be opposed to their diocesan bishop's decision to ordain women to the priesthood.

It is in the context of these provisions that women have begun their priestly ministry in the Church of England.

. . . . .

It was my husband Jonathan who insisted that I should celebrate my ordination to the priesthood with the purchase of a new stole. In the months which had followed the vote in General Synod it was as though all our celebratory instincts had been blighted like rosebuds caught by a late frost. We were encouraged constantly to be 'sensitive' to the great pain and hurt we were causing and to rejoice only in whispers and with long faces.

I did not want to buy a new stole. We owned two white stoles already. One belonging to Jonathan had been carefully designed and embroidered for his ordination to the diaconate. The other, plain and adorned only by a simple cross, belonged to a matching set of four bought when I had made the transition from deaconess to deacon in 1987. This second stole would I thought be quite appropriate. After all, I didn't want a fuss. I wanted to pretend that nothing remarkable was happening and that my ministry would continue just as before save that at last the church would recognise its priestly aspects, previously worked out in practice but unacknowledged.

How wrong I was! As the weeks wore slowly by and the cries of those opposed grew more shrill, I and I believe many other women deacons became increasingly depressed. When the first anniversary of the vote was marked by the passing of the Act of Synod, which gave in effect institutional blessing to the rejection of women's priesthood, it felt as though the baby brought to birth with such pain the year before, was now to be smothered before she had spoken her first word.

It was at this time, when I looked forward to my priesting more often with bitter tears than with joy that I worked out the symbols I wanted on the stole which Jonathan had finally persuaded me to buy. They were symbols which spoke to me of the struggle which was passing, and offered hope for the future ministry of women and men together. They were formed into a wonderful design by a woman artist friend, Linda Birch and embroidered by Lucy Hill - the same skilful woman who had created Jonathan's stole all those years before.

It is in many ways still far too soon to see clearly the implications of women's priesting in the Church of England, but the symbols which I chose provide for me some pointers to directions in which it seems that the Church has moved or is moving as a consequence of our ordinations.

The symbols I chose were these. First a seagull - and not a dove! I come of a family of several generations of sailors and so the sea is important to me personally. However beyond the personal connection I wanted in some ways to express the great 'sea-change' which I hope the priesting of women represents.

The seagull was to stand also for movement, liberation and drama. Years ago I trained as an actress and dancer. Nina in Chekhov's poignant play 'The Seagull' was the last serious role I undertook before exchanging the stage for the pulpit. I am convinced of the need for the Church to create in its liturgy new plays and new dances in which the bodies and voices of women will now partner those of men in ways we cannot yet begin to appreciate. For all these reasons I asked for a seagull to feature in the design. When Lucy came to interpret the design she decided that the single seagull was too static an image (and inclined to be mistaken for an odd looking dove!). She created a trinity of seagulls on each side of the stole, wheeling and diving as seagulls do. A sign both of movement and of strength they give me hope every time I look at them.

My second symbol was a cross - but not a traditional cross. Rather it took its shape from the cover designs for Janet Morley's now well known volume of prayers "All Desires Known".[1] It is a broken cross in which the four points do not connect in the centre. Visually it looks like a pin-drawing of a person who lacks a head and body, and has only disconnected neck, arms and legs. For me it represented negatively the broken body of the church into which women were to be ordained and all the pain and disunity we continue to endure. More positively it stood for all that Janet sought to express in that slim volume - the possibility of the naming of desire before God and of the feminisation of liturgy. It also allowed the cross to be connected not in the middle, by two lines antagonistically crossing, but by a circle around the outside, symbolising healing and the possibility of a new kind of wholeness. The nature of that wholeness and something of its implications was expressed in the two symbols used to create the circle, namely earth bringing forth ears of corn, reaching up to meet the descending arch of a rainbow. To these I will return.

First I should speak of the coins which I asked to be woven into the design. They were to stand simply for the lost coin of the parable and hence for Ann Loades book "Searching For Lost Coins"[2] which had inspired so many of us in our wrestlings with the text of the New Testament. By

---

[1] Janet Morley, *All Desires Known*, London 1992.
[2] Ann Loades, *Searching For Lost Coins*, London 1989.

extension they were to represent the whole task of feminist theology in which women have taken lamps and in the darkness of the Church's traditional interpretations searched for what may be of lasting value to them. Those meanings would I am sure have been sufficient. However Lucy insisted that they should not be embroidered coins, but real coins - pennies in fact. "They shall be pennies for Penny" she wrote in her note to me. As such they are both personalised, and sure to tarnish. They signal all that is imperfect, corruptible and earthly - everything in fact which the church has failed to acknowledge as valuable and godly.

And so to the symbol of earth and ears of corn. Aside from the obvious eucharistic connotations, and the teaching of Jesus that a grain must fall into the ground and die, these were to be a reminder of the ears of corn for which Ruth gleaned in the field. They signify all the many supportive relationships among women like that between Ruth and Naomi, and the sacrifices which women have been and continue to be prepared to make on behalf of one another. It is for me a symbol of hope of the possibility of connecting the Church with the insights and methods of Womanchurch. However it is a costly hope, symbolised unconsciously by Lucy when she beautified the earth with tiny red poppies - "just to give it a bit of colour". For the tiny red pinpoints speak to me of remembrance and of the suffering of so many women through history and across the world.

So finally to the image of the rainbow, arched between earth and heaven. Ancient symbol of the renewal of God's covenant with humanity, it promises renewal and freedom from fear. I associate it also with the peace movement and especially with those with whom I shared fellowship and prayer at the Greenham Common base when once a month a group of women would go and keep vigil while the resident women enjoyed a night of undisturbed sleep. It serves as a reminder that the ordination of women to the priesthood is such a tiny step in world terms, and a step which only has meaning in so far as it connects with all the struggles for peace and justice to which it is related.

Each of these symbols points to ways in which the priesting of women in the Church of England could open up new ways forward for women and men together. Let us therefore consider the possible implications under these categories, the Church of the Seagulls; the Church of Desire; the Church of the Lost Coins; The Church of the Gleaners and the Rainbow Church.

The Church of the Seagulls
During the years of debate around the ordination of women to the priesthood the language and forms of the liturgy, and especially eucharistic liturgy, came

under severe scrutiny from interested parties on both sides of the great divide. Questions were asked about the language and imagery being used both of God and humanity, and about the role and function of the priest presiding at the altar. Now that women finally are priests it is timely to ask "Will anything really change?" For so much energy was invested in both defending old forms and trying to invent new ones and now the work needs to be pressed forward before the practice of the first women priests ossifies for their successors into shapes no more creative than those they inherited. The seagulls need to take courage and test their wings lest they dither for ever uncertainly on the cliff's edge.

Initially of course there has been the simple pleasure of seeing women actually at the altar, moving and speaking in ways subtly different from those of men by sheer virtue of their gender and upbringing. When I asked my young children what difference if any they saw between my presidency and that of Jonathan they at once replied, "It's because your voice is like ours". Pressed a little further they volunteered "You notice us more". This attention could be construed positively or negatively - did they mean I took more time over the blessing of children (which I do, but so do other priests who are men as well as women), or was it that I was more likely to glare at them if they were making a din, I wondered!

The thrill of hearing women's voices speaking words so long reserved to men and of watching them perform actions so long forbidden has been considerable and its effects should not be minimised. It *is* wonderful that women gestating and menstruating (or otherwise) demonstrate by their physical presence the acceptability of the flesh in ways previously seemingly denied. It has implications for our understanding of the Incarnation and for our respect for the whole of Creation which can perhaps only be guessed at now. As Lavinia Byrne points out in her recent book "Women At The Altar",

> *A woman who comes to the altar as priest is a woman who moves from comparative invisibility to a place where the glory of God is recognised in her.*[3]

However at least some of that will soon become commonplace if it has not already done so, and rightly so. For while the 'just being there' factor should not be down-played, the years of waiting have opened up other patterns of creating liturgy which should now be grasped by those within the churches,

---

[3] Lavinia Byrne, *Women At The Altar*, London 1994, 1.

while those within and those now outside the established churches still remain in close contact with one another.

For the long delay in opening the priesthood to women has had its positive side. Without it we might never have considered the need for inclusive language, or named the limitations of hierarchical concepts of authority. In the time of waiting women and the men who supported them were forced to create new language, new images and new ways of performing liturgy. Even as I write Advent Sunday is approaching and Janet Morley's prayer in "Bread of Tomorrow" is apposite;

> *You keep us waiting,*
> *You the God of all time,*
> *want us to wait*
> *for the right time in which to discover*
> *who we are, where we must go,*
> *who will be with us, and what we must do.*
> *So thank you ... for the waiting time.*[4]

The lessons learnt under the pressures of struggle can now begin to be used creatively for the whole Church in ways we never dreamt of when we wrote liturgy and theology to make sense of the waiting.

So what were these lessons? First of all I would suggest that we learnt to create liturgy by *scavenging* - as all seagulls do. By this I mean that in order to express the new needs of the community of women and men in the Church, it has been and will continue to be, necessary to search through all the 'rubbish tips' of the tradition in order to pluck from it what may be nutritious. For work has been done to reveal the extent to which much Christian history and practice is little better than a rotting mass of material, much of it poisonous to women and damaging to human relating. For a long time the ideas and stories of women have been hidden and destroyed in this rotten heap, and it is only as we have recognised its nature that women have been enabled to pull from it whatever may still have value for them.

In this process however women have rarely scavenged alone. Rather the flock of seagulls pecking at the heap continues to grow, ever hopeful of tasty morsels which have been passed over. Moreover - and here the analogy breaks down - the scavengers have most often brought together their 'finds' and tried to make them into something new. Many kinds of interesting meals

---

[4] Janet Morley, *Bread of Tomorrow*, London 1992, 15.

have been made from the scraps gathered together by the other 'church' living alongside the institutional Church which in its various forms has come to be known by Rosemary Radford Ruether's designation 'Womanchurch'.

No longer buried and crushed by the weight of such tradition women are encouraging the church to glide upon the warm air currents of the Spirit. However for those of us who as priests remain within the institutional Church there remains the problem of how we integrate our experience of liturgy 'outside', with that which we are canonically bound to offer week by week in the churches we serve. For some women priests it is enough just to have been allowed across the boundary. Being there is enough and all that is sought is the ability to dance the old liturgical dances by the old score. However very many of us have learnt something of the freedom of the breeze and we have seen new dances choreographed and performed and there is no way back. Somehow the insights we have gained into the power of language to create or destroy, and the power of the liturgical iconography to shape understanding needs now to be incorporated into our regular practice.

For seagulls do not only scavenge. They also fish. In the same way we have learnt to fish in the deep waters of the Spirit for all that God gives and we should even now be seeking to reinterpret the words of Jesus to his disciples. For if perhaps we sail not secure in the great ark which once represented the Church universal, but in a flotilla of little vessels from which as fisherfolk we search the depths for food, then we shall have need of one another. We shall need to support one another in liturgies which enable all to take part and to tell their own stories of adventure upon the deep. Our liturgy needs to become less confident and more tentative, appreciating its own limits and seeking ways to articulate the experiences of all.

For the time being it seems as though we are only just beginning to learn the steps of possible new dances. For many women priests and for the male priests with whom they work two sets of experiences have followed hard on the heels of one another. The first has been that of women dancing the old dance. Women have performed the traditional steps of the eucharistic liturgy and have not stumbled. Their first attempts have been received on the whole gladly enough (even exultantly) and many have remarked as one would have hoped upon the 'ordinariness' of it all. The second however has been a sense of something lacking - of the inadequacy of the model and the need to bring to it new insights and ways of working.

Gradually I believe new patterns will emerge. Just this week I presided at the eucharist and was assisted by my male colleague who fulfilled many of the traditional roles of the deacon, but with a number of subtle differences. He assisted me in every way possible, to the extent even of holding the service book for me when necessary, but at the same time it was clear that he had a place within the liturgy which was distinct and in no sense subservient to mine. It required great trust on both our parts, for neither of us was entirely sure of what the other was going to do, but many of those who took part commented afterwards on the sense of mutuality and reciprocity which this way of working together conveyed.

Certainly it felt like trying out a new dance and having successfully twirled around the dance floor once I am committed to trying again and seeing what new variations emerge. Sometimes no doubt it will go well and we will glide upon the air currents with ease. At other times we will most probably take a nose-dive into the sea. Such must be the risks for the Church of the Seagulls, if their scavenging and fishing is to be truly liberative for all.

The Church of Desire
The Church has for centuries viewed desire of all kinds with suspicion. Sexual desire has been singled out for particularly vitriolic condemnation and permitted expression only grudgingly within heterosexual marriage. Moreover women, defined by entrapping stereotypes have been viewed as either 'desireless' in their role as virgin/mother/martyr, or 'object of improper desire', in their role as temptress/harlot. Consequently women's desires and the many issues which surround sexuality and the body have been left without articulation and the language of feeling and intimacy marginalised almost to the point of exclusion within the practice and liturgy of the churches.

Any attempt to redress this situation has tended to be met with cries of indignation and sometimes vicious attempts at repression. As Monica Furlong has pointed out, those who in the 1984 debate in General Synod spoke of women 'destroying' and 'disembowelling' the Church or as a 'virus in the bloodstream'[5] took their cue from a long tradition of scapegoating women which at its worst resulted in the persecution of women as witches. The fear of confronting that which has for so long been repressed - in this case women as full human beings in their own right is very great and it is clear that it is this fear which lies at the root of much continuing opposition to women priests, however that opposition may be otherwise articulated. For when a

---

[5] Monica Furlong, "The Guardian of the Grail", in: Sue Walrond-Skinner (ed.), *Crossing The Boundary*, London 1994, 23.

woman stands behind the altar as priest and takes in her hands the body and blood of Christ a fusion of sexuality and spirituality takes place which is deeply healing, but which can be perceived as deeply shocking by those who have been taught to keep spirituality and sexuality apart.

Hence women have been ordained into a divided church, where the voices of the fearful still receive much attention and this has had implications for us in the early months of our ministry. For not only has it muted our joy, I suspect it has also caused at least some women priests to draw back from asserting too loudly the differences they would see brought to the priesthood. Indeed there has been a great deal of emphasis on being 'just the same' as the men. For it is not just men who have framed their ministry within a dualistic understanding of sexuality and spirituality and some women are as fearful and resistant as the men towards the idea that these two driving forces of human existence can be brought together. Consequently there has been this year all too little expression of our 'desires' and the continued repression of many feelings.

Somehow the potential for healing is now present yet we hold back, afraid perhaps of the depths of its implications. If we, the women priests of this church begin at last to name our desires, where will it end?

The result has been, after so many years of speaking and writing and campaigning a most curious *silence*. Claire Herbert, one of the contributors to a volume which goes some way to breaking this silence entitled "Crossing the Boundary" writes about it like this,

> *My sense of the group of women deacons is that our prolonged adolescent period has tended to silence our dreams, because we are frightened of the anger we have been caused to feel in the past and in the present, and are scared to voice its depth. We have sought resolution for our conflict by 'privatising our dreams', being priests in secret, in home groups, friendship groups, feminist circles, and while strengthened by this action we have not dared to speak much about it in the public places of the church. This formation of identify gained through studying theology and making liturgy with other women, has led to (another) reason for silence about our future dreams. Discovering solidarity with secular feminists, and realising the depth of sexism existing still, in all our institutions, we wonder if we dare dream! Will we be so absorbed into the hierarchical structures of a patriarchalist church that we lose our identity as a people of protest and become competitive, oppressive and less in touch with our need to receive mercy?[6]*

---

[6] Claire Herbert, "A Resounding Silence", in: *Crossing The Boundary*, London 1994, 36.

The question is well put, for the danger is that those of us who have now been accepted into the male priestly caste will now simply operate within the mores of that caste. The implications of this are profound for it would involve our complicity in the continued oppression both of women and of lay people of either gender. As such it is a danger to be avoided at all costs which will demand that those of us who have been made priests do not lose our prophetic voice, but continue to speak out and be unafraid of causing division. For conflict is often the price of a lasting wholeness and it is for this reason that I believe the broken cross remains a better symbol through which to express our desires for healing than one which is intact.

The Church of the Lost Coins

For some years now women have been energetically searching scripture and tradition for their lost treasures, trying to bring to light new insights and interpretations more favourable to women and to restore some Christian 'herstory'. It has become a happy hunting ground for academics and clergy alike, much that is valuable has been discovered and no doubt there is more work to be done. Certainly there is work to be done in making this material accessible to congregations and in this the role of theological educators is crucial, for many of those offering for training at the present time have little if any understanding of the work of women theologians and tend to view anything which carries the label 'feminist' with suspicion.

It is clear that women's entry into the ranks of the priesthood has implications for the curricula of ordination courses and colleges. No longer can 'women's ministry' be regarded as a second category whose concerns can be side-lined into voluntary classes at inconvenient times. The concerns of feminist theology are now the concerns of the whole church and as such are of relevance to all ordinands regardless of gender. This means of course not only that men will be enabled to contribute to this research with greater authenticity but also that much which has been hidden from the wider church and remained a source of nourishment for women within fairly confined groupings will belong to the public domain.

The process of sharing and disseminating the insights and methods of feminist theology for the enrichment of the wider church is unlikely to be a comfortable or easy one. It is threatening both to those of us who will be required to defend our discoveries and ways of doing things, and to those who are being asked to accept a wholly new approach to the history of the Church and the interpretation of Scripture. However it is a most necessary process, which can bring fresh life to our churches. I think for example of a women colleague whose small weekly Bible Study doubled in numbers overnight when it was discovered that she was making new use of the insights of Phyllis Trible's "Texts of Terror" - most of the new membership being men, anxious to find out what heresy was being propagated and surprised in the end to find that this study was valuable to them as well.

Many of the 'lost coins' so recently rediscovered will no doubt be battered and tarnished still further in the process of their assimilation into the mainstream tradition of the Church. I do not think we should be afraid of that. For what is sought is not a treasure chest of sovereigns to be jealously guarded by the few fortunate enough to hold the key. Rather those 'coins' which are unearthed from the mire of our patriarchal history need to be woven anew into the common thinking of the whole church. Those pennies which Lucy stitched into my stole no doubt had histories of their own, quite possibly very dubious. Their value now lies not in themselves but in their place within the new whole. In the same way if feminist theology is to have lasting influence it needs to become part of the regular teaching of the wider church, while still seeking to challenge its traditions and assumptions.

It may well be that it is in terms of method rather than content that this assimilation will most easily take place, at least initially. Already the status of Practical Theology, so long the 'Cinderella' of theological syllabi, appears to be rising and this can hardly be coincidental. For Practical Theology with its emphasis upon the primary importance of the experience of the individual as the raw material for all theological reflection relates closely to the methods of feminist theology. For here too personal experience has been revalued and understood as crucial to the whole theological enterprise. Once it is accepted that theology is to be discovered in the interplay of individual experience with the tradition, rather than simply to be received as a body of established knowledge, then the way lies open for the creation of theologies which will lend meaning and purpose to the mission of the church as it enters the twenty-first century. Within such theologies the 'lost coins' may be melted down and minted afresh as women and men together create theology with the benefit of a more inclusive understanding of our traditions. We will together create theologies which are less dogmatic, in which we are not afraid to say, "I think ... I feel" (with the implication that I could be wrong) rather than "the Church teaches".

The Church of the Gleaners

Ruth gleaning in the fields stands as a potent image of the nurturing love for one another and for their families which continues to inform women's relationships with one another both within the Church and outside it. Lavinia Byrne describes it well when she writes,

> *In any human group what is the place of women? My own experience is that they are the people who have listened to me and fed me, they are people with whom I have been free to be vulnerable and free to ask questions. They have not overwhelmed me with the power and significance of their own ideas but have encouraged me to think my own thoughts and to be serious about living in terms of what I have discovered to be true. They have encouraged me when I was depressed and supported me when I was using my gifts and talents.[7]*

Over the years in which women have struggled to gain recognition for their priestly calling, those who felt themselves called and those who supported them without feeling themselves so called have gleaned together. We have prayed together, eaten together, partied together, cried together, raged together and campaigned together. Now that some of us have become priests is all that to change? Can we suddenly lay claim to an authority which we did not have before? Are our ideas suddenly to have a 'power and significance' above that of our sisters and brothers who stood alongside us for so long?

Surely not. For that would be to collude with those very structures of authority which were used to oppress women for so long and which even now retain considerable power. Rather we need to build upon all that was learnt in the wilderness of patterns of collaborative ministry, to create a priesthood which exists to enable the priestly ministry of all.

In many ways this represents a considerable shift in the perception of the role of the priest, away from an acceptance of an hierarchical model and towards an understanding of priest and people as mutually responsible for one another's nurture and walk with God. The willingness to listen to one another, to contain and respect different viewpoints within liturgy, to challenge and support on equal terms will need to be retained. Otherwise the struggle will have been in vain. For the priest presiding at the eucharist celebrates the fact that God in Jesus became human - that is to say like *all* of us, in all our incredible difference and diversity. Women so long denied entry to the priesthood on the grounds of their 'difference' need to ensure that the priesthood they now seek to shape is one in which difference is not merely tolerated but joyfully celebrated and included.

In doing this I believe they will be greatly helped by the continued

---

[7] Lavinia Byrne, *Women Before God*, London 1988, 100.

existence of groups such as Women In Theology and the Catholic Women's Network. Such critical apart communities will provide them not only with continued support and encouragement in the development of their theology and ministry but also with valuable criticism lest they be tempted by clericalism. Within the Church of England as such the Movement for the Ordination of Women has rightly begun to regroup, not just to press for women's admission to the episcopate, but to fulfil the continued need for nurture and support of those who learnt through it to live and worship in new ways. As Margaret Webster writes in the conclusion to her history of the Movement entitled "A New Strength, A New Song".

> *The different experiences described in this book have welded something stronger than just the temporary goodwill of those involved in a common task - deeper than that and not exclusive. Can the experience be fed into the Church: the suffering the waiting, the fun, the experience of conflict and dealing with it, the staying together, the valuing of each other even when views diverged? Above all, the discovering over the years of new ways of worshipping, of fresh language, of circular patterns in worship rather than always a pyramidal hierarchical structure, the symbols we used in worship - oil, yeast, grapes, flowers, rock - are the symbols of a new Christian life.[8]*

Those of us who have participated in that new Christian life will seek to take its assumptions with us into the mainstream of the Church's liturgical and pastoral practice. The result is already to be seen in shifting patterns of responsibility between clergy and lay people, in which it is no longer assumed that the priest is the fount of all knowledge from the understanding of the Trinity to the location of light bulbs! It is to be seen in the sharing of the creation of liturgy, and in the acknowledgement of the skills of the laity across the whole ambit of pastoral care. The shift is gradual of course, and the priest whether male or female who tries to introduce such patterns always runs the risk of appearing incompetent or unwilling to accept 'traditional' responsibilities. However only by so doing will the bonds of clericalism be untied, and the whole church set free to glean together in the harvest fields of the world.

The Rainbow Church
I remain hopeful for the church, despite the insidious nature of its sexism and its slowness to change. It may be that my hope is ill-founded, and that those

---

[8] Margaret Webster, *A New Strength, A New Song*, London 1994, 206.

many sisters who have left the institution behind, in favour of their own variously structured groupings, are right in assuming that patriarchy is too fundamental to Christianity for the mere acceptance of a few token middle-class women into its authority structures to have any real effect. However my experience of political life in Britain over the past fifteen years or so, suggests that the Church still has a vital part to play in challenging the oppressive structures of the state, with which women neglect to engage at their peril.

In a very real and exciting way the Church of England has chosen to recognise the potential of its women at the very time when society at large, threatened by recession, is choosing to scapegoat and repress those whom it projects as 'different', from single parents to travellers. Within its own iconography the Church is accepting the symbol of the unaccepted and unacceptable, and this should have huge implications for the way in which we relate to society at large. For if women are acceptable images of the divine, so also must be all those others whom society seeks to reject and ignore, and whom the Church seeks to serve and represent through its priesthood.

This is not to under-estimate the task before us. The giving of a voice to the voiceless is not easy, as those of us who have fought long and hard to be given a hearing will testify. However those of us who now dare to stand before God as priests, both women and men together, must attempt it, and in the attempt a new church may be fashioned, whose symbol is the rainbow. For the rainbow, sign of God's continuing love, is formed both of the strength of the sun and the weakness of waterdrops, of both feminine and masculine, and from the brokenness of light.

Penny Jones is Director of Practical Theology for the North East Ordination Course of the Church of England. She was ordained as an Anglican Priest in 1994.

Daphne Hampson

Exodus or Not?[*]

I remember as though it were yesterday standing in the kitchen of Episcopal Theological School in Cambridge, Massachusetts, when my friend Diane burst in to tell me the news. It must have been November 1971. She had been at the morning service at Memorial Church in Harvard Yard and one Mary Daly - of whom I had never heard - had delivered a sermon inviting women to exodus from the church - and women and men had poured out into Harvard Yard. History had been made; and I had been absent! Diane became a priest. Mary Daly left the church. I myself could not at that time have conceived of leaving the church and Christianity behind me. For twenty years I wanted to be ordained. But I have left.

So we are considering the fact that it is twenty years since Mary Daly's epoch-making book "Beyond God the Father" was published. It always strikes me as astonishing that the first major book in feminist theology has remained the most radical and the most imaginative. I still dialogue with it and my students are still enthralled by it. It remains as pertinent as ever. What I want to do today is to consider the theme of 'exodus'. Why leave the church? And why remain in the academy?

'Exodus' can have different meanings. Mary Daly that day left the church, as have I and others. Exodus can mean literally leaving, going out into a new existence. Over the years since the rise of feminism innumerable women have walked out on marriages in which they were being abused, jobs in which they were discriminated against, or the church in which they were unable to be ordained. 'External' exodus - as we may call it - is sometimes necessary. But there is another kind of exodus which is more subtle. Let us call it 'internal exodus'. Daly indeed hints at it when she speaks of being present, yet absent,

---

[*] This text is based on a talk given in a series in the Spring of 1994 at the University of Groningen, The Netherlands, to mark twenty years since the publication of Mary Daly's "Beyond God the Father".

at a male committee meeting, thinking one's own thoughts while physically present. Why should one - as I believe - leave the church (an 'external' exodus); yet remain within the academy, performing, when necessary, an 'internal' exodus?

One should leave the church because Christianity is necessarily sexist. It is below one's dignity to belong to a religion, or the institution which proclaims that religion, which discriminates against one. Why do I say that Christianity is, necessarily, sexist; that it cannot be reformed? That is a question which I have addressed at length in my book "Theology and Feminism" (Oxford: Blackwell, 1990) which some of you will know. The heart of the matter is this. Christianity is what I have there called a 'historical' religion. By 'historical' I mean that Christianity is not simply an idea which has arisen in history (all ideas arise within history and bear the marks of the time of their origin) but that Christians believe that God was uniquely present in a certain tradition in a certain age in a certain person, Jesus of Nazareth. Christians are those - this is a good definition - who hold Jesus to have been unique, to have been the Christ, however differently in different ages they may have chosen to express that uniqueness. To say that someone who thinks Jesus to have been a good human being with a fine moral teaching (and that is the end of it) is a 'Christian' is considerable nonsense; one could be an atheist, or Gandhi, and think that. Christians have always proclaimed not simply Jesus' message, but a message, a kerygma, about Jesus. They have not always, of course, held to Chalcedonian orthodoxy. Jesus' uniqueness has, as I have said, been understood in different ways in different ages. The earliest Christians proclaimed their belief in the catchword ICHTHUS, an acronym in Greek for the words 'Jesus Christ God's Son Saviour'. They held this of none other.

But here in this proclamation of uniqueness lies the problem for feminists. For Christians cannot but look back to this particular human being, since they believe that in him was a unique revelation of God. They must then read the (patriarchal) scriptures which tell of the history of this man and of the nation to which he belonged. They cannot just forget this period in human history, nor relate to it as one might to all other past historical epochs. Though Christians may live in the present and consider present problems, they must at some point in their discourse, if they are to be Christians, make reference to one particular past, and make reference to that past as in some way normative, as the point at which there was a revelation of God. The images and the symbols, the stories and the history of that past period will then be transposed into the present. They will be heard, in church or synagogue, as

'Scripture'. That will have its effect. It will be absorbed by the hearers, consciously or subconsciously, that women have a certain position in society and in religion and that that position is secondary to that of men. The 'concretion' of religion, as I have called it in "Theology and Feminism", is powerful.

Nor does it help to look to the stories of women in that past episode of human history. For - as feminist biblical scholars have made abundantly clear over the past decades - the position of women in that society is inferior to that of men. Why should one want to associate with those women? If what one strives for is the equality of human beings - feminism - then what we must do, men and women alike, is to move on from the past. Of course it will be useful to undertake historical scholarship; to show that women had an influence in the past, or that they were profoundly discriminated against. We cannot be free of our past. But Christians do not simply relate to the past as one might in another other discipline, drawing on the past where it is useful and leaving behind the norms of a society which have become irrelevant. Christians belong to a historical religion, a religion in which a certain past must necessarily figure. To read such literature as scripture will, at a subconscious level at least, as I have said, draw the past into the present so that it continues to have its effect. I would find it simply offensive to hear stories in which women were in inferior positions proclaimed within a religious context. Such a context is not one in which I could find God.

Moreover as a person living in an age after the Enlightenment I cannot possibly credit that God (whatever God may be) could be differently related to one age or to one people than God is related to all human beings in all ages. God is not a kind of anthropomorphic agent who intervenes in human history. I understand that in the past people could have thought that it was possible that someone could have stood in a different relation to God 'the Father' than do all other human beings. But I cannot credit that this could be the case. Thus I am not a Christian quite apart from anything to do with feminist issues. To call Jesus 'the Christ' must be a declaration of faith, and such faith is incompatible with all that we now know about the world. I find no reason to take such a step. Moreover I should have a theodicy problem were it to be the case that God had related to this person differently than to all other humans. Given what such a supposed 'revelation' has done to western history, distorting it so that men have ruled over women, I could not call such a God good. As a human being who wishes to live in the modern world, her religion compatible with all else that she believes, I must deny that Christianity can possibly be true. As one to whom an ethics of equality is fundamental, I must deny that the God of Christianity, as that God has been understood, could be called good.

It is inevitable then that I should exit from the church and from Christianity. Why? Because nothing else is intellectually honest or morally possible. If one wishes to be a religious person, not least - as I do - one must have a certain integrity. I do not admire women who try to twist Christianity to mean anything that they would have it be. Christianity must mean something. What Christians have always stood for in human history is the claim that there was a unique revelation in Jesus as the Christ. What I believe we should do in the West is to separate the question as to what it means to be a religious human being from the particular myth, Christianity, which has carried human religious consciousness in our society. For it is indeed the case, one may think - unless one is an atheist, and I am not - that Christianity has been that vehicle through which people have gained a sense as to what it is that God may be. Christianity has shaped the sense which people have had of God. The two are intricately interwoven. Yet it must be possible to say that one does believe in God (one is a theist), while considering the particular myth which has carried the sense of God in the West to belong to another age and to be mistaken. Thus what concerns me as a theologian is to think out how one should speak of God in a world in which the Christian myth can no longer serve; a theme I pursue in my forthcoming, "After Christianity".

To exit from the church is not without its effect. People notice. Once it is the case that there are women (or men, but they are mostly women) who are saying that no I am not a Christian, Christianity is a patriarchal religion, but yes indeed I count myself a religious and a spiritual person, standing within the Western tradition, that raises questions about Christianity. That religion comes to look partial. Christians have ever proclaimed that in Christ there is no East nor West; in him there is neither Jew nor Greek, there is no more male and female. Once one has said that this is not the case, that to be 'in Christ' is different for a man than for a woman, in that the second person of the trinity is wedded in one persona to the human Jesus of Nazareth who was a male in a particular society, one undermines Christology. It is no more the same thing if it is seen to be non-inclusive. Women are raising the profoundest challenge to Christology and to Christianity which has ever been raised. That challenge will not go away. Christianity is now not simply embattled, in making its claim to uniqueness, by our consciousness in this day and age of other world religions, but by women in the heart of Christianity, indeed who are theologians by profession, proclaiming themselves not to be Christians.

Why then remain in the academy? Because there is no reason to leave. The university is not, by definition, biased against women. It proclaims itself to be neutral. One has every right there to pronounce what one may think, whatever that may be. It would be extraordinarily foolish of women not to take the opportunity to do this. I realise that I am perhaps in an unusual position here. For I belong to the Divinity Faculty of an ancient university, St. Andrews, founded in the early fifteenth century, the oldest university in Britain after Oxford and Cambridge and the first Scottish university. The faculty to which I belong has taught theology, exclusively, in the same buildings, since its re-foundation in the mid sixteenth century. No one, I imagine, envisaged that one who is not a Christian would come to teach theology there. St. Andrews is however, as are all universities in Britain, a state university, not tied to the church. I am paid out of tax-payers money - and tax-payers are women as well as men (and atheists as well as Christians). Through my term as president of the European Society of Women in Theological Research, I realise how unusual is this situation. In many European countries theology faculties are tied to the church, Protestant or Catholic; and one has to see a bishop, or otherwise be licensed by the church, before one may teach. It is an invidious position for women to be in. But that is not here the case.

Given that the university proclaims itself to be neutral, one must exercise one's responsibility to say what one will: to follow truth wherever truth may lead. It is not always comfortable. For although the university in theory allows anything to be thought, it may be a very male institution. I well remember, when I was a young woman recently appointed, sitting down to a dinner with about fifty theologians which was correctly addressed by the speaker that evening 'Dear Madam and Sirs'! Recently I was sent a survey - by a man, interestingly - undertaking research on the rise of feminist theology within the academy. 'Since when has theology been taught in your institution?' 'The mid sixteenth century' I replied. 'When was the first woman appointed?' I thought back to the date of my own appointment. '1977'. That said it in a nutshell! Nor does this situation only pertain in Britain. When, in 1971, I heard of the Harvard Exodus, I was myself the only woman studying in the advanced programme in theology at Harvard Divinity School (though there had been others) and there was no woman member of staff on the faculty at Harvard. No wonder, in retrospect, I found it so difficult to express myself in seminars (and then felt discouraged as a result). It is a difficult journey that we, the first generation of women to gain a theological education, have trodden.

Here we may well speak of 'internal' exodus. Let me describe the institution in which I work. [In the lecture which I gave in Groningen I showed slides. St. Mary's College is in part a sixteenth century building. It is, almost uniquely in Britain, French renaissance, having been designed by those who came to Scotland to build Falkland Palace for Mary Queen of Scots during the Scottish-French alliance. On its tower it sports a fleur-de-lys. I showed a slide, the building in the background, with all the college assembled in their gowns, the staff including myself, seated in the front row, the students standing on a raised stand behind them. I also showed a picture of the annual boules match, an ancient tradition which has been inaugurated in recent years, since it is supposed that Mary Queen of Scots, who is supposed to have planted a tree which still survives in the quadrangle, would, through her French connection, have played boules! This amused the audience very much: it was such a happy scene of people, students and staff, again all dressed in their gowns, enjoying themselves. A third picture showed the entrance to the College with coat of arms and above it the words 'In principio erat verbum'.]

Internal exodus is a situation of extraordinary complexity. One is an outsider, and yet an insider; an outside insider. If I did not love my College, if I did not know myself to be part of this community in which I shall have spent the greater part of my working life, it would not be so complex. Were the situation simply awful, I should have had to leave many years ago. If I have found myself up against it as I stood for different values, if I have been shouted at (as I have been) and excluded, if I have at times retreated to my office to cry; this has also been the place where I have drunk innumerable cups of hot chocolate in the common room, where I have danced on Burns night, and posed for the annual college photograph. Above all it has been the students who have kept me here. What greater privilege could there be than to teach eager young minds, opening up for them something of the Western tradition and watching people learn and grow and come to express themselves articulately. There is a richness present in the classroom which revives me whenever I am low.

So internal exodus. It is that moment when one knows oneself apart; when one cannot evade the fact that one stands for different values. I will illustrate it graphically. Not long ago I was sitting in the senior common room alone, munching my sandwich, fuming at the fact that the secretary had said that we should need to get the 'permission' of 'the principal' whom she had referred to as such, in hierarchical language, about some trivial matter. I could stand no longer the photograph of the past principal of the college, in gown, bowing in deference to the Pope, likewise in costume, during his visit to Scotland. I put it in a drawer. Returning to my seat and gazing out of the window, my eye fell on a small niche which is true François I, and which would have had a statue in it when it was built. I considered François I going to the Field of the Cloth of Gold to meet Henry VIII, and wondered when that was (1520?). Then I thought, remembering that occasion, 'more men parading around in silly costumes: Plus ça change, plus c'est la même chose'. I was grinning, seated as I was on my own having lunch! It is in that moment of release that, with a sense of humour, it is possible to continue. I had taken the distance that I needed to. I had analysed the world from a feminist perspective; that which, through explaining circumstances to one, alone allows one to continue.

Simone de Beauvoir comments in "The Second Sex" that what distinguishes sexism from other forms of discrimination is that women are bound to men in the closest of bonds. They are also, she comments, often divided from one another. It is this which means that one is constantly involved in a process of negotiation with oneself. Sometimes one is just part of the company; then suddenly one looks at what transpires askance, knowing oneself to have a another judgement, a divergent ethic. As I sit in the College Hall, the fathers in their portraits on the walls looking down on me from out of their golden frames, I cannot but know that I am different. They, too, are various, from the sixteenth century to the twentieth. One, from the early nineteenth century, seems to have a bemused look on his face, for which I have often been grateful as I sat, the only woman, at Faculty Council. How should one know when to accede to what is happening, which one may think misjudged, unimaginative, or indeed discriminatory; when on the other hand must one speak up and perhaps stand alone - something which at a younger age it took all my courage to do? I have noticed over the years that it has been I who have stuck up for other women; the librarian who was about to have a wall built which would block her only window, the cleaner who is forced to clean the male lavatory. I look at the world differently, I have other connections - the world of women. 'God give me serenity to accept the things I cannot change, courage to change the things I can, and wisdom to know the difference' as that Chinese student's prayer runs. The complexity arises from the fact that I also feel myself a part of these people; I laugh with them.

What of the theology which one teaches in such an institution? I am employed as a 'systematic theologian' (the term used in the advertisement to which I responded and got the job). I should not have applied for a post in 'Christian dogmatics'. Of course one could perhaps, in a university, legitimately teach Christian dogmatics holding oneself any position. But I want to be quite clear that one should be able to speak about God, systematically, from any perspective, not simply that of Christian dogmatics. There is nothing to say that one should be Christian. I speak about God, when I speak for myself, from within the Western tradition; the tradition in which I was trained and to which I belong. Thus one has the same dialectical relation to the western theological tradition as that which I have described in relation to the institution in which one teaches. I am part of it, yet not part of it. At times I recognise in the texts of the theological heritage that other human beings loved God, as I too love God. At other times I must look at their conceptualisation of God, through the tenets of the Christian tradition, askance. Again, when one speaks of 'love of God', I must acknowledge that the power by which a person (say Jesus of Nazareth) healed so many years ago is the same power by which today I believe that people are healed from illness, whether mental or physical. On the other hand, I must acknowledge that the way in which Jesus conceptualised God, good monotheistic Jew that he was, to whom it would never have occurred that there was anything problematic about calling God 'Father', is very different from how I think that it is legitimate to speak of God. Feminists are part of the Western tradition, yet also not part of it; the excluded other. It is this to which so much of the most worthwhile feminist scholarship (think of the work of Luce Irigaray) has pointed in recent years. We must wend our way; it is indeed a dance through a minefield.

Sometimes my office has become a hotbed of revolution. Situated in the midst of that venerable institution, the door shut behind us, women have given expression to their hopes for the future and to their vision, to their frustration with their patriarchal surroundings and to their despair at male thought forms. That we are situated in such a setting gives an edge to our deliberations. If it were just plain sailing, were there feminism all around us, there would be nothing to come up against, nothing in relation to which we should define ourselves. One has to know the face of patriarchy if one is to speak to it. The contexts feminists dream up, the theology which we proclaim, would after all change our world so radically that - so one sometimes thinks - not one stone of the Western intellectual tradition would be left upon another. Monotheism, and Christianity, are not marginal to that tradition; they have been the linchpin which have held it together. They have been that which has given the ordering of society its legitimacy; which, quite literally, has given the impression that it was the will of God. Yet one cannot just jump outside that tradition, for where would one be? How could one think? I teach Schleiermacher by choice because here was a man, whom I can admire, who commenced from human awareness of God, of which I also wish to speak. In that he went on to conceptualise this awareness in Christian form, Schleiermacher took a path that I cannot follow. But his work is a starting point. I do not teach women from the past (there were no great women theologians), though I do incidentally teach the thought of some present day feminist theorists.

We live in extraordinary times. For those of us who are women belong to that generation who have consciously articulated our thoughts as women. If Adam named the world, and (it must be noted) the woman and her reality as well, women must rename it. The talk of naming I take of course from Mary Daly, who embarked on such a course twenty years ago. If it is twenty years since the publication of "Beyond God the Father", it is also only twenty years. Much water has flowed under the bridge in that time. A new generation of women has come upon the scene, a generation that does not remember what it was like to be so alone. Times change. They have changed markedly in the College to which I belong. Now there are feminist women, a whole group of them, who pursue my thoughts with me, with whom I can inter-change ideas. It is not automatically easier that there are women. Sometimes women have found it more difficult to tolerate the differences between themselves than to negotiate their divergence from men whom they expect to be different. We need to give one another space; the space that has so often been denied to women as a whole within patriarchal institutions. But most of the time it is of course greatly supportive to have other women around one.

We must seize our opportunity. Europe cannot revert, we must hope, to being Christian, the Christendom of old. If it does, women will suffer. (Look at what has happened in Poland as a result of the attempt there to institute a theocracy in place of a secular state.) We should welcome the Enlightenment and the consequent division of church and state which it has brought about in the last two hundred years. It is an intolerable situation that, in some countries, being a member of a university theology faculty is still tied to holding certain (Christian) beliefs. We see what hegemony male thought has had when the academy is in this wise enmeshed with the power of the church and of the state. Women are opening up a chink of light; they are placing a wedge between Christian thought and the question as to what it might mean to be religious or spiritual. There must, they are saying, equally be a place for them to think out how it is that they would conceptualise God. (The most difficult thing is to believe it of oneself that one has a right to be there, to think one's thoughts whatever they may be.) The changed situation which this demands we can only accomplish in unison, as there are many of us, such that we reach a critical mass.

I believe also that in this women in different disciplines can profoundly help one another. Feminist thought does hold something in common; certain modes of analysis, insights and values. I learn more from women working in feminist theory in other disciplines, which I can then transpose to my own discipline, than I do from people of a very different outlook than my own working within theology. Take for example the consideration of monotheism. How could one begin to think today about monotheism apart from the insights which have been provided by French thought into the nature of singularity, of phallocentrism, of the tendency to create a One which in turn gives rise to that which is Other to it. Again, how could one critique the fact that sin has in the West been understood primarily as pride, as hubris, were it not for the work of American thinkers who have told us of the need for women to come into their own, while men by contrast must overcome an enclosed sense of self which has set itself over against others? One is not alone, even if one feels isolated in one's discipline. Women are providing a new ethic, a new way of conceiving of the self, a new vision for one. How exciting, in such circumstances, to be working in theology; that discipline within which people have always expressed their highest aspirations.

So we should take heart. We should not exodus from theology and leave it to the men. The task before us is too important. European universities have been the citadels of power, for they have been the crucibles of new thought forms, which in turn have so profoundly affected the way in which we live. True it is tempting at times to go and do something with one's life which is more obviously needed, to work in a women's refuge or to address oneself to the many pressing problems of the world. But those of us who are attracted to the academic life, who find in abstract thought forms and in developing ideas our métier, should not despair of the relevance of our work. It may be crucial to the future of humanity. Driving away some years ago from the University of Leipzig, then in the former East Germany, my host who was a professor at the theology faculty there, repeated to me a remark that a colleague of his had just made to him, subsequent to the lecture which

I had given on 'Die Herausforderung des Feminismus für das Christentum' ('The Challenge of Feminism to Christianity'). His friend regaled him: 'Da hast du wieder eine kleine Bombe gelegt!' (There you have once again gone and laid a small bomb!). Feminism is more than a small bomb in the history of the West; it is a rather big bomb - if bomb is the right metaphor for a feminist to use. It has already begun to shake to its very foundations the world as we have known it. There is no reason on earth for us to quit. Rather should we dedicate ourselves, in our generation, to commencing on the task before us. Feminism will change theology.

Daphne Hampson is Senior Lecturer in Divinity at the University of St. Andrews, Scotland. She was the first and founding President of the European Society of Women in Theological Research.

Irmgard Maria Busch
Prozession und (k)eine Frauenkirche[*]

Mit der Kirche ist
es eigentlich ganz
einfach.
Sie geht und sie
läuft.
Manchmal hat sie
Durchfall,
manchmal hat sie
Verstopfung.
Aber hierfür gibt es
Mittel,
die bremsen oder
stimulieren,
eine Entmutigungs-
oder eine För-
derungspolitik.
Auf jeden Fall
immer
organisieren,
umstrukturieren,
erneuern.
Ohne das geht sie
nicht.
Aggiornamento
oder unbeirrbar
Richtung Zukunft

oder zurück zu den
sauberen Quellen.
Die Sache mit der
ecclesia muß einfach
laufen.

Die Kirche ist wie
eine Prozession.
Immer kommt
wieder dasselbe
heraus.
Man fängt an bei
der Kirche,
und man landet
wieder bei der
Kirche.
Der Anfang ist das
Ende,
das Ende ist immer
ein neuer Beginn.

Alles
was sich auf den
Weg gemacht hat,
alles was sich
aufhält zwischen

dem Ausgangspunkt
und der Endstation,
nennt Mann: das
Volk Gottes
unterwegs.

Jeder der mitgeht,
glaubt weiter-
zukommen.
Er hat sich bewogen
und glaubt,
daß er in einer
Bewegung sitzt.
Und so läuft das
Volk Gottes,
die eine Runde nach
der anderen.
Ihm nachfolgen, in
seinen Fußstapfen.
Der Weg ist deutlich
und liegt fest.
Von Anfang bis
zum Ende.

Es gibt einen
Hauptweg und auch

---

[*] In diesem Text werden Bilder und Analysen von Mary Daly gebraucht, die in ihren Büchern *Gyn/Ökologie* und *Reine Lust* zu finden sind. Dieser Text wurde während einer Veranstaltung der Feministischen Zeitschrift *Schlangenbrut* am 26. Mai 1990 auf dem 'Katholikentag von unten' in Berlin ausgesprochen.

Seitenwege.
Sie laufen parallel.
Die Seitenwege sind
eingerichtet für
bestimmte Gruppen.
Sicherheitshalber
sind regelmässig
Umleitungen
angelegt.
Gefährliche Wege
sind abgesperrt und
unsichtbar gemacht.
So kann kein Zwei-
fel und keine Ver-
wirrung entstehen.
Man will ja nur das
Beste für das Volk.
Wer dennoch diese
gefährlichen Wege
entdeckt
und sich nicht an
die Vorschriften
hält,
ist hoffnungslos
verloren,
sagen die Hüter der
Prozession.

Während der
Prozession werden
dauernd Menschen
eingegliedert und
aufgenommen.
Der Kreislauf hat
immer Bedarf an
frischem Blut.
Während der

Prozession werden
dauernd Menschen
ausgegliedert und
rausgesetzt.
Von den Ausgeglie-
derten erwartet
man,
daß sie sich
empören,
daß sie protestieren,
daß sie sehr traurig
sind,
weil sie nicht mehr
mitmachen dürfen.
Hierdurch entsteht
das allgemeine
Gefühl,
wie schön und selig
es ist,
wenn man mit
machen darf und
nicht zu den Aus-
rangierten gehört.
Hochpreiset meine
Seele den Herrn!
Das Ausgliedern
schliesst die Reihen
und gibt der
Prozession einen
erhebenden Anblick.

Das Eingliedern und
Ausgliedern
liefern die Kontur
und den Inhalt.
Die Reibungen der
inneren Opposition

halten alles in
Bewegung.
Bewegungen von
unten und von den
Seiten
halten die Sache in
Schwung
und lösen durch das
Tempo
die Verstopfungen
auf.

Die Prozession ist
ein Teufelskreis.

Auch im theologi-
schen Denkbereich
spielen sich die
Prozessionen ab.
Man fängt an zu
denken und zu
verkündigen,
kaut eine Zeitlang
drauf herum;
aktualisieren,
neu interpretieren,
etwas appetitlicher
machen
für die Dritte Welt,
für die Armen,
für die Frauen, für
die Umwelt und
Natur,
und dann haben wir
wieder
eine neue Runde
von demselben

gehabt.
Man ist weiter-
gekommen,
denn man ist
angekommen
wo der Ausgangs-
punkt war.
Alles dreht sich um
ihn herum.
So ist die Logik,
ganz einfach.
Immer weiter und
immer dasselbe,
regelmäßig
Spannung,
regelmäßig
Abwechslung.
Und alles geht
durch Ihn und mit
Ihm und in Ihm.
Per Omnia saecula
saeculorum.

Außerhalb der
vorgeschriebenen
Wege
fällt das ganze
Vorstellungs-
vermögen weg.
Undenkbar wird,
daß hinter den
Absperrungen,
am Ende der
Sackgassen
ganze Welten zu
entdecken sind.

Wenn der Schwung
erlahmt,

wird einverleibt und
eine neue Kanalisa-
tion angelegt.
Moderne Ketzer und
Irrlehrer werden
produziert,
die sich anstrengen
zu beweisen,
daß sie die richtige
Lehre vertreten,
daß sie es gut
meinen,
daß sie Propheten
sind
und die Kirche
retten wollen.

Mit der Kirche und
ihrer Theologie
ist es ganz einfach.
Immer wieder
Variationen auf
dasselbe Thema.
Der Ausgangspunkt
ist das Ziel,
das Ziel ist der
Ausgangspunkt.
Der Anfang und das
Ende,
ein geschlossener
Kreis,
ein Teufelskreis.

Und Frauen dürfen
auch mitmachen
in diesem Kreislauf.
Innerhalb der
göttlich gestellten
Grenzen,

innerhalb des
mystischen Leibes
halten Frauen alles
am Laufen.
Frauen regeln den
Kreislauf.
Mit viel unbezahlter
Arbeit und
grenzenloser Liebe
und Hingabe
pumpen sie die
nötigen Stoffe
und die lebens-
notwendige
Begeisterung,
bescheiden, selbst-
verständlich und
natürlich
in alle Abteilungen,
Organe und Organi-
sationen,
vor allem aber in
die Köpfe und
Häupter
des mystischen
Leibes.
Und so wie
geschrieben steht
enden hier ihre
eigenen Gedanken,
bekommen sie den
nötigen Beistand,
um voll Freude
sagen zu können:
Siehe, ich bin die
Dienstmagd des
Herrn,
mir geschehe nach
seinen Wort.

Wenn es im Inter-
esse des Gottes-
volkes ist,
wenn es der Kirche
zugute kommt,
dann dürfen Frauen
morgen mehr als
heute.
Bedingung hierfür
ist,
daß die Prozession,
der Fronleichnam
bestimmte Bedürf-
nisse hat und
daß das Zentral-
komitee
die Genehmigung
erteilt.
Die Zentrale hat die
Übersicht
und erhält und
regelt die Einheit.
Für die Erhaltung
des großen Ganzen
können Frauen
Salbungen und
Ämter bekommen,
wenn es sein muß
auch Geld.
Wenn die Zentrale
grünes Licht
gegeben hat,
können Frauen sich
ihrer Berufung
bewußt werden.
Wenn die Frau dann
vom Chef den

Segen bekommt,
wird ihr gesagt:
Selig die Frau, die
nicht denkt und
doch glaubt.

So einfach geht es
in der Kirche.

Und wie geht es in
der Frauenkirche?

Eine Frauenkirche,
die dasselbe tut wie
die richtige Kirche,
aber dann fraulich
begeistert
und mütterlich
fromm,
ist eine Variation
auf dasselbe Thema,
auf Kirche, die
organisierte
Prozession,
und kann keine
Frauenkirche sein.

Eine Frauenkirche,
die im milden und
im strengen Ton
- theologisch und
exegetisch unterbaut
- sagt: "Wir Frauen
wollen auch!
Wir gehören auch
zur Kirche!"
ist eine notwendige

Injektion
für die Belebung
und Erneuerung
des mystischen
Leibes
und kann keine
Frauenkirche sein.

Eine Frauenkirche
gebraucht den
Verstand
und ist nicht mehr
fähig
den Unsinn zu
glauben.
Eine Frauenkirche
sündigt ohne
Unterlaß
und nimmt zu an
Kraft und Weisheit.
Eine der größten
Sünden ist
der Ausbruch eines
Lachanfalls,
wenn kleine und
große Kirchenväter
Mater et Magistra
spielen,
so würdig und mit
heiligem Ernst.

Feministische
Frauen
sind sündig und
unwissenschaftlich
wenn sie
untersuchen

und dahinter
kommen,
was eigentlich
der unerschöpfliche
Gnadenbrunnen ist,
und was das Zeug
ist,
das man so
gönnerhaft
und in Gottes
Namen
austeilt.

Feministische
Frauen
entdecken Syndrome
im absurden Gang
der Dinge.
Nimm zum Beispiel
das Eucharistische
Syndrom,
ein zentral
organisierter Betrug.
Mit rituellen
Gebaren
gibt man symboli-
sches Brot zu essen,
um den Hunger zu
stillen.
Aber das Brot ist
kein Brot,
sondern ein wahrer
Leib.
Man sieht und
schmeckt das Brot,
aber in Wirklichkeit
sieht und schmeckt
man,
was man nicht sehen

und schmecken
kann.
Was man sieht und
schmeckt
ist unwirklich;
denn durch eine
höhere Gewalt
ist der Inhalt
verändert
und ist das konkrete
Wahrnehmbare
nur äußerer Schein,
keine Wirklichkeit.
Das Kommando
lautet:
"Was du siehst, das
siehst du nicht.
Erniedrige dich,
öffne dich und
deinen Mund,
Hier kommt der
Leib, die geistliche
Speise."

Dieses Ritual
ist verrückt und
lächerlich.
Aber in der
Prozession
ist dieses Ritual
logisch.
Es gehört zu einer
Praxis,
die einverleibt und
amputiert.
Die Kommuni-
kanten,
die sich den Schwin-
del gefallen lassen,

die die Lügen
gnädig empfangen
und hinunter-
schlucken
ohne Ekel und
Schluck-
beschwerden,
sind nicht mehr
imstande
mit sich selbst und
anderen
zu kommunizieren.
Mit Lügen werden
sie ausgehungert
und dann
einverleibt,
eingebracht in die
Prozession.

Feministische
Frauen sehen,
daß in der
Gesellschaft,
in der Kirche und
den Quasi-
Bewegungen
auf Kosten der
Frauen gelebt wird,
daß Frauen
mit Herz und Seele,
mit Haut und
Haaren,
gebraucht und auf-
gegessen werden.
Es scheint normal
zu sein,
daß Frauen sich
hingeben,
daß sie spirituell,

theologisch,
wirtschaftlich und
sexuell
genutzt und aus-
gesaugt
und dann weg-
geworfen werden.
Wieso, Tisch des
Herrn?
Brot und Wein
teilen?
Wer ißt eigentlich
wen auf!

Feministische
Frauen sehen,
wie die Kirche
weitermacht
mit der geistlichen
Umwelt-
verschmutzung,
umgesägte Bäume
als Kreuze austeilt,
mit Weihwasser die
dreckigen Sachen
segnet.
Feministische
Frauen sehen,
wie die Hohen-
priester
den wirklichen
Widerstand
gegen die
Vernichtung und
Gewalttaten
einverleiben,
weil der Herr doch

alles so schön
erschaffen hat.
Der Herr macht nur
saubere Sachen,
darum wollen die
normalen und
oppositionellen
Kirchenväter
auch immer alles so
sauber haben.
Mit synthetischen
Bleichmitteln
wird recycelt und
kaputtgemacht
wird die Geburt zur
Wiedergeburt,
werden die Flecken
der Jungfrauen
weggeputzt,
entsteht die saubere
Weste,
das reine Gewissen,
die gesäuberten
Texte, die reine
Lehre.

Feministische
Frauen
eignen sich einfach
nicht für die
Prozession.

Feministische
Frauen
lassen sich nicht
länger einverleiben,
sie verlieren die

Unschuld
und sündigen mit
Lebenslust.
Sie werden
allergisch
für alle Säuberungs-
aktionen.
Sie entdecken
die verschwiegene
Geschichte,
die versperrten
Wege,
die alten und neuen
Traditionen.

Mit der Kirche hat
das nichts zu tun.

Ob Frauenkirche ein
guter Name ist
für alles, was jen-
seits der Prozession
lebt,
überlebt,
wage ich zu be-
zweifeln.

Irmgard Maria Busch (1948) ist Moraltheologin und studierte an der Theologischen Fakultät in Tilburg. Seit 1986 arbeitet sie in der Erwachsenenbildung. (Arbeitsstätte: Centrum Nieuwe Ypelaar Bavel, Kloster der Paters der Heilige Harten). Sie lebte bis 1970 in Paderborn und war Industriekaufmann.

Liesbeth Huijts

Towards an Open and Bounded Space[1]: A Retrospective of the Second Dutch Ecumenical Women's Synod from an Ecclesiological Perspective

Three women responded to the appeal to act as observer during the second Dutch Ecumenical Women's Synod which was held in August of 1992. I was one of them. We walked around for five days, read papers, took part in conversations; observing how this mixed company of women at the synod, with different positions of power in society and in the church, represented their movement. On the sixth and final day of the synod, we presented our findings.

Much the same as in this article, our story focused on the way in which the woman-and-faith movement aims to shape the ecclesia of women and the incentives that the second Women's Synod provided in this process.

The Observers' Report

"... By way of public conversation and as a profession of love we would like to tell you all how we have lived these past few days. We want to tell you what we do not want to forget. What the work will look like in our opinion. And why should we object to leaving this meeting with new homework!

Mind you, we were not present everywhere; we read the papers, we conducted conversations and looked around: with our eyes. That is the way it is. We saw three tasks for the years ahead. They were all dealt with in the five clusters we worked in this week - learning, celebrating, serving, sharing and the woman-and-faith movement. We will formulate them, visualise them

---

[1] This was the title of the second Ecumenical Women's Synod. It derives from the description of the women's church by Elisabeth Schüssler Fiorenza as a 'bounded open space'. She elaborated further on this notion during the conference 'power-difference-power' in 's-Hertogenbosch in 1988. This paper was published as an article in: Elisabeth Schüssler Fiorenza, *Discipleship of Equals*, London, 1993, 332-352.

and we will sing their praises for the sake of Her, who is Merciful and Good.
In our opinion, the following three tasks are involved:
How do we let our experiences speak?
How do we want to be a religious community?
How do we compare to other religious communities?

About Our Experiences

We have all known for some time - and that is how we started - that we want
to learn, celebrate, share, and, if we must, serve as well, from our own
perspective. Our religious gatherings will have to at least be beneficial to us.
We want to be able to believe, for, through and with one another, basing ourselves also on our experiences. No longer may our laughter and tears be for
nothing, says She, our God.

But then there is the 'prism': through trial and error we discover that this
collection of experiences breaks up into many different colours. We discover
that, where changes for the better are concerned, women too have very different interests, needs and expectations and that these have to be discussed,
have to be fought over, loved and acted upon. But how do we do this: how
can we broaden our movement? Do our experiences complement each other?
Are the differences in power and helplessness too large and do they stand in
the way of collectivity?

Or must we learn to ask different questions that will make the old issues
fade? Should we not first focus and narrow our view as much as we can in
order to be able to look around? If we zoom in on the life of one woman we
can learn to see all the colours of the world. As Doreen Hazel told us even
more clearly at the opening: "Also direct your attention to coloured women
because oppression is not foreign to them." In our opinion, we will need a
funnel in order to focus our view and in order to stop ourselves from going
under in multiplicity and pluriformity; in order to distinguish between justice
and injustice and between good intentions and political plans. And we may
hope that She, our God, will show herself.

Funnel

Sanctuary for women who are unwanted in this world, who have to
remain silent in church, but are brought to speak here.
Treasury of justice for those who are dominated according to colour.
Compassion for lesbians or otherwise, heterosexuals or otherwise, with

children or without.

About Our Community
We want it so badly, and confess it again and again, a world without Jew or Greek, slave or free, 'male or female'. Because we are all one in Christ. What makes up our desire for unity, what do we think of, what vision makes us live? Can it be that here too, the old forms and thoughts darken our future; that we inherently and habitually long for a harmonious union?

Of course conflicts are unbearable and hurtful. But why? Unbearable for whom, and who will suffer when there are no conflicts? These have been the questions that were asked these past few days.

Can we find forms, create stories, share visions that do not unite our community, make it uniform. Is our unity allowed to be conflictive? Can we learn, serve, celebrate and share in a tense community, in a 'church-existence', full of new longing?

> *Wheel*
> Centre of change and democracy for those who get the short end of the stick politically and economically.
> Discipleship of equals where everyone sits around a table, shares food and drink and everything; that which is forbidden in this world but promised in the kingdom of heaven.

About Our Relationship with other Church Communities
We can be brief on this subject:
May our learning, serving, celebrating and sharing be a disgrace for the existing churches, may our gatherings be scandalous to them.

> *Apple*
> Let us not lose this:
> Put Your eyes protectively upon us, because it is Thee in particular who knows what it has cost women, what it will cost us, to get to where we are today, to rejoice in a new soul and a new body for the world."[2]

---

[2]   Included in: *Report of the second Ecumenical Women's Synod 22-27 August 1992*, 40-42. The other spies were Lidy Leussink and Willemien Boot.

What Went Before

An event is not isolated, but forms part of a historic process, and is more easily understood from a historic perspective. That is why I will go back in the history of the Dutch woman-and-faith movement; to the first Ecumenical Women's Synod in 1987.

The first synod took place at the end of a symposium which went on for several days based on the theme of 'woman and power' on the occasion of the tenth anniversary of woman-and-faith work at the Church and World training centre in Driebergen. On the day of the Synod, about forty resolutions, diverse in character, formed the basis for debates and ballots. Decisions were taken about recommendations to official bodies of the church, to political authorities and to the woman-and-faith movement. The first synod was important for the self-awareness of the woman-and-faith movement. First of all, it strengthened the self-awareness of the movement as a movement. Woman-and-faith groups often operated in relative isolation. At the synod it became clear - literally - that the movement was a very large one. It also became a political factor in the church in the Netherlands. In addition, the image of the movement as a homogeneous whole, was shown to be a false one once and for all. Coloured and lesbian women had been pointing out white heterosexism for some time, also within the movement; women on social security emphasised power differences between women as a result of their economic positions. At the synod these issues were dealt with through the agency of those same groups of women and resolutions were adopted by those present that tested oppression in its many forms.

This development was accompanied by a politicizing of the woman-and-faith movement. While until that moment language and liturgy, the position of women in oppressive church structures or religious questions had been the most important subjects in the woman-and-faith movement, political and economic issues such as racism, heterosexism, sexual violence and poverty (in society and church) have been central points on the movement's agenda since the first Women's Synod.

The first Ecumenical Women's Synod showed what vision of the ecclesia the woman-and-faith movement has in mind: an ecclesia for women where spiritual and political matters are on the agenda; where power differences between women are taken seriously and where they, who are unequal in this world, practice a 'discipleship of equals'. This term was coined by Schüssler Fiorenza, who was introduced in the Netherlands in November 1987 with the publication of the Dutch translation of her book 'In Memory of Her', and it was used by a number of theologians as a political-theological model for the woman-and-faith movement; as such it was recognised and adopted by many women in the movement.

In everyday life it often was difficult to live with the differences and to endure the confrontations. In the years following the first synod difficult and often endless discussions about differences in power were sometimes solved with a pragmatism that is typically Dutch: 'In the end we all stand for the same thing so let us not waste all our energy and time on each other but instead let each of us fight the battle on our own terrain.' The conviction that "that which is done to one member of the community - ecclesiologically speaking - touches everyone"[3] seemed in danger of being lost. By the way, the result of this pragmatic attitude was a movement that brimmed over with activity.

Looking for a Tense Community

It was at that moment in history that the second Ecumenical Women's Synod took place. During the preparations for the event there were attempts to find ways to combat the threat of fragmentation that faced the movement (see above). It was clear that the second synod had to emphasise solidarity again while, at the same time, differences should not be glossed over. To this end three steps were taken.

First of all, the synod decided to work on a plan of action for the woman-and-faith movement for the next five years. It was decided that the following method would be used. During the first four days the participants worked out themes in workshops and prepared plans of action. On the fifth day these plans were worked out further and formed the basis for the plan of action that was drawn up. Participating women and women's groups committed themselves to parts of this plan of action. On the final day, the plan was presented to each other and to people who could only attend that particular day and would pass the plan on to their supporters. In addition, it was taken for granted that the synod would be supported from the first preparations to the final day by the groups in the woman-and-faith movement. A core group was established to create conditions in which these groups could prepare and shape the synod together. However, it was inevitable that in creating

---

[3] Will Verhoef, "Will she be there, my sister?", in: *Eighty May Post* 9 (1994) 3, 6.

conditions, decisions were made with regard to contents as well. This regularly caused tension between the core group and woman-and-faith groups around the country. The second synod is characterised by the fact that women have remained in this area of tension and, also when solutions could not be found directly, did not withdraw nor exert their powers. During this synod it became evident that participants wanted to look for forms of solidarity, also in situations in which the atmosphere was not happy and relaxed.

The third step concerned the subject-matter of the synod. With the aid of the advisory committee, which consisted of fifty women, the core group looked for a framework within which it would be possible to work toward a feeling of solidarity among women that does not blur power differences. To this purpose, the core group sought the advice of two theologians from the United States of America: Elisabeth Schüssler Fiorenza and Delores Williams. Schüssler's concept of women's ecclesia as an open rhetorical space that is bound together by its struggle against multiplying forms of oppression seemed to suit this purpose. In order to make the feeling of solidarity tangible, the group relied on Delores Williams.

Williams argues that, in our attention for everything that is concerned with the justified existence of women, we should not forget what it means to be a 'church' or a 'community'. She uses the traditional functions that the church has in the areas of learning, serving and celebrating to develop activities that create communities, and adds other functions including 'sharing'.[4]

These four functions of the community - learning, celebrating, serving and sharing became the pivots that were to lead to an open and bounded space. That is to say: the fact that women's groups categorised their activities under one of the four functions, might make it possible to look for links between social issues without obscuring their social meaning. Indeed, there were some surprising collaborations as a result. For example, members of the lesbian network 'Verkeerd Verbonden', a representative of the Islamic organization Nisa and the women's group SIEN of the *Basisbeweging Nederland* organised a joint workshop with the title 'Love is multi-coloured'.

---

[4] Annelies Knoppers,"A conference for and by women. The ideas behind the second Ecumenical Women's movement", in: *Mara* 5 (1992) 3, 36.

At times it seemed impossible to find links based on the four functions of the community. While the workshops were being prepared, black women discovered that white women were less than willing to consider racism as a matter for discussion. Thereupon they decided to organise their own workshop.

> ... we had decided at first to stay away, but love is profound, we are here anyway, but now on our own terms. And whether we will have a community depends on you, my white sisters, and not on us. Although our workshop is closed to white women, our hearts are not.[5]

With this decision, they succeeded in getting white women to put the issue of power differences between black and white women on the agenda after all. In the end, a number of white and black women jointly formulated action items.

Learning, Celebrating, Serving, Sharing.
These four functions of the community served to support the search for links and solidarity without glossing over differences. It will be clear that this process was not always easy. Sometimes positions of power were used to force an agreement. Sometimes women wondered in despair whether it would be possible to work together at all. But in general, a feeling of determination to get on with each other emerged during the synod. This revealed itself in the joint development of plans of action; in the mutual support shown during the drawing up of these plans; in the determination to engage in confrontations. Whereas the first synod put the issue of differences on the agenda of the woman-and-faith movement, it was the second synod that made the search for forms of commitment, regardless of power differences, a major point on the movement's agenda. Learning, celebrating, serving and sharing are concepts that did not really come alive for women during the second synod. They were probably too controversial. Opinions were divided as to the use of these concepts from the Christian tradition.

The four concepts met with criticism similar to that which greeted the concept of 'synod' five years earlier. They were said to be too ecclesiasti-

---

[5] Doreen Hazel in her introduction "In the name of love" during the opening of the Women's Synod, in: *Verslag* 1992, 13.

cal, too connected with the established churches. Women feared that these concepts would reintroduce the traditional androcentric meanings of community.

Despite this criticism, the concepts were maintained for the same reasons that had led to the choice, five years earlier, to keep using the concept of 'synod'. It showed 'that women are most definitely able to take the initiative to create their own definitions of words'.[6] By using words such as learning, celebrating, serving and sharing, women again claimed their tradition and the political and theological right to interpret that tradition. To provide an answer to the criticism, it was decided during the second synod to investigate how participants would interpret the four functions of the community: namely learning, celebrating, serving and sharing. This was the true task of the observers whom I referred to at the beginning of this article.

About the World in Our Midst.
During the preparations for the second synod, the question as to how we want to shape the ecclesia of women was formulated as follows: how do we want to give shape to the solidarity among women without glossing over the differences between them? This question was recognised and acknowledged during the second synod as an ecclesiological question for the woman-and-faith movement. An answer was sought during and after the synod. This was not always an easy process; it seemed, at times, like an obstacle course. A number of the obstacles that women were faced with were discussed in this article. The core group of the second Women's Synod wrote in a letter that it sometimes seems that the dialogue in the woman-and-faith movement is more of a conversation about each other than a conversation with the world in our midst, than a conversation in which various options and analyses concerning the injustice in this world are possible, and arguments can take place about adequate strategies and views which can bring about new realities.[7]

But it was during the synod that women also experienced that the ecclesia of women sometimes briefly takes on a shape during the process

---

[6] Knoppers 1992, 33.
[7] The board of the Ecumenical Women's Synod foundation (the core group) in an open letter to the woman and religion movement. *Newsletter Women's Synod,* nr.11, July 1993.

of looking for a community that is full of tension: it takes shape in collaboration, in mutual support, but particularly in confrontations where participants continue to look one another in the face. Women learned and are learning that new questions can break through old dichotomies and reveal new issues. For example, during a conference in February 1994, organised by the committee for 'power inequality between men and women' of the May Eighth Movement, participants managed to leave out of the discussion the question as to whether women should occupy themselves with such structural church issues.[8] Taking into consideration the practices of women in the discussion about functions in the churches other functions became visible. Shepherds for example: women who call together the community, function as binding forces and exert power whenever social differences threaten to drive us apart. Or the function of prophetesses: women who, for example, lodge complaints against sexual assault in pastoral relations and warn that this type of violence endangers the community.

The second Ecumenical Women's movement has profited because, after a period in which power differences between women were justifiably emphasised, we are searching once again for that which binds us together without losing sight of these differences. The discussions about and the practices of the ecclesia of women have been given new incentives as a result. The task which the name of the second Ecumenical Women's Synod entails: 'Towards an Open and Bounded Space', still determines the agenda of the woman-and-faith movement.

There will be much discussion, struggle, love and action for the sake of a community that will be and is, at times, already tangible.

(translation: Brigitte Planken)

Liesbeth Huijts is manager Unie KBO, the Dutch Association of Catholic Societies for Senior Citizens. Researcher at the Dominican Centre for the Study of Theology and Society in Nijmegen at the time of the synod.

---

[8] The Eighth May movement is a platform for Roman Catholic organizations for the renewal of church and society. A number of women's organizations, the woman-and-faith groups among them, at work in Roman Catholic bishoprics or of Roman catholic origin, are affiliated to this movement.

Michaela Moser

Working on Creating Space for Each Other.
Towards the First European Women's Synod

It was Dutch women who started having 'Synods' and who set on fire women in other parts of Europe. The stories about their Synods were inspiring and seductive and this led to women in Austria, Germany and Switzerland organising and holding their own Synods. Each of them was quite different from the others, focusing on different main items according to the situation in the particular country.

At the same time the idea of holding a European Synod has taken root and in 1992 an international committee started to meet in the Netherlands to prepare this open-access, six-day event for a thousand women, which will take place in Austria in July 1996.

By holding on to the name 'Women's Synod' the organisers desire to proclaim that women want to gather, to draw authority from their collective decisions and to take responsibility for their own leadership and action. In addition they want to reclaim the term in its old meaning of a coming together of like-minded people to achieve goals together. In order to realise this project they are coming together from different parts of Europe twice a year and are putting a lot of time and energy into the preparation of this event. During their work over the last years they have had to learn that organising a European event with almost no money to start with is quite an experience, involving a lot of challenges. involved.

Europe - A Coat of Many Colours
Looking at a map, it becomes quite obvious how the shape of Europe has changed within the last couple of years. Dramatic developments have occurred since 1989 and pressing new problems have emerged. Despite the 'fall of the iron curtain' Europe is still a split continent. Wanting to become 'the world's richest club' the European Union has been quite successful in building a 'Fortress Europe', separating the 'members of the club' from all 'the others', who may well be European. Based on exclusion and exploitation

the Union tries to build a new European identity, continuing Europe's history of violence.

It can be shown historically how European identity has been created in differentiation from those of other geographical areas, people defined physically different and culturally inferior. Robert Miles recounts how Greco-Roman cartographers mapped on to the unexplored margins of their world mythical tribes of one-footed or dog-headed creatures.[1]

The history of Europe has been violent from the very beginning, which - as it is told in the foundational stories - started with Europe being raped by Zeus. And the construction of a seamless European cultural identity has always been "a sexist myth, built as it is on the invisibility and exclusion of women from its structures and foundational thinking".[2] Although Europe or at least parts of Europe are the world's richest parts, there have always been people suffering within Europe and there has always been discrimination and division.

At the moment there is an ongoing war in former Yugoslavia in which women are abused as a special kind of 'war material'. In Eastern Germany and other former communist states women are struggling against unemployment. More and more women in all parts of Europe are suffering from poverty and a lack of social policies. Not to mention the fate of refugees. At the same time the extreme Right Wing Movement is increasing, showing different faces in different countries. The situation is serious and it is the awareness of this seriousness together with a growing responsibility for how Europe is acting within the world community which pushes women towards holding a European Women's Synod. There is an urgent need to build networks that move towards transforming actions without re-writing the old myths of a common identity, but looking carefully at differences instead. Because instead of being a 'seamless garment' Europe is "a coat of many colours"[3] and there are lots of differences waiting to be made visible and dealt with.

---

[1] Cynthia Cockburn, *In the Way of Women. Men's Resistance to Sex Equality in Organizations, Basingstoke*, London 1991, 208; See also: Robert Miles, *Racism*, London 1989.

[2] Mary Grey, "Till they have Faces. Europe as a Sexist Myth and the Invisibility of Women", in: *Concilium* 8(1992)2, 12-19.

[3] Ibid., 17.

The Differences Between Us

One of the significant things about all the Women's Synods held so far has been their ability to bring together women from quite different backgrounds. At the Austrian Synod for example, women from different denominations as well as from different organisations such as the traditional Catholic and Protestant women's organisations and the feminist theologian's network came together in large numbers to discuss their places in churches and society. As the experience of the 2nd Dutch Synod shows, a coming together of different groups of women, although heading towards all sorts of common goals, can also highlight pain and troubles. Participating as an outsider at the 2nd Dutch Synod it did not seem to me at all that the Dutch women have reached a point beyond difference, but I have been impressed with their way of expressing their differences. Looking toward to the first European Synod I hope that we will be able to follow the example of our Dutch sisters. Because before being able to work together as European women we have to become aware of our various differences and dare to make them visible and heard.

East and West

Some of the differences that in my experience are quite tricky to deal with are the differences between women from the East and the West of Europe. First of all there is most of the time a language problem. Not only do very few of the Western women speak Polish, Hungarian or Romanian, but words that we are able to translate and that exist in both cultures may have a very different meaning and can be an important source of misunderstandings.

> *The concepts 'left', 'emancipation', 'politics', 'solidarity', 'socialism', and even 'women's equality' are not used normatively by post-communist women, but as descriptive terms appropriated by an authoritarian, repressive socialism, referring to disturbing realities imposed by that system. (...) 'Feminism' itself has a completely different set of associations, and is often regarded with hostility, as many authors discuss. Indeed, not only abstract concepts are misunderstood, but banal and yet extremely important terms such as 'restaurant', 'daycare', 'shopping', and 'housework' ...*[4]

But problems of communication "are just a microcosm of the problems in

---

[4] Nanette Funk, Introduction, in: Nanette Funk/Magda Mueller (eds.), *Gender Politics and Post-Communism. Reflections from Eastern Europe and the Former Soviet Union*, New York/London 1993, 4.

any meeting or dialogue between Eastern and Western women".[5] Western feminists have distorted the situation of women in Eastern and Central Europe in many different ways and there are a lot of prejudices and stereotypes from both sides. For these reasons there is a real need to make meetings possible in order to talk to each other and to be able to get beyond stereotypes to express the real differences. It should also been borne in mind that there are as many differences between Eastern women as there are between women from the Western European countries and if we speak about 'Eastern European women' we have to realise that we are speaking about millions of women living under various circumstances in countries with very different histories.

"Look at the Black Woman ..."
Finally all we have to face the fact that there are no monolithic experiences at all. There isn't even anything that we could identify as 'The Hungarian Experience' or 'The Dutch experience' or 'The Austrian experience'. At the Dutch Synod, Black Women showed clearly that the time is not yet ripe to go beyond differences. Rather we have to learn to live with differences and contradictions.

The Dutch Synod showed that it is important that different groups within a movement focus on different and only build alliances only if absolutely necessary. Nevertheless we must also be aware of the danger lying in this.

Splintering into different political factions and special interest groups has erected unnecessary barriers to Sisterhood that could easily be eliminated. Special interest groups lead women to believe that only socialist feminists should be concerned about class; that only lesbian feminists would be concerned about the oppression of lesbians and gay men; that only black women or other women of color should be concerned about racism.[6]

When Black women at the Dutch Synod decided to have their own workshop which was closed to White women they tried to demonstrate this to White women in a very specific way. They told them, that they are not longer willing to be the only ones who bring questions of racism into consideration. They showed that they are fed up with always having to make themselves visible and heard, having always to react, of making White

---

[5]   Ibid.
[6]   Bell Hooks, *Feminist Theory from Margin to Centre*, Boston 1984, 61f.

women aware that once more they didn't consider the different and various kinds of circumstances under which women are living. They have had enough of the fact that white heterosexual women are still perceived as the norm. Therefore the Womanist theologian Doreen Hazel challenged the participants of the Dutch Synod to look at the Black woman and to realise that no kind of oppression is strange to her when she explained why the Black women decided to have their own workshop.[7]

However the Dutch women are likely to have moved forward together in some ways by realising that there are ways to work together without ignoring differences.

Working on Creating Space for Each Other

According to Annelies Knoppers, the project worker of the Dutch Synod the experiences of the Synod have revealed how far away the goal of solidarity is. Rather than speaking about solidarity she therefore suggests using the term community, meaning a "working on creating space for each other".[8] What women who want to transform society need at this stage is space. Space to meet each other, to talk to each other, to discuss their concerns and to exchange experiences and strategies. Looking at the map of Europe we have to recognise "that transforming action demands broadly-based coalitions. However difficult it is to achieve, the power of change is solidarity."[9] According to the Black feminist writer bell hooks the idea of sisterhood is false if it is based on the idea of common oppression. Hooks therefore suggests that instead of assuming common oppression which is "mystifying the true nature of women's varied and complex social reality"[10], there would be a real chance for solidarity by thinking about shared strengths and resources.

The first European Women's Synod might be a chance for women from all over Europe "to find ways of working together that respect the diversity of women's life experiences. Across the boundaries of culture and ethnicity, of language and history and religious affiliation, of class and education and

---

[7] See Doreen Hazel, "In naam van de Liefde", in: *Verslag 2e oecumenische vrouwensynode*, 22-27 augustus 1995.

[8] Annelies Knoppers, talk given to the international preparatory committee.

[9] Alexina Murphy, "European Women's Synod 1996", in: *Chrysalis*, January 1994, 11.

[10] Hooks, *op. cit.*, 44.

income, of different abilities and life-styles, different choices, different orientations, women can listen to each other".[11]

Women with different backgrounds and experiences might be able "to hear each other into speech"[12] and to listen to their stories of various kinds of oppressions as well as to the stories of resistance and solidarity. The stories of the Women in Black demonstrating for peace on the streets of Belgrade every week. The stories of the women of Chernobyl, working hard to improve the life of themselves and their suffering children. The stories of British women participating in the strong women's peace movement of their country. The stories of all those women who are concerned about the ecological crisis of our planet. The stories of all the women exploring their spirituality in different ways and different places. The various stories of griefs and of strengths, of nightmares and dreams.

If the participants of the European Women's Synod succeed in providing space for each other and hearing each other into speech the Synod might become what it is meant to be:

A Women's Synod is a gathering, which enables women to create space for each other. Women are sharing their different experiences and are taking responsibility for the realisation of their visions and dreams. They are exchanging strategies for translating their ideas into action and for grasping responsibility in churches, economics and politics.[13]

Michaela Moser is a member of the international preparatory committee of the European Women's Synod. She studied theology in Innsbruck/Austria and Nijmegen/NL. She worked as a teacher in primary school and within adult education projects. Since September 1994 she studies at LSU-College, Southampton, GB, doing research for her doctorate.

For further information about the European Women's Synod contact:

European Women's Synod	Initiativgruppe
attn. Joke Koehler	Frauensynode
c/o Kerk en Wereld	Canisiusgasse 16
Postbus 19	A-1090 Wien
NL-3970 AA Driebergen	Austria

---

[11] Alexina Murphy, *op. cit.*, 11.
[12] It was Nelle Morton who introduced the model of "hearing into speech" to Feminist Theology. See Nelle Morton, *The Journey is Home*, Boston 1985.
[13] Flyer of the European Women's Synod.

Elzbieta Adamiak

Feministische Theologie in Polen?
Ein beinahe unmögliches Thema

Bei der Suche nach einer meiner Ausbildung entsprechenden Stelle, habe ich einen Theologieprofessor (einen Priester) gefragt, wie er die Möglichkeit einer Anstellung an seiner Fakultät einschätze. Seine Antwort lautete: "In ein paar Jahren muß sich die Situation ändern". Er meinte damit, daß auch Frauen Theologie lehren dürften. So ungefähr läßt sich auch die Situation der feministischen Theologie in Polen beschreiben: "Vielleicht in ein paar Jahren..."

Zwar war in Polen - anders als in den meisten kommunistischen Ländern - die theologische Ausbildung auch vor 1989 für Laien zugänglich. Es gibt sogar 47 promovierte Theologinnen! (Soweit ich weiß, sind alle Katholikinnen; davon sind 27 Ordensfrauen, die im Vergleich zu Lainnen bessere Möglichkeiten für Studium und Anstellung haben). Nur fünf lehren an theologischen Fakultäten (davon vier Ordensfrauen). Ich brauche wohl nicht hinzuzufügen, daß es bisher keine Theologieprofessorin gibt (auch keinen Laienprofessor in Theologie). Das wichtigste Problem der Theologinnen in Polen ist also: Wie sie als Theologinnen tätig sein können, in einer Kirche, die das nicht ermöglicht... Die Theologie bleibt für viele nur eine Freizeitbeschäftigung. Die bekannteste polnische Theologin ist Frau Stanisława Grabska, die im Jahre 1973 als erste Frau an der theologischen Fakultät in Louvain-la-Neuvre promoviert hat. Sie ist auch diejenige, die im Verlauf der Zeit immer wieder Aufsätze zum Thema: "Frau - Kirche" veröffentlicht hat.[1]

---

[1] S.Grabska, "Kobiety w Kościele" [Frauen in der Kirche], Więź 8(1965)6, 45-52; dies., "Przyszłość kobiet w Kościele jutra" [Die Zukunft der Frauen in der Kirche von morgen], Więź 19(1976)2, 60-67; dies., "Spóro miejsce kobiety w Kościele i społeczeństwie" [Die Auseinandersetzung um den Platz der Frau in der Kirche und Gesellschaft], Więź 36(1993)1, 24-31.

Sie wurde aber jahrelang von keiner Fakultät angestellt, sondern war in einem Zentrum der katholischen Intellektuellen tätig (um die Zeitschrift "Więź") und hat da Bücher publiziert. In den letzten Jahren hält sie Vorlesungen am religionswissenschaftlichen Institut der Warschauer Universität. In Hinsicht auf die Frauenproblematik in der Theologie ist noch ein Name zu nennen: Ewa Durlak, die 1986 zum Thema "Die Theologie der Frau im Licht des Zweiten Vatikanischen Konzils" ("Teologia kobiety" w świetle Soboru Watykańskiego II. Studium dogmatyczno-pastoralne, Lublin 1985, Manuskript) an der Katholischen Universität in Lublin promoviert hat. Nach ihrem Eintritt in den Orden hat sie aber nicht viel veröffentlicht.[2] Zuletzt ist meine Doktorarbeit zu nennen, die erste zu einem feministisch-theologischen Thema in Polen.[3]

Um die bisher erschienenen polnischen Aufsätze zum Themenbereich Frau/Kirche skizzieren zu können, muß man auf den gesellschaftlichen Kontext hinweisen. Es gibt nur sehr wenige feministische Gruppierungen, und deren Stimmen erklingen besonders laut in der Abtreibungsdebatte. Es sind sehr wenige Publikationen im allgemein feministischen Sinne erschienen.[4] In den Kirchen gibt es fast keine Gruppen, die ihre Interessen feministisch nennen. Da es vor 1989 verboten war, sich frei zusammenzuschließen, gibt es in Polen eigentlich keine traditionelle Frauenarbeit und -verbände in den Kirchen. Es gab (und gibt) zwei offizielle Institutionen seitens der Kirchen: Eine Unterkommission der polnischen Bischofskonferenz für Frauenseelsorge und den Frauenrat beim Polnischen Ökumenischen Rat (dem die römisch-

---

[2]   E.Durlak, "Polskie publikacje teologiczne po Soborze Watykańskim II na temat kobiety. Przegląd bibliograficzny" [Polnisch theologische Publikationen über die Frau nach dem Zweiten Vatikanischen Konzil. Eine bibliographische Übersicht], in: *Ateneum Kapłańskie* (1988)474, 258-275; E.Durlak/R.Szmydki, "Feminizm" [Feminismus], in: *Encyklopedia Katolicka*, Bd.5, Lublin 1989, 115-116.

[3]   E.Adamiak, *Maryja w feministycznej teologii Cathariny Halkes* [Maria in der feministischen Theologie von Catharina Halkes], Lublin 1994.

[4]   S. de Beauvoir, *Druga płeć* [La deuxième sexe], Kraków 1972; eine Auswahl feministischer Texte: *Nikt nie rodzi się kobietą* [Niemand wird als Frau geboren], Hg. T.Hołówka, Warszawa 1982; M.Humm, *Słownik teorii feminizmu* [Dictionary of Feminist Theory], Warszawa 1993. Das einzige mir bekannte Buch, das die eigene feministische Reflexion präsentiert, ist: *Głos mają kobiety* [Die Frauen haben das Wort], Hg. S.Walczewska, Kraków 1992. Es ist auch die erste Nummer einer polnischen feministischen Zeitschrift erschienen: *Pełnym głosem* [Mit voller Stimme], besonders interessant ist der Aufsatz von B.Limanowska, "Dlaczego w Polsce nie ma feminizmu?" [Warum gibt es in Polen keinen Feminismus?], Pełnym głosem (1993)1, 3-24.

katholische Kirche nicht angehört). In den letzten Jahren sind zwei christliche
Frauenorganisationen von unten entstanden: eine katholische (Polski Związek
Kobiet Katolickich [Der polnische Verband der katholischen Frauen], 1990)
und eine ökumenische (Związek Dziewcząt i Kobiet Chrześciajńskich
[polnische YWCA], 1991 - sie ist die einzige, die in ihrem Programm die
Verbreitung der feministischen Theologie in Polen erwähnt). Beide Frauen-
verbände sind jedoch vorwiegend auf die praktischen Probleme von Frauen
ausgerichtet.

Die bisherigen polnischen Publikationen zum Thema Frau/Kirche könnte
man unter einen Nenner bringen: "Theologie der Frau".[5] Ein wichtiger Teil
polnischer Positionen beschäftigt sich mit der Lehre von Papst Johannes Paul
II. über die Rolle der Frau in der Kirche - hier gibt es eine Reihe von
Diplomarbeiten.[6] Es gibt auch Übersetzungen, meistens aus dem Französi-
schen.[7] Diesen Publikationen ist gemeinsam, daß sie von einer gewissen

---

[5] Neben den oben genannten Arbeiten von S.Grabska und E.Durlak, hier noch andere: Rola
kobiety w Kościele *[Die Rolle der Frau in der Kirche]*, Lublin 1958; E.Ehrlich, "Biblia o
kobiecie" [Die Bibel über die Frau], in: *Ruch Biblijny i Liturgiczny* 28(1975)6, 245-252; dies.,
"Problem kobiety w Piśmie świętym" [Das Problem der Frau in der Heiligen Schrift], in:
Znak 28(1976)262, 463-473; A.Jankowski, "Maryja - biblijne synteza powołania kobiety"
[Maria - die biblische Synthese in der Berufung der Frau], in: *Znak* 28(1976)262, 474-486;
J.Banak, "Nobilitacja kobiety w Nowym Testamencie" [Die Erhöhung der Frau im Neuen
Testament], in: *Chrześcijanin a współczesność* (1986)2, 17-22; H.Wistuba, "Kobieta w
Kościele i świecie" [Die Frau in der Kirche und in der Welt], in: *Ateneum Kapłanskie*
114(1990) 487, 407-417.
[6] L.Kleszcz, *Maryja wzorem chrześcijańskiego życia w nauczaniu Jana Pawła II w latach 1978-
1985* [Maria als Vorbild des christlichen Lebens in der Lehre von Johannes Paul II. in den
Jahren 1978-1985], Lublin 1985; A.Maciaszek, *Rola i miejsce kobiety w Kościele według
Karola Wojtyły, Biskupa i Papieża w latach 1962 - 1987* [Die Rolle und der Platz der Frau
in der Kirche nach Karol Wojtyła, Bischof und Papst in den Jahren 1962-1987, Lublin 1988;
M.Braun-Gałkowska, *Nauczanie Jana Pawła II o kobietach* [Die Lehre Johannes Paul II. über
die Frauen], Warszawa 1989; M.Adaszkiewicz, *Znaczenie listu apostolskiego Jana Pawła II
"Mulieris dignitatem" dla duszpasterstwa maryjnego w Polsce* [Die Bedeutung des
Apostolischen Briefes "Mulieris dignitatem" von Johannes Paul II. für die marianische
Seelsorge in Polen], Lublin 1992 (alle sind Manuskripte).
[7] F.Heer, "Kobieta w Kościele" [Die Frau in der Kirche], in: *Więź* 5(1962)1, 44-50; J.Vinatier,
Kobieta w Kościele [Die Frau in der Kirche; La femme dans l'Église], Warszawa 1976;
K.Rahner, "Maryja i chrześcijański obraz kobiety" [Maria und das christliche Frauenbild],
in: *Novum* (1976)10, 58-66; N.Échivard, *Kobieto, kim jesteś?* [Femme, qui es-tu?], Poznań
1987; H.U. von Balthasar, "Godność kobiety" [Die Würde der Frau], in: *Kosmos i człowiek*.

Empfindlichkeit gegenüber der Einseitigkeit männlich geprägten Kultur geprägt sind. Die meisten benutzen einen engen - und vielleicht deshalb negativen - Begriff von Feminismus als Kampf um die Gleichberechtigung der Frau. Er wird als Vermännlichung der Frau abgewiesen. In geringem Maße betrachten sie die Kirche als eine Institution, die auch zur Frauenunterdrückung beigetragen hat/beiträgt. Die Heilung dieser Situation sehen sie in einer idealisierten Vision von Weiblichkeit, deren Vorbild Maria darstellt.

Nach dieser kurzen Darstellung kann es nicht verwundern, daß die ersten Publikationen, die sich *explizit* mit der feministischen Theologie beschäftigen, von Männern stammen. Der erste, sehr kurze Aufsatz (3 Seiten) ist in der ökumenischen Zeitschrift der reformierten Kirche "Jednota" erschienen und präsentiert zwei Strömungen der feministisch-theologischen Reflexion (nach der Unterscheidung von E.Moltmann-Wendel): Die radikale und die reformorientierte. Der Verfasser bemüht sich, die Vorurteile dem Feminismus gegenüber auszuräumen, indem er die reformorientierte Richtung als ausschlaggebend darstellt und ihre Grundziele nennt.

Das Büchlein von Pater Prof. A.Nowak (OFM) "Kobieta kapłanem?" ([Die Frau, ein Priester?] Lublin 1993) handelt faktisch über die feministische Theologie. Jedoch stellt der Verfasser diese äußerst verkürzt dar. Das Buch ist in einer Weise geschrieben, die ein Gespräch unmöglich macht.[8]

Meinen Aufsatz "O co chodzi w teologii feministycznej?" [Worum geht es in der feministischen Theologie?][9] verstehe ich als eine knappe Einführung ins feministisch-theologische Denken. Nach einer kurzen Darstellung ihrer Entstehungsgeschichte erkläre ich einige Grundbegriffe aus dem feministischen Vokabular, die in Polen echte "Fremdwörter" sind (Unterscheidung zwischen Emanzipation und Feminismus, Androzentrismus, Sexismus, Patriarchat). Danach nenne ich Grundströmungen feministischer Theologie und ihre Hauptvertreterinnen. Zum Schluß habe ich versucht, Einsicht in die

(Kolecja Communio), Poznań Warszawa 1989, 258-264; P.Evdokimov, *Kobieta i zbawienie świata* [La femme et le salut du monde], Poznań 1991; G.Blaquiere, *Łaska bycia kobietą* [La Grace d'etre femme], Kraków 1993; dies., "Misja kobiety w Kościele" [Die Mission der Frau in der Kirche], in: *W drodze*, (1988)2, 54-64.

8 Um dies zu veranschaulichen, reicht es, ein krasses Beispiel zu zitieren: "Die Formulierungen vieler Vertreterinnen der sogenannten feministischen Theologie, wie z.B. D.Sölle, M.Daly, E.Moltmann-Wendel, U.Krattiger, B. von Wartenberg, haben einen häretischen Charakter. Sie streben die Vernichtung der Familie an, interpretieren die Offenbarung, das Christentum in sexuellen Kategorien" (S.19).

9 *Więź* 36(1993)1, 68-77.

Fragen und Folgerungen zu geben, zu denen feministische Anliegen in der Bibelinterpretation, Gotteslehre, Christologie und Anthropologie geführt haben. Mein Artikel ist also eine Darstellung der Tendenzen, die in der westlichen feministischen Theologie entstanden sind und (noch) keine Reflexion, die Fragen aus unserem Kontext entstehen läßt, sie zu benennen und zu beantworten versucht.

Einen solchen Versuch hat K.Wiśniewska-Roszkowska unternommen, die mehrere Bücher aus dem Grenzgebiet Medizin/Ethik geschrieben hat. Die Verfasserin des Buches "Feminizm zreformowany" ([Der reformierte Feminismus] Wrocław 1993) unterscheidet sich von anderen AutorInnen darin, daß sie ausdrücklich eine Vision entwickelt, die sie selbst feministisch nennt. Nach der Lektüre bleibt aber zu fragen, ob nach der Reform überhaupt noch etwas Feministisches in ihrem Denken geblieben ist. Sie betrachtet das Problem im Spiegel der Sexualethik und konzentriert sich auf die Aufgaben der Frau in der Familie, vor allem der Mutterschaft. Feminismus stellt sie mit der "sexuellen Revolution" gleich und die bedeutet für sie "die sexuelle Häresie" (S. 37-44; 119-120). Die Ergebnisse der Frauenforschung in der Theologie bezeichnet sie als "kuriose Ideen, die sogar die Feminisierung des Herrgottes anstreben" (S. 121). Sie weiß übrigens nichts über feministische Theologie, die von Katholikinnen betrieben wird. Obwohl also die Autorin versucht, eine Art Einführung ins feministische Denken geben, vertritt sie eine biologistische und sexuell zentrierte Sicht, die mit dem Hinweis auf die 'Andersartigkeit' der weiblichen Natur und mit Mutterschaft verbundenen Funktionen endet... Um ein volles Bild der auf polnisch erschienenen Literatur zur feministischen Theologie zu skizzieren, muß noch auf einige Ausnahmen hingewiesen werden. Das sind zuerst zwei Aufsätze, die ausländische feministisch-theologische Publikationen präsentieren[10], und zwei Übersetzungen: Der einzige auf polnisch erschienene feministisch-theologisches Text - von Catharina Halkes[11] - und ein Artikel von Wolfgang

[10] J.Eska, "Antyfeminizm w Kościele?" [Antifeminismus in der Kirche?], in: *Więź* 13(1970)10, 3-13 (über das Buch von M.Daly, The Church and the second Sex); S.Grabska, "Przyszłość kobiet w Kościele jutra" [Die Zukunft der Frauen in der Kirche von morgen], in: *Więź* 19(1976)2, 60-67 (über J.M.Aubert, La Femme. Antiféminisme et christianisme, und ein Artikel von G.Thils).

[11] C.Halkes, "Pieśń protestu Magnificat" [Das Protestlied Magnificat], in: *Więź* 36(1993)1, 78-81.

Beinert, der bald erscheinen wird.[12]

In den polnischen Publikationen *über* feministische Theologie stehen zwei Problembereiche im Mittelpunkt: Familie und Frauenordination. Familie soll die erste und wichtigste Lebensaufgabe der Frau sein und das wird tatsächlich von vielen so gesehen. Feminismus wird dagegen eher als Familienfeind angesehen. Die Frauenfrage im kirchlichen Bereich wird auf die Frauenordination reduziert und damit abgelehnt. Es gibt in Polen keine öffentliche Diskussion über Frauenordination, d.h. es gibt keine Frauengruppen oder Persönlichkeiten aus kirchlichen Gremien, die Frauenordination öffentlich fördern würden. Die meisten Publikationen diskutieren also mit Argumenten, die in westlichen Theologien erarbeitet wurden.

Wie ist die Frage zu beantworten: Warum gibt es in Polen keine feministische Theologie? Wenn die wesentlichen Faktoren, die zur Entstehung der feministischen Theologie in West-Europa beigetragen haben, die zweite Welle der Frauenbewegung, die ökumenische Bewegung und die nachkonziliare Reform in der römisch-katholischen Kirche[13] sind, so kann man ihre Abwesenheit leicht mit der geringen Relevanz der drei genannten Bewegungen erklären. Sie bilden nicht die entscheidende Strömung des gesellschaftlichen und kirchlichen Lebens in Polen. Es wurde schon auf das Fehlen der feministischen Gruppierungen im gesellschaftlichen Kontext hingewiesen. Man kann wohl sagen, daß die zweite Welle der Frauenbewegung Polen nicht erreicht hat. Schon aufgrund der konfessionellen Landschaft (die vorwiegende Mehrheit der Bevölkerung ist römisch-katholisch) spielt die ökumenische Bewegung und Theologie eine geringe Rolle. Eine nachkonziliare Reform könnte schon aus politischen Gründen nicht in vollem Maße verwirklicht werden. Das gilt besonders für die Situation der Laien(theologInnen). Für sie gibt es mit Ausnahme des Religionsunterrichtes fast keine Möglichkeiten, in den kirchlichen Strukturen beruflich (d.h. nicht ehrenamtlich) zu arbeiten. Politische Gründe waren es auch, die die Kontakte mit westlichen Theologien verhindert haben. Dadurch ist ihre Kenntnis nur Experten vorbehalten. Es gab und gibt zu wenig Diskussionen über die historisch-kritische Methode und ihre Folgen für Exegese und Theologie. Die Richtungen der modernen

---

[12]   W.Beinert, "Teologia feministyczna. Powstanie - istota - oddziaływanie" [Die feministische Theologie. Entstehung - Wesen - Wirkung], in: *Studia teologiczno-historyczne Śląska Opolskiego* 14(1993), 71-95.

[13]   Vlg. H.Meyer-Wilmes, *Rebellion auf der Grenze*. Ortsbestimmung feministischer Theolgie, Freiburg/Basel/Wien 1990, 19-41.

Theologie, die mit feministischer Theologie verwandt sind, bleiben für viele unbekannt. Es gibt sicher tiefere Gründe, die sich aus der polnischen Geschichte und Tradition ergeben, die einen echten Dialog mit feministisch-theologischen Themen erschweren. Man muß zuerst die Vorurteile und das Unverständnis aufräumen...

Elzbieta Adamiak ist 1964 in Poznan (Polen) geboren. Studium der Theologie in Lublin. 1994 erste feministisch-theologische Dissertation in Polen über die Mariologie in der feministischen Theologie. Verschiedene Studienaufenthalte im Ausland, u.a. in Nijmegen bei 'feminisme en christendom'. Momentan arbeitet sie als Verlagsmitarbeiterin.

Anne-Marie Korte

High Standards: Ideals and Reality of Feminist Theology as a 'Different Academic Discipline'

The Situation in the Netherlands as a Case in Point

Embarassed by the 'struggle within the institutions'? I have noticed that the 'struggle within academic institutions' is only rarely discussed whenever feminist-theological developments in different countries and different contexts are described. Moreover, the information that is publicised, is mainly restricted to news of women being made redundant or being refused appointments in the academic circuit[1], or to autobiographical stories by women which by now are classic examples of being excluded or relegated to marginal situations.[2] A much more structural, but also much more abstract approach towards the 'struggle within the academic institutions' is found in the analyses of the exclusion of women and other 'outsiders' from the prevailing academic policy[3], analyses based on Virginia Woolf's "Three

---

[1] See also Janice Raymond, "Mary Daly: A Decade of Academic Harassment and Feminist Survival", in: Mary Spencer, Monika Kehoe, Karen Speece (eds.), *Handbook for Women Scholars: Strategies for Succes*, San Francisco: Center For Women Scholars - America's Behavioral Research Corporation, 1982, 81-88.

[2] See also Mary Daly, "Autobiographical Preface to the Colofon Edition" and "Feminist Postchristian Introduction", in: Mary Daly, *The Church and the Second Sex. With a New Feminist Postchristian Introduction by the Author*, New York 1975, 5-51; Marga Bührig, *Spät habe ich gelernt, gerne Frau zu sein*, Eine feministische Autobiografie, Stuttgart 1987; Annie Lally Milhaven (ed.), *The Inside Stories. 13 Valiant Women Challenging the Church*, Mystic, Connecticut 1987.

[3] See also Jo Anne Pagano, *Exiles and Communities. Teaching in the Patriarchal Wilderness*, Albany 1990; Christine Schaumberger, "Kennis is macht: Perspectief van een binnen/buitenstaanster", in: Hedwig Meyer-Wilmes & Lieve Troch (eds.), *Over hoeren, taarten en vrouwen die voorbijgaan. Macht en verschil in de vrouwenkerk*, Kampen 1992, 73-94; Kathleen O'Brien Wicker, "Teaching Feminist Biblical Studies in a Postcolonial Context", in: Elisabeth Schüssler Fiorenza (ed.), *Searching the Scriptures. A Feminist Introduction*, New York 1993, 367-380.

Guineas"[4] as their prototype.

When we attempt *in concreto* to pin down the actual battlegrounds and the processes of change that determine our theology in our own situation and context, we apparently prefer to discuss 'the struggle at the base', rather than the struggle within the academic institutions. We come up with the problems and struggles of women in, and on the fringe of, the church and depict the daily conflicts and structural social problems facing various groups of women. We show how themes that are central to our feministtheological work are involved with this struggle at the base.[5]

Why do these feminist-theological (self)presentations hardly, if ever, mention our struggle *within* the academic institutions? Is this incompatible with our model picture of feminist-theological struggle? It has now become the approved procedure for us, feminist theologians, to present our credentials in terms of our backgrounds and social positions. Surprisingly, we hardly ever dwell on our academic training and the battle we have fought to be able to participate in it, to finish it, and partly to adjust it according to our own ideas, let alone reveal what it has cost us, literally and figuratively. Do we consider our efforts for other training and research programmes, for paid research in the field of theological women's studies, for having our questions included in current training and research too down to earth, too individual - or perhaps too much of a 'luxury' problem? Or are we at a loss or ambiguous about our *own* academic ambitions? Why do we indicate the danger of becoming estranged from the struggle at the base through our work as scholars,[6] but omit to point out the danger of not giving or asking for sufficient mutual support *within* the academic institutions?

---

[4] Virginia Woolf, *Three Guineas*, New York 1966.

[5] See also Lieve Troch, "The Feminist Movement on the Edge of the Churches in the Netherlands. From Consciousness-raising to Womenchurch", in: *Journal of Feminist Studies in Religion* 5(1989)2, 113-128; Id., "A Method of Conscientization. Feminist Bible Study in the Netherlands", in: Elisabeth Schüssler Fiorenza (ed.), *Searching the Scriptures*, Volume One: A Feminist Introduction, New York 1993, 351-366; Chung Hyun Kyung, *Struggle to be the Sun Again. Introducing Asian Women's Theology*, Maryknoll NY 1991; Anne Brotherton (ed.), *The Voice of the Turtledove. New Catholic Women in Europe,* New York 1992; Ursula King (ed.), *Feminist Theology from the Third World*, Maryknoll, NY 1994.

[6] See also Elisabeth Schüssler Fiorenza, *Bread Not Stone. The Challenge of Feminist Biblical Interpretation*, Boston 1984, xxiii-xxv; Catharina Halkes, "Feminisme en de hele bewoonde wereld", in: *Mara* 7(1994)3, 9-18.

The Situation in the Netherlands: Rapid Advance
In my opinion the Dutch situation provides an interesting example to examine the matter in greater detail.[7] The rapid and exemplary advance of feminist theology in academic institutions is characteristic of the Netherlands. In no other country did feminist theology make such fast and firm headway in the academic world as in the Netherlands. Not only was a strong network of feminist study and action groups established within the Dutch universities in the 1975-1985 period, but there also appeared a complete, institutional structure for theological women's studies, consisting of specially appointed lecturers, compulsory courses, programmes of study, graduation projects, training-incentive posts, etc.[8]

In hindsight this success story of women's studies in theological education appears to have been due especially to the enormous growth in the number of women studying at theological educational institutions. The number of women studying theology at Dutch universities increased between 1975 and 1985 from 5% to 50% of that student population. Because of the 'women's studies' programme many women did not only start reading theology, but they also graduated. Women's studies created 'a room of one's own' for women in the academic theological study programme. The investments of the universities in the structural incorporation of women's studies proved their validity almost instantaneously because many more women finished their studies.

Strangely enough, a similar advance of the programmed and institutionally incorporated *research* in the field of theological women's studies did not materialise, although this was originally certainly expected.[9] Actually it was

---

[7] The following exposition is based on two publications on the state of feminist-theological research in the Netherlands. See Anne-Marie Korte, "Stromen en stremmingen. Structurele inbeddingen van het vrouwenstudies theologie onderzoek in Nederland", in: Freda Dröes, Anne-Marie Korte, Marian Papavoine, Jonneke Bekkenkamp, (eds.), *Proeven van vrouwenstudies theologie*, III, [IIMO Research Publication; 36], Leiden/Utrecht, IIMO/IWFT, 1993, 243-266; Id., "The Birth of Aphrodite", in: Fokkelien van Dijk-Hemmes & Athalya Brenner (eds.), *Reflections on Theology and Gender*, Kampen 1994, 71-86.

[8] See Jonneke Bekkenkamp, Freda Dröes, Anne-Marie Korte (eds.), *Van zusters, meiden en vrouwen. Tien jaar feminisme en theologie op fakulteiten en hogescholen in Nederland* [IIMO Research Pamphlets; 19], Leiden/Utrecht: IIMO/IWFT, 1986; Anne-Marie Korte & Jonneke Bekkenkamp, "Die fliegenden Holländerinnen. Feministische Theologie an Fakultäten und Hochschulen in den Niederlanden", in: Christine Schaumberger, Monika Maassen (Hg.), *Handbuch Feministische Theologie*, Münster 1986, 94-115.

[9] In 1986 an overview of the development of feminist theology in Dutch academic theological

not until a few years ago that initiatives in this field were taken, with results only just beginning to show. A number of theological educational institutions have drawn up and presented interdisciplinary research progammes for theological women's studies[10], and women's studies have been integrated into a few theological research programmes.[11] A project committee 'Theological Women's Studies' has been established within the national organisation for financing theological and philosophical research; this committee has been directed to promote submission of more and qualitatively better applications for research grants in the field of women's studies. It also provided financial support for a four-year inter-university research programme for research in theological women's studies and religious studies, called 'Corporality, textuality and contextuality', which started at the end of 1993.

It is, however, a cause of great concern that once again the existence of

---

institutions was published. This was based on final papers and incipient research for doctoral theses, from which lines were pursued to numerous research programmes. The optimistic tenor of the overview indicates that these research programmes were expected to get off the ground as quickly and dynamically as the study programmes. The endowed rotating professorship for 'Feminisme en Christendom' (Nijmegen), established in 1983, also under-pinned these expectations. (See Bekkenkamp e.a. (eds.), *Van zusters, meiden en vrouwen*.) But in the article "Feministisch-theologisch onderzoek in Nederland", in: Jonneke Bekkenkamp e.a. (eds.), *Proeven van vrouwenstudies theologie*, II, [IIMO Research Publications; 32], Leiden/Utrecht: IIMO/IWFT, 1991, 247-266 summarising the current state of affairs, Marian Papavoine had to acknowlegde the fact that only the start of research in theological women's studies with specific modes and themes of their own was found in the different theological faculties.

[10] These research programmes were developed within the framework of working groups (interdisplinary 'departments') established for theological women's studies. Participants in these groups were lecturers and researchers of theological faculty or university from different disciplines. For details of such a programme see Fokkelien van Dijk-Hemmes, "Toward a Women's Studies Research Program in the Faculty of Theology, Utrecht University", in: Van Dijk-Hemmes & Brenner (eds.), *Reflections on Theology and Gender*, 9-19.

[11] Such integration entails more than incorporating just one individual women's studies research in a theological research programme. A case in point is the theological faculty of the University of Amsterdam, where women's studies have only 0,5 job on the strength, which is not sufficient for a research programme of its own. Gender- specific issues have therefore been integrated into the theological research programme ('De erosie, decentrering en transformatie van de westerse canon'). Besides the lecturer in women's studies two AIO's (trainee research assistants) and a post-doctorate researcher involved in explicit women's studies projects are taking part in this programme.

women's studies research is completely ignored by the new organisations that are now being established for the financing and concentrating of research within the world of Dutch theology. Neither in the AIO-netwerk Godgeleerd-heid (Netherlands Network for Advanced Studies in Theology) nor in the Onderzoeksschool Theologie en Godsdienstwetenschappen (Netherlands School for Advanced Studies in Theology and Religion), that are now being set up, is one single thought given to women's studies, neither structurally nor thematically. Even after this has been brought to their attention, the governing bodies of these new research organisations have seen no reason to adjust their policies in this respect. Where has all the initial consideration towards feminist theology gone? Why is it becoming problematic for feminist theologians to get a firm footing within academic theological institutions at the very moment that research is mentioned? I do not consider this a matter of sheer coincidence, nor due to a lack of research ambitions or research competence on the part of individual feminist theologians. On the contrary, it is a matter of diverse, more structural hurdles and pitfalls, as I shall illustrate below. But my objective is, of course, wider: what policy, what strategies and solutions can be found to remedy the situation?

Radical Ambitions

In my opinion a major reason why institutional incorporation of theological women's studies is such an uphill struggle, is the radical academic self-definition of theological women's studies. By this I mean its very critical attitude towards 'current' and 'prevailing' research.[12] I hasten to add that this critical stance is not restricted to theological women's studies, indeed, it is found in women's studies in all other disciplines. Based on their far-

---

[12] See also Judith Plaskow, "The Coming of Lilith. Toward a Feminist Theology" [1st ed. 1972], in: Carol P. Christ and Judith Plaskow (eds.), *Womanspirit Rising. A Feminist Reader in Religion*, San Francisco 1979, 198-209; Mary Daly, *Beyond God the Father. Toward a Philosophy of Women's Liberation*, Boston 1973, 1-12; Katie G. Cannon (e.a.), *God's Fierce Whimsy. Christian Feminism and Theological Education,* New York 1985; Kwok Pui-Lan, "Mothers and Daughters, Writers and Fighters", in: Letty M.Russell, Kwok Pui-Lan, Ada María Isasi-Díaz, Katie Geneva Cannon (eds.), *Inheriting Our Mothers' Gardens. Feminist Theology in Third World Perspective*, Philadelphia 1988, 21-34; Elisabeth Schüssler Fiorenza, "Commitment and Critical Inquiry. Harvard Divinity School 1988 Convocation", in: Id., *Discipleship of Equals. A Critical Ekklesia-logy of Liberation,* London 1993, 275-289; Ivone Gebara, "Women Doing Theology in Latin-America", in: King (ed.), *Feminist Theology from the Third World*, 47-59.

reaching ambitions in this respect, women's studies have interpreted their duties from the very beginning as 'practising academic scholarship in a totally different way'.[13] The fact that women are becoming both subjects and objects of learning has been interpreted as an absolute academic revolution, a paradigm change, and the creation of a new 'discourse'. Such a critical stance requires a thorough revision of almost all academic basic principles. As put by the feminist philosopher Sandra Harding, the problem is not that women practising women's studies would not know how to deal with women's subjects in an academic way, or how to pose feminist questions in an academic setting. The crux is that because we deal with women's subjects and pose feminist questions, current scholarship itself has become a problem.[14] A daunting prospect. If this is taken seriously, it will give rise to a flood of epistemological questions, presenting themselves, moreover, with an urgency that brooks no delay.

The Dutch dissertations in the field of theological women's studies of the past years show without hardly any exception how imperative and demanding the discussion of these kind of epistemological matters is, with the result that in a number of cases, dealing with these matters occupied the greatest part of the research.[15]

---

[13] Cf. Gloria Bowles & Renate Duelli Klein (eds.), *Theories of Women's Studies*, London and New York 1983; Sandra Harding & Merill B. Hintikka (eds.), *Discovering Reality. Feminist Perspectives on Epistemology, Metaphysics, Methodology, and Philosophy of Science*, Dordrecht/Boston/London 1983; Evelyn Fox Keller, *Reflections on Gender and Science*, New Haven/London 1985; Seyla Benhabib & Drucilla Cornell (eds.), *Feminism as Critique. On the Politics of Gender*, Minneapolis 1987; Nancy Tuana (ed.), *Feminism and Science*, Bloomington and Indianapolis 1989; Sneja Gunew (ed.), *Feminist Knowledge. Critique and Construct*, London/New York 1990.

[14] Sandra Harding, *The Science Question in Feminism* , Milton Keynes 1986.

[15] See also Hedwig Meyer-Wilmes, *Rebellion auf der Grenze. Ortsbestimmung feministischer Theologie,* Freiburg/Basel/Wien 1990; Grietje Dresen, 'Preface', to *Onschuldfantasieën: Offerzin en heilsverlangen in feminisme en mystiek,* Nijmegen 1990, published in: Bekkenkamp e.a. (eds.), *Proeven van vrouwenstudies theologie,* II, 271- 274; Anne-Marie Korte, *Een passie voor transcendentie. Feminisme, theologie en moderniteit in het denken van Mary Daly,* Kampen 1992; Annelies van Heyst, *Verlangen naar de val. Zelfverlies en autonomie in hermeneutiek en ethiek,* Kampen 1992; Jonneke Bekkenkamp, *Canon en keuze. Het bijbelse Hooglied en de Twenty-One Love Poems van Adrienne Rich als bronnen van theologie,* Kampen 1993. See also the discussion on methods in theological women's studies in: Jonneke Bekkenkamp e.a. (eds.), *Proeven van vrouwenstudies theologie,* I, [IIMO

Thus, in practice it takes a lot of time to create the framework, the phrasing of the actual questions and the appropriate discussion climate that are required when attempts are made to practise learning in such a fundamentally 'different' way. The implications of this radical position can by no means be appreciated and fully understood in advance. Only gradually does it become evident how much epistemological research is required, research which is also very time-consuming. In many cases the importance and relevance of this 'methods business' by no means speaks for itself to outsiders - to say nothing about speaking to the imagination. The internally-focused character of this research certainly does not facilitate its institutional incorporation.

Besides, due to this epistemological 'alertness', the general and topical question about the academic status of theology and its own identity is encountered much faster and more directly within theological women's studies, probably much earlier and more inevitably than in other theological research. This is an issue that is considered theoretically the most important preliminary question in theological research at the moment, albeit that there is definitely no consensus about it.[16] The need to enter fully into this 'what is theology?' issue - or to avoid it altogether - is not conducive to a fast tying up of research in theological women's studies with existing programmes in theology and religious studies.

Research Publications; 25], Leiden/Utrecht: IIMO/IWFT, 1989; Els Maeckelberghe, "Proeven van feministische theologie", in: *Lover. Literatuuroverzicht voor de vrouwenbeweging* 16(1989)4, 212-217; Bekkenkamp e.a. (eds.), *Proeven van vrouwenstudies theologie*, II.

16 See also Edward Farley, *Theologia. The Fragmentation and Unity of Theological Education*, Philadelphia 1983; Mark C. Taylor, *Erring. A Postmodern A/theology*, Chicago/London 1984; H.J.Adriaanse, H.A.Krop, L.Leertouwer, *Het verschijnsel theologie. Over de wetenschappelijke status van de theologie*, Meppel 1987; Jürgen Moltmann, *Was ist heute Theologie? Zwei Beiträge zu ihrer Vergegenwärtigung* [Questiones Disputatae; 114], Freiburg/Basel/Wien 1988; David Tracy, *Blessed Rage for Order. The New Pluralism in Theology*, San Francisco 1988; Id., "The Uneasy Alliance Reconceived. Catholic Theological Method, Modernity and Postmodernity", *Theological Studies* 50(1989), 548-570; Hans Küng and David Tracy (eds.), *Paradigm Change in Theology. A Symposium for the Future*, Edinburgh, 1989; Gavin D'Costa, "The End of Systematic Theology", *Theology* 95 (1992), 324-334.

University Cutbacks

A second reason why institutional incorporation of theological women's studies is lagging behind is, I think, an external matter that might come under the heading of cyclical factors, factors determined by economic situations. I have already mentioned the new organisational fabric for a (more concentrated) financing of theological research that is at present being established in the Netherlands.

Actually there has been a constant flow of academic reorganisations since 1985, caused by the national policy of drastic cutbacks in higher education. Overwhelmingly fast changes in the organisation and financing of academic research are the result. Research should be better, more efficient, more streamlined, 'internationally competitive' and yield qualitatively higher results. All this, of course, for less money. Criteria for applying and granting finances for research purposes are continually changing. The dynamic aspects of such a policy might promote innovative research. But to get a grip on these changing structures is difficult for 'non-established' fields of research like women's studies. There are still very few women in higher places in academe. Since, relatively speaking, women are far more often saddled with temporary and part-time jobs than men, it is also more difficult for them to move on to tenure or higher positions. Consequently they are the first to lose their jobs when mergers or reorganisations appear on the horizon.[17]

Moreover - and this may be the negative side of their large investments in the theological women's studies programmes - the theological study programmes have invested next to nothing in structural investments in research in this field.[18] Where women's studies are concerned theological

---

[17] In more than a third of all Dutch theological educational instertions there were no women holding permanent appointments on the academic staff at all in 1989, in about one third this varied from 1 to 4%, in the other third it varied from 5 to 9%. See A.H.Smits e.a., *Rapport van de Verkenningscommissie Godgeleerdheid* I, Den Haag: Ministerie van Onderwijs en Wetenschappen, maart 1989, 92-93, for a survey of the number of women on the academic staff of the theological educational institutions and the nature of the appointments they held.

[18] De Verkennningscommisie Godgeleerdheid (The Theology Exploratory Committee), commissioned in 1989 by the Dutch government to investigate the theological faculties and universities, also met with the problem of disproportionate investing in (conditions for) education compared to investing in research. The Committee warned the universities against the ambiguity in their endeavours to promote women's studies: appointing lecturers for theological wommen's studies but not granting them sufficient time for doctorate research.

institutions have no research policy. Enabling individual women to obtain a doctorate is a *sine qua non*, but in itself not sufficient for developing longer-term visions on - and making concrete investments in - research in theological women's studies as part of a university's overall policy.

A View from the Grass Roots

Fortunately there is also another story to be told about the organisation and incorporation of research in theological women's studies in the Netherlands. This becomes clear when we look at the achievements of feminist theologians in the field of research cooperation, by 'working their way up' as well as by 'mutual assistance'. Much has been set in motion during the last decade. In 1986, for example, the Onderling Promotie Promoting Netwerk ('Mutual Promoting of Obtaining a Doctorate' Network) was founded. Its members are working for their doctorate and encouraging each other in small working parties and annual conferences. The European Society for Women in Theological Research, with a strong Dutch Committee, was also founded in that year. Around the same year the "Proeven van vrouwenstudies theologie" series was started. Women writing their doctoral dissertation can publish part of their research in this series. These are all initiatives from below, to promote that more theological research is undertaken, exchanged, and brought into the open by women.

Informal and mutual initiatives like this do not only stimulate building a network of one's own, but also affect the established institutional structures. This becomes apparent when we look at research in theological women's studies as it is presently executed in the Netherlands, and the way it has in actual fact been institutionally classified. When we look at the official research surveys, such as academic annual reports of theological institutions, it is curious to see that not much research in women's studies appears to be done. When, on the other hand, explicit enquiries are made, a far greater number of theological researchers than expected indicate that they are working in this particular field. This is most surprising and raises the question as to what exactly 'women's studies' is,[19] but also indicates a

---

The theological faculties and universities were admonished to face their responsibilities in this respect and to relieve the lecturers from an overdose of lecturing and administratieve duties until after their doctorate. "Only then a situation can be averted where the one hand doles out trendy gifts, wich are actually taken back by the other". Smits e.a., *Rapport van de Verkenningscommissie Godgeleerdheid* I, 92.

[19] Obviously there is little consensus in theological institutions as to what feminist-theological

research climate in which - however incidental and indirect - the relevance of women's studies questions in a wider sense is gradually being taken up.

It will cause no surprise that most research in women's studies nowadays is done on an individual and temporary basis. This is also connected with the nature of such research. Between 1985 and 1995 doctorate research in the Netherlands was predominantly an individual matter, in accordance with the age and position of most feminist-theological researchers. Owing to research planning and cooperation 'at the grass roots' this individual research is, however, increasingly incorporated in current research programmes on its own merit. More and more feminist-theological researchers are taking part with their own research in theological, philosophical, ethical and other research programmes within or among the theological institutions. Their contribution to the research programmes of centres for research in women's studies, such as the Belle van Zuylen Instituut in Amsterdam, the Anna Maria van Schuurman Centrum in Utrecht, or the Centrum voor Vrouwenstudies in Nijmegen is also increasing.

A major problem remains the fact that despite this influence from below, research in theological women's studies still remains relatively invisible and does not have a distinctive face of its own. Joint research planning and programming by women researchers in theological women's studies are highlighted far too sporadically and shown as a concerted effort. To a large extent this is due to the fact that the past period has been so strongly

---

research actually is. But is consensus indeed required, and if so, what positive effects would it have? Devoting special attention to the position of women can, of course, not be compared with, for instance, developing a feminist-theological form of hermeneutics. However, is it really necessary to establish a clean borderline between 'truly feminist' research and research which 'only' treats gender as a relevant academic category? (See also Elisabeth Schüssler Fiorenza, "The Ethics and Politics of Liberation. Theorizing the "Ekklesia" of Women", in: Id., *Discipleship of Equals*, 332-352; Rosi Braidotti, "What's Wrong With Gender?", in: Van Dijk-Hemmes & Brenner (eds.), *Reflections on Theology and Gender*, 49-70.) The fact that 'gender' is becoming increasingly visible and accepted as an academically relevant category is probably an indication that the term as such has lost its exclusively and unambiguously feminist power and bite. But this does not warrant the conclusion that the category as such would no longer be able to play an important role in the battle to broach women's issues. On the contrary, the strugggle over the divergent use of the 'gender' category actually fans the fire. Instead of disqualifying research starting from the 'gender' category actually it would seem much more sensible to engage in a broad-based debate and discussion, based on the factual and diverse appeal made to this category.

dominated by the individual dissertation research of women researchers. Now that a considerable number of women has recently obtained their doctorate in the field of theological women's studies or will shortly do so, a new situation has, in fact, arisen. I consider it a *sine qua non* for the further development of research in theological women's studies in the Netherlands that 'independent' research programmes will be established. Inter-university programmes should be initiated, as well as local research, linked to one particular institution. Such local programmes are also of great importance to maintain contact with the (local) colleagues for research that is practice-based and practice-oriented.

It should be prevented at all costs that research in theological women's studies remains an 'undercurrent' affair. This implies, at a structural level, that we must continue our battle for the appointment of women in higher academic functions. It implies, above all, that regular professorships - i.e. not founded by special appointment or endowed by private institutions or foundations - in theological women's studies must be established in the Netherlands. More than ten years ago it was a big leap forward when a rotating endowed professorship for Feminism and Christianity was established in Nijmegen - the very first in this discipline in the world. Now this kind of chair no longer meets the requirements, because of its low level of continuity and its inadequate position, and the Netherlands is even liable to lose her pioneering role in this respect!

Creating a Higher Profile
Research in theological women's studies will also become more 'visible' when we give its contents a higher profile. Inherent in the fact that a great deal of this research is individual and temporary is the danger of its being relegated to the fringe and disappearing from sight within, or compared to, larger-scale research programmes. Moreover, much research in women's studies goes beyond the existing boundaries and divisions of theology. Notably inderdisciplinary research does not dovetail with theological or women's studies research. And fairly often this interdisciplinary research - taking place in the borderland of systematic theology and women's studies in literature, philosophy, history, or social sciences -involves very interesting and promising research.

It is bad luck for theological women's studies that they are suffering from the 'unknown, unloved' syndrome in the research circuits of theology on the one hand, and women's studies on the other. I don't believe in solving this problem by ignoring theological women's studies' own identity or by representing them as resembling as closely as possible non-feminist theology or non-theological women's studies. A clear profile of its own for theological women's studies is not only important for the continuation of this research as such, but also for theological research as a whole.

Theological women's studies should make no secret of their views on theology, but propound and present it as their own, meaningful answers to the 'what is theology' discussion, if only because fundamentalism and neo-orthodoxy do not augur well for women. At the moment the strongest movements trying to revitalise theology appear to come from neo-orthodox and fundamentalist quarters. In the western world feminist theology is one of the few, truly vital, religious movements in which the clash between Christian faith, modernity, and secularity is not assimilated in a fundamentalistic or neo-orthodox way. Feminist theology has new views on theology and these must be set out far more explicitly.[20] I make a strong plea for not speaking too implicitly about theological moments and aspects thereof when we are profiling research in theological women's studies.

Conclusion

Feminist-theological training and research is pervaded with the ideal of 'doing research in a different way' - and rightly so. This ideal as such is, I think, no problem, and there is every reason to continue honouring it. But it is of the utmost importance to recognise the high demands of its practical implementation and the pitfalls it involves. I hope that my survey of recent developments in the structural incorporation of feminist theological training and research in the Netherlands - and I assume that this situation applies to many western countries at this moment[21] -has explained why the major problem now is not so much the realisation of 'other training', but especially the realisation of 'other research', and how this can be solved.

Today the organisation and financing of research is the academic

---

[20] See also Anne-Marie Korte, "De religieuze bronnen van de compassie. Feministische theologie als kritische cultuur-theologie", *Tijdschrift voor Theologie* (1994), 357-380.

[21] This assumption is confirmed by the above-mentioned article by Elisabeth Schüssler Fiorenza, "Commitment and Critical Inquiry", which does mention succesful results achieved in changing programmes of study in Havard, but does not record ny changes made or being made in the field of research.

battleground *par excellence* in the Netherlands. This is the place where the survival of academic theological institutions and appointments is fought. Consequently there is no longer any question of noble gestures towards women's studies on this front. One might ask whether, in the light of such increased resistance, it would not be important for feminist theology to engage battle here. I think the answer should be a clear 'yes', because doing research within an academic setting is relevant for feminist theology as such, as it enables feminist theology to explore its own questions in depth, and at the same time to enter into an ongoing discussion with other research in theology and women's studies.

The Dutch example shows why informal and mutual cooperation between feminist theologians engaged in research is of such importance. Mutual support, working your way up from the bottom, and forming networks are the actual 'basis', and absolutely vital for the creation of other/one's own research programmes, for paid research in the fields of theological women's studies, and for the incorporation of our questions in established training and research. This does not mean that I am playing down the importance of acquiring positions of power within the established academic structures and institutions. What it does mean is, that I want to emphasise that such positions should be and remain - closely related to the 'struggle from the grass roots', inside the academic institutions and in the world outside.

(translation: Lysbeth Croiset van Uchelen-Brouwer)

Dr. Anne-Marie Korte, born in 1957 in Bussum, studied theology and philosophy at the Roman Catholic University of Nijmegen. She worked as a researcher for the project 'Feminism and Theology' at the University of Nijmegen. Currently she works as a lecturer for Women' Studies Theology at the Roman Catholic University of Utrecht. Her doctorate is entiteld, *A Passion for Transcendence. Feminism, Theology and Modernity in the Thinking of Mary Daly*, Kampen 1992. She is editor of the series *Proeven van vrouwenstudies theologie* and writes for various journals particulary around the theme of embodiment as an hermeneutical category within feminist theology.

Adriana Valerio

La parole influente:
Domenica da Paradiso (1473-1553)

Aperçus biographiques

Domenica Narducci naquit le 8 décembre 1473 à Florence dans le bourg appelé 'Paradiso',de parents maraîchers, François et Constance Narducci.[1] Précocement consciente de sa vocation religieuse, Domenica fit de multiples tentatives pour entreprendre un chemin de foi répondant aux exigences de sa propre spiritualité. Son penchant pour la vie érémitique et contemplative, associée au service des pauvres, le choix de vivre comme une 'béguine', comme une laïque, donc sans devoir se lier aux obligations d'une congrégation religieuse quelconque, constituent les étapes significatives d'une recherche de liberté intérieure qui va constamment caractériser son existence.

Les exploits du Savonarole ont provoqué un tournant décisif dans l'anxiété religieuse de Domenica.[2] Abandonnant la maison familiale, elle s'établit dans la ville de Florence en décembre 1499. Là, grâce à ses dons prophétiques et mystiques, mais aussi à sa forte personnalité, elle devint vite un point de référence pour un nombre croissant de croyants et croyantes, qui constituèrent autour de sa personne un cénacle, centre de vie spirituelle et politique enraciné dans la réalité florentine.

Certaines de ses disciples se joignirent à elle, pour former une 'communauté' dans une maison achetée en 1505. Mais elle ne voulu pas se lier à aucun ordre religieux, ni se sentir engagée par la 'direction' d'un père spirituel unique. Cette façon d'agir la rendit rapidement suspecte aux yeux de beaucoup, et mal vue par les dominicains, dont pourtant elle se sentait

---

[1]   Voir Adriana Valerio, *Domenica da Paradiso. Profezia e politica in una mistica del Rinascimento*, Centro Studi altomedioevali di Spoleto, Spoleto 1992.

[2]   Lorenzo Polizzotto, "When Saint Fall out. Women and Savonarolan Reform in Early Sixteenth-Century Florence", in: *Renaissance Quarterly* 3 (1993), 486-525.

particulièrement proche. Obligée de choisir une obédience institutionnelle pour elle-même et les disciples qui partageaient sa vie, elle ne renonce pas à son esprit indépendant et veut que ses consoeurs travaillent, "parce que ses filles doivent être dégagées de tout patronage". Elle revêt l'habit dominicain, (reçu des mains de Sainte Catherine de Sienne, lors d'une extase) choisissant la voie privée du Tiers Ordre et ne voulant jamais prononcer aucun voeu solennel, si ce n'est au moment de sa mort, en 1553, à l'âge de 80 ans.

Une communauté religieuse aussi insolite, fondée par elle avec l'approbation du pape Léon X en 1515, devint un lieu significatif de rencontre à Florence, pour beaucoup de chrétiens et chrétiennes, qui trouvent un guide spirituel éclairé en la personne de Domenica. Non seulement ses consoeurs s'adressent à elle, mais aussi des laïcs, des religieux, des ecclésiastiques, des théologiens, et ses propres confesseurs, envers lesquels elle adopte une attitude libre, qui ne coïncide pas avec les canons traditionnels de l'obéissance féminine. C'est ainsi qu'elle renverse souvent les rôles, exerçant la fonction de guide, et non de disciple.

Son engagement religieux pour la réforme de l'Eglise (*Renovatio Ecclesiae*) se complète d'un engagement intense dans le secteur politique; elle se veut protagoniste des évènements sociaux et politiques de l'époque. Paladine, mais sans fanatisme, de la liberté républicaine florentine, elle estime essentiel d'harmoniser le difficile mariage entre raison et foi dans le renouveau de la société, avec un passage nécéssaire du plan de la rhétorique à la réforme pratique.

La crise des années '40 représente un virage ultérieur dans sa vie. Le pouvoir 'dur' de Côme Ier dans la principauté des Medicis, les inquiétudes créées par la crise protestante, le climat inquisiteur de plus en plus pressant de la Contre-réforme, amènent Domenica à limiter ses propres interventions publiques.

Elle meurt le 5 août 1553, en 'odeur de sainteté', grâce à ses prophéties et à ses miracles. La grande duchesse Christine de Lorraine introduira, après 1611, les Actes pour la canonisation de Domenica. Cause maintes fois reprise et jamais conclue: dans l'*Index Causarum* Domenica est cataloguée comme 'vénérable'. Le monastère de la Crocetta qu'elle fonda existe toujours à Florence, et les soeurs conservent pieusement son souvenir.

Parole prophétique[3]

Les lettres, sermons, visions, révélations et 'traités' conservés dans les archives du monastère florentin, nous révèlent une femme en laquelle cohabitent, avec un rare équilibre, mystique et engagement dans le monde, direction spirituelle et administration conventuelle.

En parcourant la vie de Domenica da Paradiso, on est frappé par le profond désir d'indépendance qui se manifeste tout au long de cette vie. Les interrogatoires qu'elle eut à subir durant le procès qu'on lui intenta en 1500, "femme scandaleuse et suspecte d'hérésie", manifestent bien son attitude d'autonomie à l'égard de toute autorité, qu'elle soit paternelle ou religieuse. Pour sa défense, elle se réfère au Christ même, qui ne la veut assujettie à aucun pouvoir, y inclu celui du 'père spirituel'.

Cette liberté, enracinée dans une profonde expérience d'union à Dieu, lui donne l'audace de s'adresser directement au pape, pour le rappeler à ses propres responsabilités pastorales; elle lui permet aussi de se référer sans réticence mais avec une certaine désinvolture, à ses 'directeurs spirituels'. Elle lui donne enfin la franchise de dialoguer avec Dieu comme avec un ami unique. Liberté de parole (la *parrhésia* biblique) qui se traduit en mots forts, pleins d'autorité, à travers les modalités de la prophétie, de l'enseignement, de la prédication et de la vision mystique.[4]

Son expérience religieuse est très étroitement liée et mise au service des actions qu'elle mène dans le contexte historique qui est le sien, et aussi à son activité prophétique, qui exhorte, secoue, incite au repentir, dans le cadre plus vaste de ce que l'on appelle alors la Réforme de l'Eglise. Mère 'cigale', comme elle aimait à se définir ironiquement, elle est très consciente de l'influence de sa propre parole, qu'elle doit adresser là où la situation l'exige, pour réconforter, réprimander ou 'dresser'; consciente peut-être aussi, comme la culture érémitique s'affirmait durant ces années-là, que ceux qui possèdent la *parole* ne sont pas sujets au destin, puisque l'intelligence et la parole ont valeur d'immortalité.

---

[3] Signalons: Gabriella Zarri, *Le sante vive. Profezie di corte e devozione femminile tra '400 e '500*, Rosenberg & Sellier, Torino 1990; Adriana Valerio, "L'esperienza profetica femminile nei secoli XIV-XVI", in: *Rassegna di Teologia* 6 (1994); Adriana Valerio (ed.), *L'altra rivelazione. Percorsi storici della profezia femminile*, D'Auria, Napoli 1995.

[4] Adriana Valerio, *Cristianesimo al femminile. Donne protagoniste nella storia del cristiane-simo*, D'Auria, Napoli 1990.

Prédication[5]

C'est au nom de cette même liberté que lui donne la foi que Domenica prêche publiquement, provoquant ainsi les soupçons des autorités ecclésiastiques.

Dans un domaine humaniste, il n'est pas rare de trouver à l'époque des femmes qui lisent et interprètent l'Ecriture, ce qui nous permet aujourd'hui de retrouver des mots féminins insolites et féconds. S'agit-il d'une lecture dirigée et soutenue par l'étude? Ou bien plutôt assimilée oralement, à travers la liturgie et la prédication? Est-ce une compréhension similaire à la compréhension masculine, ou conduit-elle à une compréhension personnelle et originale? Les expériences singulières de Macrina, dans la culture biblique, de Mélanie, philologue et exégète, par Demetriade, Marcella, Paola, les disciples de Saint Jérôme, occupées à l'étude de la Sainte Ecriture, quelle importance, quelles répercussions ont-elles eues dans le christianisme féminin, là où des contestations favorables provoquaient de toutes façons un choc entre une "culture du soupçon" et une lecture de la Bible liée à la stricte interprétation des autorités hiérarchique?

L'histoire de l'*exégèse féminine* n'a pas encore été écrite... Je voudrais seulement mettre en évidence l'enrichissement de la sensibilité scripturaire dans le domaine humaniste qu'a permis l'accès des non-clercs au livre saint, en dehors donc de la tradition de la grande culture monastique. Je pense à Marguerite d'Angoulême (1492-1549), à Vittoria Colonna (morte en 1547), à Caterina Cybo (m. 1557), qui travaillèrent et raisonnèrent sur la Bible.

Domenica elle-même, illettrée et analphabète, connaît la Sainte Ecriture: elle la cite, et ses oeuvres en parlent sans cesse, conjugant son interprétation biblique personnelle et allégorique avec sa proclamation explicite et courageuse. Tout comme le feront ensuite la mexicaine Juana Inès de la Cruz (m. 1695) ou la Quaker Margareth Fell (m. 1702), Domenica interprète 1 Cor 14,34 ("Les femmes doivent se taire dans les assemblées") comme un appel à s'exprimer en public que la libre volonté de l'Esprit Saint fait aux femmes. Son horizon théologique lui permet également, dans son commentaire de la parabole du bon grain et de l'ivraie, de trouver là les fondements de la tolérance, alors qu'au contraire l'interprétation courante de cette même page de l'Evangile voulait y voir la légitimation de l'élimination des

---

[5] Adriana Valerio, "Donne e Scrittura. Per una storia dell'esegesi femminile", in: *Gli specchi delle donne. Per una teologia al femminile*, Cens, Milano 1994, 55ss.

hérétiques.

C'est donc une exégèse alternative que celle de Domenica, proche de la pensée d'Erasme, mais issue surtout de la sensibilité propre à la mystique féminine, qui donne la suprématie à l'amour, et dans laquelle la Parole devient présage de miséricorde.

Parole mystique

Les dons mystiques de Domenica naissent de l'expérience d'un rapport d'union intime avec le Seigneur, dans une foi emprégnée d'une tendresse qu'on dirait conjugale. La révélation dynamique de Dieu lui-même dans le plan de l'histoire est profondément ancrée dans son esprit, mais elle a été cultivée à travers un langage analogique, qui inclut à l'égalité les deux genres, et dans lequel les aspects symboliques du masculin alternent avec ceux du féminin, pour mieux approcher la mystérieuse réalité divine. Ainsi, le discours sur Dieu change l'image de Dieu, parce que le Dieu Père sévère est en même temps Mère qui nourrit, mère qui rassemble ses poussins sous son aile; Dieu de tendresse, parce que Père de miséricorde, sein accueillant, mamelle nourricière, mère féconde. La 'matrice' de Dieu dont il est question dans le language biblique pour indiquer l'amour, fruit de la compassion, est récupérée symboliquement par Domenica, dans l'image de Jésus amoureux, époux passionné.

Nous nous trouvons donc en présence d'une théologie que j'aime définir comme *théologie de la tendresse*. Une théologie, riche d'un langage poétique, qui naît à partir d'émotions, d'expériences de communion, qui ne détient pas la vérité, mais la cultive plutôt dans les fragments de l'expérience, qui ne discute pas sur Dieu mais raconte la stupéfaction de la rencontre avec l'amour. Il s'agit donc d'une théologie a-dogmatique, consciente des limites de la raison et du langage, dans la codification de la réalité divine, et relativisant les solutions intellectuelles qui veulent circonscrire le transcendant, afin que la personne humaine s'ouvre à l'étonnement du mystère. Dans l'union mystique, le processus de divinisation pousse Domenica à s'identifier au Christ. Elle est l'*alter Christus*, parce qu'elle se conforme au Christ des douleurs. La femme peut donc être *Imago Dei*.[6]

---

[6] Kari Elizabeth Børresen (ed), *Image of God and Gender Models*, Solum Forlag, Oslo 1991; Kari Elizabeth Børresen, *Le Madri della Chiesa. Il Medioevo*, D'Auria, Napoli 1993.

Nous nous trouvons en présence d'une divinisation de la femme (de telles femmes étaient appelées *Mères divines*) et il ne s'agit pas d'un mythe rare dans l'histoire chrétienne. L'incarnation de Dieu sous les apparences féminines (songeons à Guglielma de Milan, à Prous Boneta, à la vierge vénitienne, annoncée par Guillaume Postel, à Marta Fiascaris) ne se borne pas seulement à une autre approche de la vieille question de l'*imago Dei*, mais elle met aussi en évidence le besoin spirituel d'adoucir l'image sévère du transcendant, pour en exalter la sollicitude maternelle.[7]

Mais dès que change le climat de la Contre-réforme, Domenica, ainsi que d'autres femmes, seront ramenées au silence. La lecture de la Bible leur sera interdite et elles devront, muettes, suivre un chemin difficile à la recherche de Dieu. "Brèves paroles et longs silences" pour utiliser un oximore de Marie Madeleine de Pazzi (m. 1607).

Personnalité innovatrice

Mysticisme et prophétie, abandon en Dieu et engagement dans le monde, désir de vie spirituelle et participation aux évènements socio-politiques de son temps sont les deux faces de la spiritualité complexe de Domenica da Paradiso, mère spirituelle mais aussi administratrice avisée, fondatrice d'une communauté religieuse tout en étant laïque, prédicatrice savante bien qu'analphabète.

Son expérience religieuse évoque l'élan créatif du mysticisme flamand, la liberté intérieure des béguines, le caractère entreprenant des femmes prédicatrices laïques, la solitude des ermites médiévaux, le zèle missionnaire des prophétesses. Une conscience historique vit profondément en elle, et elle se manifeste dans sa façon laïque de s'ouvrir au monde, avec une intelligence politique; dans l'usage de critères éthiques s'adaptant avec souplesse aux différentes situations; dans l'attention qu'elle porte aux problèmes de la vie d'une humanité concrète; dans l'exercice d'un rôle prophétique, qui lui fait découvrir un transcendant accessible dans la contingence des évènements; dans l'affirmation et la pratique du droit à la parole publique, qui lui donne conscience de ce que cette parole féminine n'est plus superflue mais nécéssaire; dans la liberté de l'insoumission, pour faire des choix difficiles;

---

[7] Peter Dinzelbacher/Dieter R. Bauer, *Religiöse Frauenbewegung und mystische Frömmigkeit im Mittelalter*, Boehlau, Köln 1988; Adriana Valerio, "Una chiesa al femminile. Guglielma da Milano", in: *Cristianesimo al femminile* cit, 111-125.

dans l'abolition de toute médiation ecclésiastique pour établir un contact direct avec Dieu.

Lorsque Domenica critique une théologie orgueilleuse et arrogante qui n'est plus à la recherche de Dieu, nous pouvons percevoir le processus de la mystique féminine, opposant à l'*intellectus fidei* d'une spéculation religieuse froide et décadente, l'*intellectus amoris* d'une foi qui naît d'une expérience unique, et qui sait conjuguer une vie de foi et engagement dans le monde. En même temps qu'elle donne une visibilité et une incisivité transformatrices à cette façon féminine différente de parler de Dieu.

Adriana Valerio est chercheuse en Histoire de l'Eglise à l'Université de Naples, Italie. Ses livres *Christianesimo al femminile* et *Domenica da Paradiso. Profezia e politica in una mistica del Rinascimento* ont pour sujet deux questions très importantes dans la reconstruction de l'Histoire des femmes: les fonctions de prophètes et de prédicatrices.

Bruna Peyrot

L'identité des femmes chez les Vaudois du Piémont

Au Moyen-Age

Les réflexions qui suivent ont pour fil conducteur le rôle des femmes chez les Vaudois du Piémont, la plus ancienne minorité protestante d'Italie. Son histoire commence au Moyen-Age, vers la fin du douzième siècle. En l'an 1174 environ, un riche marchand, dit Vaudès ou Valdès, après une grave crise spirituelle qui, comme d'autres protagonistes des mouvements héréticaux des douzième et treizième siècles, l'amena à se libérer de ses richesses, se voua entièrement à la prédication de l'Evangile dans la langue du peuple.

Autour de lui se groupèrent bientôt de nombreux disciples, hommes et femmes, qu'on appela 'les pauvres de Lyon', parce qu'ils habitaient surtout cette moderne ville française. D'ici, le mouvement s'étendit tout d'abord au sud de la France, puis s'unifia avec les 'pauvres' de la Lombardie et continua sa diffusion au sud, dans l'Italie méridionale et au nord, vers l'Europe septentrionale et orientale, jusqu'en Autriche et en Bohême.

Parmi les principales caractéristiques du mouvement vaudois on peut mentionner: la pauvreté, l'insistance sur la libre prédication de l'Evangile par tous les croyants, laïques et écclesiastiques, le refus de liens unissant l'Eglise et l'Empire. Exigence fondamentale pour les Vaudois: l'obéissance rigoureuse au Sermon sur la Montagne et la résistance au système hiérarchique féodale et, enfin, le refus de la violence.

Les historiens du Moyen-Age admettent que la presence des femmes prédicatrices dans les premiers groups vaudois est attestée par les sources de l'époque. Mais quelques décennies plus tard, les femmes perdront leurs positions et retourneront au silence des rôles traditionnels.

Cela se passe toujours comme cela dans l'histoire: les périodes révolution-naires ouvrent aux femmes des nouvelles voies, comme si l'insurrection les rendait tout simplement visibles; au contraire, quand le mouvement social s'arrête et vise à se transformer en institution, à formuler des règles précises et à prendre en charge une tradition qui doit être transmise aux nouvelles générations, alors les femmes ne sont plus reconnues, et par conséquent, elles sont renvoyées à leur cocon domestique.

Dominique Godineau le dit bien, par exemple à propos de la Révolution française. Les femmes participent au début des révoltes, elles mettent le feu aux poudres, mais très vite, elles se limitent à soutenir les hommes. Autrement dit, l'économie insurrectionnelle privilégie le monde masculin au moment où la nécessité d'une organisation collective devient prioritaire dans le contexte révolutionnaire.

Un autre exemple nous propose une analogie supplémentaire: dans le christianisme primitif, une première phase donnait aux femmes une place importante; une autre période a suivi, dans laquelle la femme sera exclue de tous les rôles institutionnels et de tous les ministères.

Mais pour ce qui concerne les Vaudois du quatorzième siècle, si la femme n'apparaît plus sur la scène publique, cela ne signifie nullement son absence au service social de la communauté des fidèles. L'historien du Moyen-Age Grado G. Merlo a très bien expliqué l'action et la figure des "misérables petites sottes qui prêchaient" dont parlent les abbés et inquisiteurs, souvent en termes méprisants. On les considéraient en effet comme des incontrôlables méchantes, doublement hérétiques, en tant que femmes et comme *pauperes Christi*.

Répression et persécutions

Les femmes vaudoises furent souvent confondues avec les sorcières et comme elles brûlées sur les bûchers, qui constituaient un spectacle sur les places publiques. Nous n'avons pas beaucoup de souvenirs des femmes comdamnées par l'Inquisition. Le silence descend sur elles et sur toute l'histoire d'une minorité, les Vaudois, très encombrants pour la culture dominante italienne.

Pendant les treizième, quatorzième et quinzième siècles, les Vaudois vivaient presque en clandestinité. Bien vite la répression se déchaîna contre leurs groups et, en peu de temps, le mouvement fut anéanti dans bien des parties de l'Europe; il ne survécut pratiquement qu'en Bohème, où il fut absorbé par le mouvement hussite et dans les vallées dites encore aujourd'hui 'vaudoises', aux confins de la France et de l'Italie, au sud-ouest de Turin, en Piémont. Ici les Vaudois restèrent emprisonnés dans une sorte de ghetto, souvent persécutés et soumis à de cruelles vexations. Ils réussirent à sauvegarder leur autonomie de foi et de loi jusqu'au jour où se leva l'aube de la Réforme.

L'adhésion à la Réforme protestante amena la reconnaissance de l'égalité spirituelle des femmes, mais refusa leur admission au ministère pastoral et au service diaconal. Les sources vaudoises des seizième et dix-septième siècles ne parlent des femmes que pour citer leur action auprès des personnes âgées, des jeunes garçons et filles, qu'elles aident et protègent. Ou alors, lorsqu'elles prêchent le Seigneur dans quelque cavernes ou anfractuosités rocheuses bien cachées, pour permettre aux hommes de fuir et d'échapper aux poursuites des mercenaires à la solde des souverains piémontais de la Maison de Savoie.

Au temps de la Réforme les Vaudois découvrirent qu'ils n'étaient plus seuls dans leurs convinctions de foi. Au Synode de Chanforan (vallée d'Angrogne), en 1532, en présence des deux réformateurs venus de Suisse (Farel et Saunier), ils décidèrent d'adhérer à la Réforme et, depuis ce moment-là, le mouvement vaudois se transforma peu à peu en Eglise Réformée. Ils décidèrent aussi de traduire la Bible en français, à leurs frais, et la traduction fut faite par Pierre Robert, dit Olivétan, cousin de Calvin.

L'adhésion à la Réforme marque le début de nouvelles persécutions déchaînées contre les membres de la 'Religion Prétendue Reformée' par les ducs de Savoie, par le roi de France et par les papes de l' église romaine. Une des plus terribles persécutions fut celle du 1655, dite 'Les Pâques piémontaises'; elle souleva l'indignation de tout le monde protestant d'Europe, et en Angleterre tout particulièrement celle de Cromwell et du poète Milton. Un autre génocide se produit en 1686. Après la Révocation de l'Edit de Nantes, les vallées vaudoises du Piémont furent envahies par les troupes du duc de Savoie. Les Vaudois furent contraints à l'exil et trouvèrent un accueil fraternel en Suisse. De là, à la suite d'une mémorable expédition sous la conduite du pasteur-condottiere Henri Arnaud, ils réussirent a reconquérir leur terre.

Il faut dire que cet événement est devenu le fondement de la mémoire collective vaudoise, transmise de génération en génération parmi l'histoire des familles qui en maintenait le souvenir, avant la création des musées et des lieux de mémoire historique mis en place par l'institution de l'église vaudoise.

Le mémoire des femmes

Et les femmes, dans toute cette période? Aujourd'hui, on s'en souvient comme d' héroïnes, épouses, mères ou filles de ces hommes qui ont su résister aux papes et aux rois. Au dix-septième siècle surtout, la femme vaudoise est identifiée avec 'celle qui a été violée'. Et cela est certainement justifié, car le viol faisait partie de la persécution. Mais il n'y a pas eu que cela. Les siècles des guerres de réligion parlent beaucoup de l'histoire des répressions à l'égard de la minorité protestante, mais il n'y a pas une parole spécifique sur les femmes de cette minorité. De plus, puisque toutes les archives des églises vaudoises avaient été jetées aux bûchers, la mémoire des femmes plongea dans le silence, en même temps que l'histoire de la vie quotidienne des paroisses des vallées vaudoises.

On en a gardé cependant quelques traces. On sait, par exemple, que Giovanello, le héros populaire de la résistance vaudoise du 1655, avait une femme du nom de Caterina Durand, du village de Rorà. Elle fut emprisonnée, mais elle n'a jamais abjuré. L'historiographie vaudoise lui a attribué des qualificatifs mérités également par la plupart des femmes vaudoises de cette époque: courageuse, avisée, fidèle compagne de son époux.

Au dix-huitième siècle, le point de vue des femmes est encore moins connu. Les persécutions terminées, les 'hérétiques' vécurent dans le 'ghetto' - la terre qu'on ne pouvait quitter sans permission du Duc de Savoie - sans aucune possibilité d'acheter des terres nouvelles, d'exercer des professions liberales, privés des droits civils qui en auraient fait de vrais citoyens. Ceux qui désideraient poursuivre des études devaient le faire à l'étranger. Beaucoup d'entr'eux choisissaient d'y rester; d'autres revenaient au pays avec une femme étrangère qui devenait, aux yeux du peuple des vallées, la 'dame', porteuse en fait d'une culture d'au delà des Alpes, élément de première importance pour transmettre aux vallées les coutumes européennes.

On sait très peu de choses, finalement, sur les femmes de cette époque, que ce soit de la 'dame' des salons bourgeois, ou bien de la paysanne, maîtresse de la petite maison que sa famille partage avec le bétail qu'elle posséde et tous les outils de travail.

Nous avons tout de même retrouvé un document datant de 1757, dans lequel on décrit le trousseau d'une femme du pays de Prali (Val Germanasca) qui avait été volé, et qui comportait "des lingeries et ornements de femme", pour une somme de 80 lires. La vie de cette femme serait restée parfaitement anonyme s'il n'y avait eu ce vol qui transmit à l'histoire quelques généralités à son propos: son nom d'abord, Jeanne Richiarda, et aussi l'énumération de ses pauvres vêtements, le tout enregistré dans les archives du Tribunal de la vallée San Martin (aujourd'hui val Germanasca).

Des noms de femmes se trouvent aussi dans les *Actes des Synodes des églises vaudoises* de 1692 à 1854. C'est la première documentation officielle écrite après le retour de l'exil suisse des Vaudois (1689). Les *Actes* sont des décisions prises par les députés des communautés vaudoises des vallées lors de leurs Synodes. Ce Synode etant la plus importante assemblée délibérative pour la vie et l'organisation de l'institution écclésiastique.

Surtout pendant les premières décennies du dix-huitième siècle, tous les efforts des Vaudois étaient centrés sur la reconstruction de la vie quotidienne, là où la destruction et la mort avaient sévi. Chaque décision prise visait à redonner des règles à la société civile dans laquelle était aussi enracinée la société religieuse vaudoise. Les Vaudois se sont occupés avant tout des écoles, des temples et de la Discipline. La Discipline peut être définie comme la 'Constitution' de l'église, le code règlant les comportements des hommes entre eux, pour les 'lier' dans l'avertissement, et les 'dénouer' en donnant le pardon, sous le regard des anciens et des diacres de l'église.

Enfin, les Actes traitent beaucoup de questions de femmes. On les invite à se réconcilier avec leurs époux, et en même temps les maris sont invités à 'tenir en amitié' leurs épouses. On les écoute quand elles viennent demander 'réparation' pour une promesse de mariage non-tenue, ou révéler le nom du père de l'enfant illégitime qu'elles ont eu, et pour lequel les anciens de la communauté rechercherons un vrai père... Quelquefois, ce sont aux femmes elles-mêmes à juger d'autres femmes, comme dans le cas de Camille Vertu, accusée par son mari d'être incapable de 'commerce avec un homme'; deux femmes 'dignes de foi' seront alors chargées de procéder à des examens intimes de Camille, et déclareront finalement n'avoir rien constaté de "différent et d'opposé à son sexe" (acte 11 du 1708). D'autres fois encore, des femmes comparaissent, au titre de mère ou de veuve, pour demander une aide financière afin que leur fils puisse continuer ses études pour le ministère pastoral.

Par les Actes des Synodes, nous pouvons comprendre l'engagement vaudois dans la construction d'une société protestante au sein des vallées du Piémont, là où ils étaient autorisés à résider, dans un petit carré de terre difficile à cultiver, à rendre productive pour eux et pour les générations de l'avenir.

Dans les Actes, on peut aussi constater la volonté de prendre en compte l'égalité entre hommes et femmes. Tous sont appelés à se présenter devant Dieu, à ne pas l'offenser, à ne pas profaner le jour du Seigneur, mais à le célébrer au contraire avec leurs enfants bien élevés.

Il n'y a pas de discours spécifique sur les femmes au dix-huitième siècle:

elles semblent accepter le rôle qui leur est attribué et n'apparaîssent que parmi les noms et prénoms des dynasties pastorales vaudoises, en qualité de mère, fille, soeur et épouse de pasteurs. Leur discours est communautaire, témoignage de leur présence collective. Elles semblent ainsi poser les bases de cet univers anonyme, afin que dans les siècles à venir, la capacité des femmes à se retrouver ensemble, à avoir un même discours social puisse être plus concrètement visible.

Forces féminines

Le dix-neuvième siècle, en effet, va offrir aux femmes vaudoises l'occasion de s'unir en différentes formes d'organisations ecclésiales, qui les verront tricoter et étudier la Bible en communauté. En 1848 les Vaudois purent pour la première fois jouir des mêmes droits civiques que leurs concitoyens. L'édit d'émancipation du 17 février 1848, promulgué par le roi Charles Albert, n'était pas une vraie reconaissance de la liberté religieuse, mais il assurait aux Vaudois le droit de s'organiser librement dans leurs vallées et d'en sortir, avec des droits égaux à ceux des autres sujets du royaume.

L'histoire 'sans qualités' du dix-septième siècle, même si elle fut très héroïque, ou l'histoire sans protagonistes féminines du dix-huitième siècle préparent l'histoire du dix-neuvième siècle, où les femmes vaudoises se retrouvent dans un lieu privilégié: les Unions des femmes, présentes dans les communautés des vallées et dans les villes italiennes aussi, là où étaient nées de nouvelles églises vaudoises, après l'émancipation civile.

Les Archives nous donnent des témoignages importants sur l'activité des femmes dans les Unions. Les procès-verbaux de leurs réunions indiquent un schéma répété d'actions: chants, prière, quête, étude biblique, informations sur la vie communautaire de leur paroisse, chants et salutations finales. Le chant et la méditation biblique déterminent le style d'être ensemble, des relations interpersonnelles, habituant le corps et l'ésprit à une discipline mentale qui, maintes fois, semaine après semaine, modèle l'identité de la personne. Le chant est un acte physique parce qu'il permet la manifestation de l'âme dans le présent. On chante avec l'émotivité et les pensées heureuses ou pénibles du moment existentiel vécu. On chante en pensant aux mots du psaume qui toujours offrent un mot particulièrement évocateur pour la personne qui les chante. On chante enfin, sentant la force du groupe qui entoure l'individu, et qui est en train d'exprimer une communion spirituelle dans une même recherche de Dieu. Chants et méditation biblique: cette dernière est le point central des réunions de femmes. Introduite par "madame la Présidente de l'Union" (bien souvent la 'dame' du pasteur local) elle cherche à répondre aux questions principales qui se posent aux croyants du temps. Les thèmes médités sont typiques du protestantisme libéral de l'époque: appel à la conscience personnelle, découverte du rapport direct avec Dieu, sans aucune médiation, conscience d'être pécheur/pécheresse.

Cependant, la piété vaudoise du dix-neuvième siècle ne comprenait pas seulement une dimension de vie intérieure: pour les femmes, comme pour les hommes d'ailleurs, la spiritualité devait se concrétiser à l'extérieur, par un comportement de 'service' envers le prochain. Le 'service' pour la Vaudoise et pour le Vaudois a été toujours le fondement de la pensée et de l'action, devenant une façon de vivre, de penser, de réaliser des projets individuels et collectifs. Le 'service' devient une idée théologique: aimer le prochain signifie aimer Dieu; une idée sociologique: faire quelque chose pour ceux qui ont besoin, près de nous ou loin de nous; une idée anthropologique enfin: le 'moi' se rapporte constamment aux autres.

Pour les femmes, le 'service' signifia rendre publics leurs devoirs privés: s'occuper de l'éducation réligieuse des enfants à l'école du dimanche, soigner les vieillards, réconforter les souffrants, se livrer à l'enseignement et tricoter pour les bazars des missions. Pour les femmes vaudoises, la première sortie du cercle familial s'accomplit soit dans le domaine du service volontaire, soit dans le choix d'un travail payé, sous le double signe de l'exemple religieux et de la métaphore maternelle: les femmes portent dans le social leur capacité de se prendre soin des autres.

Tout le dix-neuvième siècle met en action les forces féminines, que ce soit dans le monde catholique ou dans le monde protestant. Mais si dans le premier on privilégie les formes mystiques, dans le monde protestant naît le concept de 'l'individu engagé'. En Europe, le mouvement pour l'émancipation des femmes porte leur voix hors du foyer familial, et c'est publiquement qu'elles réclament les droits civiques et politiques égaux à ceux des hommes.

Identité de personne
Les femmes vaudoises continuèrent à assurer leur présence dans l'espace du foyer familial et du social-religieux, sans pour autant réfléchir à leur identité de femme. Elles ne réclamèrent jamais aucun droit 'en tant que femmes'. Elles se perçoivent avant tout comme des personnes, elles s'expriment surtout en tant que femmes croyant en Dieu, à la recherche d'un service qui leur soit accessible. L'idée de 'personne' qui est la leur ne comprend toutefois pas la

différence entre masculin et féminin, entre hommes et femmes. C'est une idée 'neutre', ce qui présente à la fois des limites et des avantages. Les limites d'abord, puisque est ignoré l'importance de l'identité sexuelle, qui conditionne un grand nombre d'inégalités sociales dans la vie et la société. Quand on parle seulement de 'personne', on ne peut pas reconnaître la domination réelle que l'homme peut exercer sur la femme. Les avantages ensuite: le caractère 'neutre' de la personne favorise la transformation de la catégorie du 'genre' en personnalité juridique, fondant la différence sur des droits sûrs.

Les femmes vaudoises n'ont pas prétendu à une reconnaissance spécifique, mais seulement aux droits qu'avaient les hommes. Jusqu'en 1903, elles n'ont pas eu le droit de vote; elles obtinrent celui d'être élues en 1930. Enfin, en 1962, elles acquirent le droit de devenir pasteure d'une église, 'pastora' dit-on aujourd'hui. Et pour la première fois en 1962, deux femmes vaudoises furent consacrées 'pastore' au Synode. En 1976 naquit la Fédération des Femmes Protestantes Italiennes, encore en function aujourd'hui et bien engagée dans les politiques des femmes.

Les femmes vaudoises ont donc fait un long chemin, caractérisé par un désir associatif et un engagement dans le 'service' envers les autres. Si elles n'ont pas donné priorité à la recherche et à l'affirmation de leur identité de femme, cela ne signifie pas qu'elles se soient désinteresseés de 'la condition des femmes'. Mais nous le redisons, elles ont préféré chercher une identité de 'personne'. C'est seulement depuis les dernières décennies du vingtième siècle que les femmes vaudoises ont reconnu leur condition de femmes et ont entamé une réflexion et une discussion à ce sujet, dans le monde vaudois et protestant italien, mais aussi avec les autres femmes.

Bibliographie

Actes des Synodes des églises vaudoises. 1692 - 1854, (a cura di Teofilo Pons), Torre Pellice, Società di studi valdesi, 1948.

Hugon Augusto Armand, *Storia dei valdesi*, vol.2, Claudiana: Torino 1974.

Pierre Bolle, *Le Protestantisme en Dauphiné en XVII siècle*, Curandera: Poët/Laval 1983.

Emidio Campi, *Protestantesimo nei secoli. Fonti e documenti I. Cinquecento e Seicento*, Claudiana: Torino 1991.

Arturo Genre, Oriana Bert, *Leggende delle valli valdesi*, Claudiana: Torino 1977.
Dominique Godineau, "Sulle due sponde dell'Atlantico: pratiche rivoluzionarie femminili", in: George Duby, Michelle Perrot, *Storia delle donne, l'Ottocento*, Laterza: Bari 1991.
Anne Marie Käppeli, *Sublime croisade. Ethique et politique du féminisme protestant (1875 - 1928)*, Zoè: Genève 1990.
Giovanni Grado Merlo, *Valdo e valdismi medievali. Itinerari e proposte di ricerca*, Claudiana: Torino 1984.
Giovanni Grado Merlo, *Identità valdesi nella storia e nella storiografia*, Claudiana: Torino 1991.
Bruna Peyrot, *La roccia dove Dio chiama. Viaggio nella memoria valdese fra oralità e scrittura*, Forni: Bologna 1990.
Bruna Peyrot (con G. Bonansea), *Vite discrete. Corpi e immagini di donne valdesi*, Rosenberg & Sellier: Torino 1993.
Anna Doria Rossi, *La libertà delle donne. Voci della tradizione politica suffragista*, Rosenberg & Sellier: Torino 1990.

Bruna Peyrot est née à Luserne Saint Jean (Turin) en 1951. Directrice d'école, elle fait à la fois de la recherche d'histoire sociale, surtout par rapport à l'histoire et la culture protestante en Italie et à l'identité des territoires alpins. Elle est membre de la Société Italienne des historiennes et dirige cours de formation sur la didactique de l'histoire. Elle a publié, *La roccia dove Dio chiama. Viaggio nella memoria valdese fra oralità e scrittura*, Forni: Bologna 1990; *Vite discrete. Corpi e immagini di donne valdesi*, Rosenberg & Sellier: Torino 1993; *Oltre le nuvole. Storia di una curatrice d'anime*, Giunti: Firenze 1994.

Dagny Kaul

Femmes-pasteurs et théologie féministe au sein de 'l'association norvégienne des théologiennes'

Historiquement et objectivement parlant, il existe une corrélation, réelle encore que problématique, entre la théologie et le ministère ordonné. Cette interaction entre la théologie comme discipline universitaire enseignée aux étudiants de la faculté et la vie paroissiale telle qu'elle est modelée par le contenu de la foi à travers les ministères ecclésiastiques n'est pas sans faire question. La tension entre théologie et ministère est encore plus sensible dans le cas des femmes en passe de s'insérer dans les structures androcentriques de l'église et de la théologie.

Dans les pays nordiques, depuis déjà des dizaines d'années, des femmes-pasteurs ont, dans le cadre des Eglises d'Etat de confession évangélique-luthérienne qui sont les leurs, recueilli le fruit de leurs expériences et constitué des traditions. L'ordination de femmes-pasteurs date au Danemark de 1948, en Suède de 1959, en Norvège de 1961, en Islande de 1982 et en Finlande de 1992. En Norvège il existait une 'association norvégienne des théologiennes' (NKTF) dès 1958. Elle compte aujourd'hui 210 membres et regroupe des femmes-pasteurs et des théologiennes qui au niveau des hautes écoles et des universités s'occupent de théologie feministe. La tension signalée entre le ministère exercé par les femmes et leur théologie a marqué l'histoire de NKTF depuis sa fondation.

La question que je pose dans cet article est la suivante: L'ordination de femmes a-t-elle, à quelque degré que ce soit, contribué à atténuer l'androcentrisme dans le ministère et la théologie? Je vais tenter de répondre à la question en faisant l'analyse de NKTF. Je retracerai quelques traits fondamentaux de l'évolution de l'Association en me concentrant sur l'ordination de la première femme-pasteur (1961) et de la première femme-évêque (1993). Nous esquisserons les quelques présupposés juridiques et théologiques de ces ordinations, et nous donnerons une idée de la manière dont les femmes ont su exploiter cette conjoncture. Nous insisterons surtout sur les perspectives ouvertes et les problèmes suscités par la solidarité féminine créée par NKTF: dans quelle mesure cette solidarité a-t-elle fait évoluer les ministères de l'église et sa théologie dans le sens d'une libération des femmes?[1]

La première femme-pasteur: implications théologiques

NKTF a commencé comme association de prières et sa première assemblée générale date de 1958, trois ans avant l'ordination de la première femme. La presque totalité des théologiennes de Norvège en faisait partie à cette époque. Les réunions, avec leurs conférences et leurs discussions sur des sujets théologiques, contribuaient à développer le sentiment de communauté entre théologiennes, à favoriser la prise de conscience de leur identité et le respect qu'elles se portaient à elles-mêmes. En ces années-là, le nombre de théologiennes diplômées augmentait rapidement. La situation suscitait de grandes espérances, mais non sans alimenter les réticences contre l'ordination de femmes au ministère.

C'est en 1956 que le gouvernement travailliste de Norvège écarta les derniers obstacles juridiques interdisant aux femmes l'accès à certaines fonctions publiques, y compris le ministère pastoral. Deux conditions canoniques subsistaient en matière d'ordination. 1. Il revenait à chaque paroisse de décider si oui ou non elle voulait se donner une femme comme pasteur. 2. Chaque évêque avait le loisir de porter son choix sur qui il voudrait ordonner. Plusieurs femmes avaient fait savoir qu'elles étaient prêtes à se faire ordonner, mais elles se laissèrent retarder par des tractations relatives à un ministère particulier pour les femmes.

Une femme d'un certain âge, Ingrid Bjerkås, trancha le noeud gordien. Elle usa du même argument que le gouvernement et le mouvement féministe: le principe égalitaire. En possession de la même compétence formelle que les hommes-théologiens, elle se considérait aussi qualifiée qu'eux pour le

---

[1] Je cherche à discerner les possibilités dont disposent les femmes-pasteurs et les théologiennes d'une église d'Etat évangélique-luthérienne en vue de contribuer à transformer *de l'intérieur* une église androcentrique. Ces possibilités tendent à diminuer dans la mesure où l'église actuellement prend ses distances vis-à-vis d'un pouvoir séculier socio-démocrate qui a oeuvré pour l'égalité des sexes. Je pense, d'accord en cela avec R. Radford Ruether, que les femmes-pasteurs et les théologiennes dans les églises protestantes ont réciproquement besoin les unes des autres. Rosemary Radford Ruether, *Womenchurch. Theology and Practice,* San Francisco 1985, 39.67.

ministère pastoral.[2] Elle présenta à un évêque sa demande qui fut acceptée. Grand-mère ayant atteint la soixantaine, elle devint la première femme-curé du pays. La paroisse qui lui était confiée était l'une des plus austères, sur la côte la plus septentrionale, avec l'Atlantique-Nord comme plus proche voisin. A cette population de pêcheurs elle se donna généreusement. Son mari, retraité, assumait les tâches ménagères.

Sur quelle théologie se fondait son ministère? Ingrid Bjerkås avait été femme au foyer dans une banlieue d'Oslo jusqu'à ce qu'elle entreprît à l'âge de 50 ans des études de théologie. A 39 ans, alors que les Allemands occupaient Oslo, elle avait vécu une forte expérience religieuse. Dieu lui était apparu comme très proche et soucieux de sa vie quotidienne et de celle de sa famille. Cette expérience de la proximité de Dieu et de sa providence - d'avoir contact avec Dieu - devint déterminante pour sa vie. Mais elle avait du mal à se situer par rapport à l'action divine telle qu'elle l'expérimentait: Comment se plier aux directives de Dieu tout en ayant les pieds sur terre? La seule personne qui la comprît vraiment, était une chrétienne qui l'encourageait dans son évolution religieuse. Elles dirigeaient de concert une école du dimanche et une amitié pour la vie s'était nouée entre elles.

L'évolution religieuse d'Ingrid Bjerkås eut cette conséquence que jamais elle ne se chercha de place au sein des traditions théologiques patriarcales. Certaines doctrines centrales dans le luthéranisme sont absentes de sa théologie, en particulier la faute et le péché conçus comme rupture avec Dieu. Le principe même de la justification lui semble sans importance. Elle récuse les représentations de l'enfer et de la damnation, en dépit de sept années d'études théologiques. Ce qui la soutient sa vie durant, c'est la foi en ce Dieu qui s'est révélé à elle dans une expérience religieuse décisive. Son rêve était de pouvoir ouvrir à ses paroissiens l'accès à cette vie en Dieu.

La première femme-pasteur semble avoir personnifié un point de vue de théologie féministe, même si le mot alors n'existait pas encore. Sa théologie plongeait ses racines dans des expériences qui sont caractéristiques du rôle de la femme au foyer; son évolution religieuse s'est nourrie essentiellement d'un échange entre âmes-soeurs. Le fort accent qu'elle met sur la proximité de Dieu et le soin qu'il prend de nous dans le quotidien souligne des valeurs présentes dans la vie de la femme à la maison. Mais il n'existait pas de

---

[2] Ingrid Bjerkås, *Mitt kall*. Cappelen, Oslo 1966.

langage ou de théologie pour articuler ou transcrire l'expérience religieuse d'une maîtresse de maison. De ce fait, sa théologie peut paraître simpliste. On la considérait pieuse et fortement motivée dans sa vocation, mais on l'accusait de manquer de théologie. Sa base théologique s'avéra toutefois assez forte pour défier la mentalité patriarcale régnante et ouvrir l'accès de la fonction pastorale aux femmes dans notre église.

Le débat sur l'ordination des femmes provoqua une scission au sein de NKTF. Une fraction non négligeable était opposée à l'ordination. Elle souhaitait que les femmes veillent sur leur spécificité, leur aptitude á cultiver les relations de proximité, le souci du prochain et les valeurs de coopération. Leur argumentation théologique était de tendance conservatrice: les textes de la Bible relatifs à la soumission de la femme au titre de l'ordre de la création. La fraction qui souhaitait que des femmes soient ordonnées se réclamait d'une exégèse historique, critique et libérale: rien n'empêchait alors l'ordination de femmes. Cet argument négatif était complété par des considérations sur la théologie luthérienne des ministères et l'image que les femmes se faisaient de ce que l'église devrait être. NKTF continua d'exister comme association théologique, mais perdit progressivement de son importance. Elle était privée de son élément moteur du fait qu'elle se refusait â soutenir activement la requête des femmes-pasteurs.

Nouvelles impulsions féministes: réorganisation de NKTF

L'élément radical n'avait pourtant pas dit son dernier mot. Il reparaîtra, mais cette fois dans un contexte théologique et politique. Stimulées par la première série de cours sur la théologie féministe à l'Université d'Oslo en 1975, les étudiantes constituèrent un groupement féminin qui se donnait pour tâche de réorganiser NKTF. L'Association se donna des statuts favorables aux femmes-pasteurs et donna accès dans son sein à des étudiantes approchant du terme de leurs études. Chercheuses et étudiantes devaient être représentées dans le comité directeur de l'Association. Un réseau de relations entre les membres fut mis en place dans chaque diocèse. NKTF organisa annuellement une conférence. La première conférence de théologie féministe, tenue en 1979, rassembla 113 participantes.

Sous sa nouvelle forme, NKTF s'est choisi deux priorités: 1. promouvoir les intérêts des théologiennes dans la pratique et la théologie de l'église. 2. soutenir les efforts en cours pour faire place à des femmes dans tous les organismes ecclésiaux et dans l'enseignement de la théologie.

- NKTF a des représentantes dans le comité directeur de l'Association des pasteurs. Cette association est orientée vers la théologie, mais fait fonction également de syndicat professionnel des pasteurs de l'Eglise de Norvège.

- NKTF a obtenu de figurer sur la liste des instances à consulter officiellement par le Ministère des Cultes et l'Association des pasteurs.

- NKTF a, dès que possible, lancé le nom de Rosemarie Køhn comme candidate possible à l'épiscopat et par là-même habitué l'opinion publique à concevoir une femme-évêque. Rosemarie Køhn a été par la suite élue présidente de NKTF.

- Des actions ont été menées pour confier à des femmes la formation théologico-pratique et pastorale des futurs pasteurs. En liaison avec la préparation d'un nouveau livre de hymnes, un projet a été mis au point avec le souci d'utiliser de préférence un vocabulaire applicable aux deux sexes. Un groupe de travail s'était donné pour tâche de relever tous les cas de vocabulaire privilégiant le genre masculin, signe patent de la prédominance masculine. Un commentaire de ce travail a été présenté en même temps que des contre-projets non-discriminatoires.

- Une motion fut adressée à la Conférence des évêques (de l'Eglise de Norvège) pour attirer son attention et celle de l'opinion publique sur les mauvais traitements dont les femmes ne sont que trop souvent victimes. Les évêques firent alors une déclaration soulignant l'incompatibilité de la violence et du mariage. Cette initiative du groupe eut également pour conséquence la publication d'un livre "Violence dans le mariage" et la mise au point d'un programme de recherche. On est en train d'instaurer un centre de soins et de réconfort spirituel destiné aux femmes victimes de la violence. Le thème des mauvais traitements et de la violence sexuelle est inscrit au programme de la formation diaconale dans l'église.

La joie de mettre sur pied quelque chose en commun a pris des dimensions internationales. Les femmes-pasteurs des pays nordiques se sont réunies pour la première fois en Norvège, mais ont par la suite organisé des rencontres tous les deux ans dans les différents pays à tour de rôle.

Un nouveau pas en avant fut fait quand NKTF sollicita d'envoyer un 'visiteur' à l'assemblée générale du Conseil Oecuménique des Eglises à Vancouver en 1983. Ce 'visiteur' avait pour mission de promouvoir devant le Conseil la cause des théologiennes. Grâce à l'aide inappréciable de Connie Parvey qui connaissait tout le monde du fait de son travail au C.OE.E., il fut possible d'organiser une réunion à Vancouver qui rassembla 25 théologiennes de la plupart des continents. L'objectif de la réunion était de les faire se rencontrer dans l'espoir de favoriser le développement des réseaux et de faire progresser la théologie féministe.

Il y a un lien entre Vancouver et le groupe qui a pris l'initiative de lancer l'Association Européenne des femmes pour la recherche théologique (European Society of Women in Theological Research = ESWTR). Joann Nash Eakin, attachée au Département de l'éducation théologique du C.OE.E, a posé les bases d'un développement systématique de la théologie féministe en Europe et lui a assuré le premier fonds économique. Soutenue par Bärbel von Wartemberg, elle a réalisé le séminaire de théologie féministe de Boldern où ont été élaborés les premiers linéaments de ESWTR. Notons également que Ruth Epting en jouant un rôle d'intermédiaire a permis à l'ESWTR de pousser des racines en Suisse et dans le monde bancaire.

Cette période de réorganisation portait l'empreinte de la collaboration entre pasteurs, théologiennes de métier et étudiants de deux facultés rivales, ce qui rendait possible d'aborder des tâches réparties sur un éventail très ouvert.

La première femme-évêque

Les années 80 virent les femmes accéder à presque tous les niveaux de la vie de l'église et de son administration. Profitant de la décennie oecuménique de la femme, l'Assemblée de l'église (de Norvège), tenue en 1988, décida de mettre le thème de la femme à son ordre du jour. L'Assemblée exhorta les femmes à postuler les postes de curé et de doyen. Elle était favorable à la nomination d'une femme au poste d'évêque. Sous l'égide du Conseil de l'église (de Norvège) des cours de formation aux postes de direction furent proposés aux femmes.[3] A l'approche de 1990, les femmes constituaient environ 12% de la totalité des pasteurs et environ 30% des pasteurs travaillant pour des institutions. Des couples se partageaient ici ou là une responsabilité pastorale. Deux femmes exerçaient la fonction de doyen.

Rosemarie Køhn assura la présidence de NKTF de 1984 à 1989. Elle avait assumé précédemment des fonctions pastorales, mais durant les années en question, elle occupait un poste de professeur associé à l'Université d'Oslo. Elle enseignait l'Ancien et le Nouveau Testament. A partir de 1989, elle était

---

[3] Gunvor Lande (responsable du groupe chargé par le Conseil de l'église de son projet de former des 'leaders' parmi les femmes), *Leiarutvikling for kvinner* dans la publication *Den Norske Kyrkja*, édition revue de 1966.

recteur du séminaire de théologie pastorale à l'Université d'Oslo. C'est ce séminaire qui met la dernière main à la préparation des pasteurs de l'église à leurs tâches pastorales. Au sein de NKTF, les femmes-pasteurs sont actuellement en majorité. Et ce qui les concerne est en voie de polariser les activités de l'association. Les conférences annuelles, situées à l'origine dans un week-end, ont été déplacées et sont tenues en semaine. NKTF, consulté, s'est exprimé officiellement sur deux questions importantes: 1. Une nouvelle loi déterminant le statut légal de l'église, fut mise en place ouvrant la porte à un développement d'organismes de direction autonomes dans l'église. Les liens avec l'Etat se sont détendus. 2. Une loi entra en vigueur réglant l'exercice de la fonction pastorale.

Une préoccupation constante de NKTF a été la collaboration entre les femmes-pasteurs et les opposants. La tradition, bien norvégienne s'est établie d'éviter les confrontations violentes et de chercher plutôt des compromis souples. Le but a été atteint par la distinction nette entre le niveau pratique de l'administration et le niveau spirituel. Il n'en résulte pas moins qu'un certain nombre de femmes se sentent privées d'évêque.

Le vingt-cinquième anniversaire de la première ordination de femme a été fortement marqué par NKTF, sous la forme de célébration liturgique festive à la cathédrale d'Oslo. La longue procession de femmes-pasteurs au début de la cérémonie fit en particulier une forte impression. Pour fêter le jubilé, les sermons prononcés par la première génération de femmes-pasteurs furent rassemblés et un certain nombre d'entre eux publiés dans un volume intitulé "Le pont de l'arc-en-ciel".[4]

NKTF contribua à renforcer la compétence et l'assurance de ses membres en organisant des cours d'entraînement à l'efficacité personnelle. Ces cours visaient surtout à développer et renforcer chez les femmes-pasteurs leur identité de 'leader'. Ces cours étaient financés par le Ministère des Cultes.

Rosemarie Køhn conçut pour NKTF une nouvelle stratégie: il s'agissait de susciter l'intérêt des femmes-pasteurs en faisant des travaux de sociologie religieuse. Les connaissances acquises serviraient de base à une activité professionnelle et à une politique ecclésiastique. Le premier projet utilisait une méthode sociologique quantitative pour mettre à nu les conditions de

---

[4] Rosemarie Køhn (réd.), *Regnbuebroen. En samling prekner, andakter og essays av kvinnelige prester,* Trondheim 1986.

nomination et de travail pour les femmes exerçant les fonctions de pasteur. Cette enquête 'de l'extérieur' sur la situation des pasteurs dévoila le besoin d'approfondir les problèmes et de concevoir comment le ministère pastoral est vécu 'de l'intérieur'. Ceci suscita une enquête par mode d'interrogation - cette fois-ci qualitative - auprès de 40 pasteurs et 10 présidents de conseils paroissiaux - les deux sexes étant représentés à égalité - et 5 évêques.[5] Køhn était assistée dans ce projet de deux pasteurs et deux étudiantes. Une meilleure compréhension de leur propre situation stimula les pasteurs à mettre l'accent sur l'aspect professionnel de leur tâche et à promouvoir leur solidarité. La réalisation de ce projet contribua également à renforcer la position de Rosemarie Køhn dans l'esprit des femmes-pasteurs et des organes directeurs de l'église.

Dès le début des années 80, NKTF avait élaboré des stratégies pour faire accéder une femme au collège des évêques. En 1993, Rosemarie Køhn fut proposée comme évêque de ce même diocèse où la première femme-pasteur avait été ordonnée. Rosemarie Køhn vint en troisième position quant au nombre de voix sur la liste dressée selon les règles du droit et devant aboutir sur la table du ministre des Cultes auquel il revenait de choisir. Rosemarie Køhn était, parmi les pasteurs, la candidate réunissant le plus grand nombre de suffrages. Et l'un des évêques s'était prononcé en sa faveur. Du coup le Ministère pouvait s'écarter du classement résultant de la consultation des organismes de l'église. Il nomma Rosemarie Køhn évêque. Les femmes dans le pays entier accueillirent cette nomination comme un signe de bon augure. Des femmes qui précédemment s'étaient fait rayer des listes de l'église, s'y sont fait réinscrire.[6]

La nomination fut suivie d'un choc en retour pour NKTF. Au moment même où la première femme siégeait au collège des évêques, l'accès aux autres postes-clés de l'église étaient bloqué pour les femmes-pasteurs. L'Association des pasteurs ouvrit le feu en se choisissant pour président un opposant au ministère pastoral des femmes. Puis cette même association se donna un secrétaire général également opposé à ce ministère. A la réunion suivante de l'Assemblée de l'église un adversaire de l'ordination des femmes fut élu membre du Conseil de l'église sur proposition sauvage d'un membre

[5] K. Almås, A.L. Brodtkorb et al., *Presterollen. En kvalitativ interviewundersøkelse om det å være prest i Den norske kirke,* Trondheim 1988 (NKTF 1988).
[6] L'église évangélique luthérienne du Danemark eut sa première femme-évêque en 1995: Lise-Lotte Rebel (44).

de l'assemblée, barrant ainsi la route à une femme-pasteur. Cette exclusion avait été obtenue de façon démocratique, et elle scandalisa les membres de NKTF.

Les pasteurs ont besoin de théologiennes

Provoquée par ce choc en retour NKTF se choisit une présidente plus explicitement féministe, se recentra sur la spiritualité féminine et mit en place une structure moins pyramidale. L'assemblée annuelle constitua des groupes chargés d'assumer la responsabilité des différents secteurs de travail: La conférence annuelle, l'exploitation politique des affaires traitées au sein de l'Association des pasteurs, l'Assemblée de l'église et le Ministère des Cultes, le bulletin des réseaux "Sainte Sunniva". Les dirigeantes prirent contact avec les trois facultés de théologie au sujet de la situation des femmes-pasteurs. Près de 50% des étudiants en théologie sont des femmes. Cette évolution est révélatrice. Le besoin se fait sentir au sein de NKTF d'intensifier les rapports professionnels entre de (potentiels) pasteurs féministes et les théologiennes qui, au niveau des universités et des hautes écoles, s'occupent de théologie féministe. NKTF a été longtemps une association pour les femmes-pasteurs, ce qui a détendu les liens de l'association avec les autres théologiennes. Les succès remportés pour promouvoir les intérêts des pasteurs l'ont été en partie au détriment du débat nécessaire sur les problèmes et les tensions d'ordre théologique. La théologie féministe controversielle a dans l'ensemble été tenue à l'écart. Des signes manifestes indiquent toutefois que les femmes-pasteurs ne dépasseront pas une certaine frontière tant qu'elles s'orienteront à partir d'une théologie androcentrique. Il s'avère difficile pour les pasteurs d'exprimer clairement ce qui les concerne comme femmes sans être étayées par la théologie dont les axiomes sont issus de points de vue féministe. Nous le voyons dans trois contextes.

Pour NKTF, le débat dans les médias relatif à la femme-évêque s'est soldé par un échec. Des membres nombreux de NKTF souhaitaient un soutien officiel de l'association à la candidature de Rosemarie Køhn, ce que le bureau directeur pour de bonnes raisons se refusait à faire. Une lettre ouverte fut bien adressée, couverte de signatures, au Ministre des Cultes, mais trop tard pour infléchir le processus.

Quand sa candidature apparut comme sérieuse, Rosemarie Køhn fut sommée - beaucoup plus que n'importe quel candidat masculin - de préciser ses convictions sur des thèmes aussi controversiels que la vie commune hors du mariage ou l'homophilie. Elle fut violemment prise à partie à cause de ses positions théologiques. Il était difficile pour NKTF de prendre sa défense de ses points de vue en ces matières, parce que les membres de l'association étaient très divisés sur ces points.

La direction, raisonnant à partir du principe de l'égalité des sexes, estimait qu'il était loisible de nommer Køhn puisqu'elle était compétente, quoi qu'il en soit de son sexe. En conséquence il parut superflu de discuter ce point. NKTF était dans l'impossibilité de préconiser que cette égalité soit encouragée aussi longtemps que les prémisses sont celles d'une église dominée par des hommes et estompent ce qu'il y a de particulier dans la situation des femmes. C'eût été en fait compromettre la nomination de Køhn.

Les opposants se réclamèrent aussi du sexe de la candidate. Etant une femme, elle ne pouvait pas être ordonnée. Elle était 'spirituellement invalide'. Les actes de son ministère furent déclarés invalides par ses opposants. Les pasteurs ordonnés par elle ne seraient pas des vrais pasteurs. NKTF était dans l'impossibilité de triompher des arguments visant à la disqualifier en raison de son sexe biologique considéré comme pertinent en matière d'ordination. Cela aurait supposé une théologie moderne des ministères au courant des dernières recherches sur le genre (en anglais *gender*), et l'intégration de ces théories dans une nouvelle interprétation des fonctions de l'homme et de la femme. Une telle théologie des ministères n'a pas encore vu le jour.- L'impuissance théologique mise à nu dans ce débat est cause d'un sentiment de frustration parmi les membres de NKTF.

Le grand projet relatif au rôle du pasteur fit sentir le besoin d'une théologie orientée d'un point de vue féministe. Il suffit de se reporter à la tension manifeste entre les parties du projet qui sont sexuellement neutres et la description des différences entre les sexes. Celles-là font le tableau du comportement du prêtre tel qu'il est et de la manière dont il vit sa situation. Les réponses fournies par des femmes comme par des hommes s'harmonisent bien dans ce contexte en sorte qu'il est impossible d'isoler certains traits sexuellement distinctifs. Les deux sexes participent à part égale à dessiner le rôle du pasteur.

Le reste du projet analyse le matériel recueilli par interviews dans le but de discerner s'il n'y aurait pas ici ou là des traces de quelque chose qui soit 'typiquement' féminin ou masculin. Certaines différences sont mises en évidence aussi bien dans la manière de conduire le travail que dans la conception par le pasteur de sa fonction. L'on considère comme caractéristique que la méthode de travail des femmes soit orientée vers la personne et consiste à transmettre le message en s'engageant dans les processus qui sont ceux de l'interlocuteur. Les hommes sont davantage orientés vers les faits et leur prédication est plus directement liée à leurs fonctions ecclésiastiques. La différence entre les sexes est résumée lapidairement ainsi: Les femmes vivent le message, les hommes le transmettent (NKTF 1989 p.241, 269). Les résultats de l'enquête montrent que les femmes visent à se distancer de la traditionnelle et masculine image du pasteur; elles cherchent à déterminer leur propre rôle de pasteur en accord avec leur identité et leur situation féminines[7]. Il en résulte que les hommes se sentent interpellés sur leur rôle à eux, ce qui fait supposer un potentiel de modification et de créativité en matière de rôle pastoral.

Le projet conclut que le rôle du pasteur est affecté d'un 'signe négatif' et est considéré comme 'un poids'. Le pasteur a un travail dur et il éprouve le sentiment qu'on attend beaucoup de lui dans une culture séculière en évolution rapide. - Peut-on envisager que le 'signe négatif' du rôle pastoral supposé sexuellement neutre, soit ressenti plus fortement par les femmes en raison des problèmes particuliers qu'elles rencontrent dans une église à prédominance masculine? La question ne peut recevoir de réponse que si l'on utilise les critères d'analyse qui tiennent compte du sexe et que la recherche féministe a élaborée.

Le projet conclut en outre que l'aspect religieux du ministère pastoral - et aussi bien de la réflexion théologique - ne s'expriment que faiblement dans les réponses à l'enquête - Peut-on envisager que le silence sur ce point soit lié à la situation des femmes-pasteurs? S'il est vrai que les femmes - par suite de leur identité féminine - s'efforcent de modeler de nouveaux rôles pastoraux donnant la priorité dans les relations à la sollicitude, il faut s'attendre à ce que se crée une fissure par rapport à une pastorale et à une théologie centrées sur l'homme. Comment des femmes-pasteurs pourraient-elles exprimer des relations de sollicitude à l'aide d'une théologie qui est fondée sur les principes d'autonomie et d'autorité? Le projet décèle que les femmes-pasteurs éprouvent le besoin d'une théologie qui s'harmonise avec

---

[7] Ulrike Wagner-Rau, *Zwischen Vaterwelt und Feminismus. Eine Studie zur pastoralen Identität von Frauen*, Gütersloh 1992, 72; L'ouvrage introduit aux thèmes de théologie pastorale féministe qui, à l'instar du projet sur le rôle du prêtre, met l'accent sur les différences sexuelles. Cf. Else-Britt Nilsen, *Gjennom prestenes briller. Om eksteskap og kirkens vigselspraksis,* Universitetsforlaget: Oslo 1991.

leurs priorités.

On peut dire la même chose du recueil de sermons composés par des femmes-pasteurs. Les sermons visent à décrire la situation dans laquelle le message est proclamé, mais il n'y a que fort peu de considérations dogmatiques. Le personnage de Jésus et l'image de Dieu sont partiellement revêtus de traits féminins, mais sans que soit articulé le caractère problématique de cette interprétation. Le recueil de sermons manifeste le besoin d'avoir une théologie susceptible de faire correspondre l'expérience que les femmes ont de leur situation avec le contenu théologique de la prédication.Les femmes-pasteurs ont besoin de l'interprétation que donne des symboles chrétiens, dans la liturgie, les sacrements, la prédication et la cure d'âmes, une théologie féministe. Tout cela doit être mis en relation avec la situation des femmes.[8]

Les théologiennes ont besoin des pasteurs

S'il est vrai que les pasteurs de NKTF ont besoin de théologiennes, la réciproque est tout aussi vraie. L'interaction entre femmes-pasteurs et théologie feministe est à la racine du principe herméneutique d'où est issue la théologie féministe: les conditions sociales et la théologie s'impliquant réciproquement, il faut voir comment et en quel sens. La situation culturelle, politique et économique n'est pas la même pour les deux sexes. Comme groupe social, les femmes sont au cours de leur croissance intégrées à la société selon un autre modèle que les hommes - dans un univers où la plupart de ceux qui exercent le pouvoir sont des hommes. De ce fait, les théologies émanant de ces groupes sociaux distincts ne sont pas identiques. Une théologie ne saurait être adéquate pour les femmes si elle n'émane pas de la position effective qui est la leur dans la société et la culture: elle est féministe. Mais elle est également prophétique: le mouvement théologique féministe international accorde la priorité à la justice et à la vérité dans les rapports des sexes entre eux et des sexes avec le Très-Haut.

Au sein des facultés de théologie, les femmes adonnées à la recherche se heurtent d'entrée de jeu à la même ambivalence que les femmes pasteurs dans l'église. Elles sont écartelées par la nécessité de s'adapter à des structures

---

[8] Il est généralement admis - on l'a prouvé - que les femmes du fait de leur type d'expériences peuvent enrichir la théologie pratique de points de vue nouveaux, mais l'opinion est sceptique en ce qui concerne leurs apports à la théologie comme inventaire d'un contenu de la foi. Kristin Molland Norderval, *Mot strømmen. Kvinnelige teologer i Norge før og nå,* Oslo 1982, 174-176.

androcentriques tout en préservant leur intégrité comme femmes et croyantes - en solidarité avec les autres femmes.[9] Cette tension circonscrit les possibilités de développement de la théologie féministe positivement et négativement. La côté négatif de la situation est renforcé du fait que la vie ecclésiastique et la théologie androcentrique tendent à marginaliser la théologie féministe qui se développe à partir de cette tension dans la vie de foi des femmes.

Aussi longtemps que la théologie féministe sera tenue à l'écart de la vie religieuse de l'église, elle risque de se développer en deux directions qui ont ceci de commun qu'elles portent préjudice à l'église. 1. En créant une communion religieuse-sacramentelle hors des églises établies. 2. en se réduisant à un mouvement éthique profane qui lui-même se dissout dans le mouvement du féminisme politique.[10] Dans les deux cas, l'église et les femmes-pasteurs sont privées du potentiel de renouvellement de la vie religieuse et de la communion dont le mouvement féministe prophétique est prégnant.

L'histoire de NKTF montre que les femmes ont trouvé leur premier accès dans l'église en acceptant les prémisses androcentriques de la théologie et de la vie des communautés chrétiennes. Mais la pratique pastorale qui s'en est suivie a fait germer le besoin de refondre la théologie et le ministère à partir des prémisses féminines elles-mêmes. Les femmes-pasteurs accueillent la théologie de leurs con-soeurs et s'engagent dans un dialogue et une collaboration centrés sur la théologie féministe.[11]

---

[9] Depuis que Rosemarie Køhn a accédé à l'épiscopat, elle peut sans avoir à en demander l'autorisation utiliser la liturgie dite du 8 mars et par conséquent l'expression "Dieu comme Père et Mère".

[10] La manière dont Schüssler Fiorenza met l'accent sur l'aspect éthique du christianisme au détriment de son aspect sacramentel et symbolique, est sujette à caution. "Women's Church" comme paroisse du discours moral (en allemand: "Gemeinde des moralischen Diskurses", in: *Brot statt Steine,* Fribourg 1988, 137; Cfr. *In Memory of Her. A Feminist Theological Reconstruction of Christian Origins,* New York 1985, 345-346).

[11] NKTF peut être considéré comme "Women's Church" au sein de notre église dans la mesure où l'association repose sur les mêmes objectifs:
1. Critiquer l'élément patriarcal dans l'église et la théologie; 2. Mettre en lumière les femmes dans le christianisme; 3. Reconstruire l'église comme une église de femmes: modifier le rôle du pasteur; 4. Donner aux ministères, à l'organisation ecclésiastique et à la vie de foi, des justifications nouvelles et inspirées par la théologie féministe. NKTF peut sur ces différents points servir de base pour une transformation de l'église. En ce qui concerne "Women's

Cette évolution nous fait espérer l'avènement d'une théologie féministe s'enracinant dans la vie liturgique de l'église. Le côté sacramentel de la liturgie de l'église et le côté prophétique de la théologie féministe peuvent s'alimenter réciproquement en sorte que la théologie féministe conserve son caractère religieux et son caractère explosif dans la vie de l'église et sa théologie. Il sera passionnant de suivre les évènements et voir si NKTF connaît l'heure de sa visite.

(Traductien: Pater Albert Raulin O.P.)

Dagny Kaul fait depuis 1975, des conférences sur la théologie féministe, comme professeure assistante, chercheuse associée à l'association, sous différentes fonctions. Elle consacre sa recherche actuelle à la relation entre 'morale' et 'vérité' dans le processus de construction d'une théologie.

Church", Hedwig Meyer-Wilmes ("Kirche", in: *Wörterbuch der feministischen Theologie,* Gütersloh 1991, 214) souligne la connexion avec le mouvement féministe, mais n'aborde pas la signification du ministère pour la libération; ibid. *Rebellion auf der Grenze. Ortsbestimmung feministischer Theologie,* Freiburg/Basel/Wien 1990. Sur le ministère et les femmes dans l'église catholique voir: Ida Raming, *Frauenbewegung und Kirche,* Weinheim 1989. Radford Ruether insiste sur la corrélation entre une pratique de libération et la réflexion théologique sur les contenus de la foi dans "Women's Church", par exemple dans R. Radford Ruether, *Womenchurch,* 73.

Athalya Brenner

Women's Traditions Problematized: Some Reflections

> In truth, tradition that is not the defense of what has been handed down but the continual shaping of the ethical life in general constantly depends upon raising awareness, which takes over in freedom.
>
> H.-G. Gadamer, Wahrheit und Methode

In recent years, feminist criticism has attempted to combat the androcentrism of our cultural production by introducing new concepts into cultural criticism. These concepts are differentiated by gender, as against older modes of criticism that claim a universal, non-gendered status while in effect representing male views. Two of the major concepts introduced in the 1970's and 1980's are 'women's traditions' and its close relative, 'women's experience'. These terms, and the concepts underlying them, are still questioned by mainstream scholarship --be it in theology, Bible criticism, literary criticism, psychology, sociology, anthropology, history, or other fields. On the other hand, the terminology and concepts alike have been embraced by feminist critics and readers with great enthusiasm, to the point that they are accepted nowadays as maxims that are hardly problematized, although they should be problematized. Womanly readers are not critical enough any more: they have become de-sensitized by/concerning the two concepts. In accepting them with less questioning than we should, we run the risk of emptying them of meaning and usefulness while, paradoxically, at the same time canonizing them. We tend to overlook that to speak of 'women's traditions' in literary texts (especially texts produced in the past) is to refer to a construct of our own making, much like Bible scholars refer to constructs such as 'priestly traditions', 'wisdom traditions' and so on. The present paper is addressed to current practices of using women's 'traditions' and 'experience' and the quest for finding them in the Hebrew Bible (HB), in the hope that more caution is introduced into quest and terminology alike.

What Do We Mean by 'Tradition'?

Lexicographic definitions are often a convenient point of departure. The Webster Dictionary has a simple definition for 'tradition': customs, beliefs, opinions etc. that are handed down from generation to generation, be they respected (as in 'traditionalist attitudes') or modified. In the Concise Oxford Dictionary (1979), 'tradition' is an opinion, a belief or custom borne out of accumulated experience and/or continuous usage, handed down from ancestors to future generations orally and by praxis. A distinction is made between theological, artistic and legal traditions. Theological traditions may be doctrines, with a claim for an underlying divine authority ('truth'). The examples given for the linguistic usage of 'tradition' within the theological context imply that written records are excluded from this concept.[1] In the contexts of art and law, though, insistence on the unwritten transmission of tradition is abandoned, and the elements of experience and continued practice are emphasized. The etymology is traced to classical Latin, with the denotation of 'impart', 'hand over', 'transmit' or 'bequeath'.[2] The Thesaurus section of my computer word-processing program[3] offers a compromise. 'Tradition' is synonymed by the following chain: custom, convention, habit, practice, manner, fashion, way, observance. And 'traditional' is divided into two sections: 'conventional' (conservative, inherited, common, typical, established, sanctioned) and 'handed down' (unwritten, oral, historic, ancestral, classical).

What Do We Mean by 'Women's Traditions'?

So much for lexicography and common usage. My immediate response to these lexicographic notations, in the context of the present paper, is: How do we want to define women's traditions? If we wish to address unwritten materials, then we draw an immediate blank - at least for the Israelite/ Hebrew biblical world. And if we wish to recognize women's traditions in written sources, canons and scriptures, and to adopt/adapt them to our contemporary requirements, then we face severe problems emanating from

---

[1]   The Jewish oral Torah; teachings by Jesus and his disciples not recorded in writing in the NT; Muhammad's oral teaching, not included in the Qur'an.

[2]   I chose these two dictionaries simply because they are on my shelves. The fact that their definitions of 'tradition' differ is enough, in my opinion, to justify, a re-examination of this seemingly familiar and transparent term.

[3]   English-Hebrew Word for Windows (1994).

the enveloping maleness of those texts. I would like to explore the implications of 'tradition' for current feminist inquiry in theology precisely from this perspective of definition and ensuant epistemology. My source material and examples will be from the Hebrew Bible, although any other canonico-scriptural text can be used for this purpose.

Indeed, when we deal with ancient theological texts, written tradition is all we have to go by. In other words, if we follow the Oxford Dictionary definition, then we must conclude at the outset that we have no direct access to ancient Hebrew/Judaic women's traditions. We can safely assume that oral materials were and are transmitted and swapped in pre-literate and non-literate societies[4]; women participate in the creation and transmission processes of any culture.[5] Hence, traditions must have been created, continued, modified and transmitted also by ancient Israelite women.[6] There is also no reason to reject the notion of literacy for at least some ancient Israelite women. But when we include presumably female, oral or written, literate/literary sources under the superordinate term 'tradition', then we must face up to the fact that such sources were altered and effectively murdered- -by the mostly male scribes, narrators and editors; by M (male/masculine) oriented contexts; by M-dominated transmission and exegesis. There must have been women's traditions in ancient Israel: how can it be otherwise? But, if any of those were incorporated in the HB, they have become embedded, enveloped and smothered. The question should therefore be formulated as follows. Given the circumstances of the preservation of women's traditions, inasmuch as they exist in the Bible at all, and in the absence of live informants, what makes such written-down oral traditions -- or, for that matter, also literate traditions --specifically female/feminine (F), and just how do we come to recognize them as such?

Women's Traditions in the Hebrew Bible: Criteria for Recognition

My late friend and colleague Dr. Fokkelien van Dijk-Hemmes examined the Hebrew Bible in order to find traces of 'women's texts' in it[7]: She proceeded

---

[4]   W.J. Ong, *Orality and Literacy. The Technologizing of the World,* London/New York 1982.

[5]   See my Introduction in: A. Brenner and F. van-Dijk-Hemmes, *On Gendering Texts. Female and Male Voices in the Hebrew Bible,* Leiden 1993, 1-5.

[6]   S.D. Goitein, "Women as Creators of Biblical Genres", in: *Prooftexts* 8 (1988), 1-33; translated from the *Hebrew Studies in Scripture,* Tel Aviv 1957, 248-317.

[7]   In her Ph.D. dissertation, *Sporen van vrouwenteksten in de Hebreeuwse Bijbel* (Utrecht,

from the assumptions that women are silenced or at least muted by the dominant male culture, but their culture can be excavated out of the written texts.[8] She defined texts as F (female/feminine) compositions when:

(1) women play a dominant role in them;
(2) they are about or attributed to women;
(3) they reflect women's experience; and
(4) the F elements in them are muted by the dominant (M) culture, hence the reflected women's discourse may be double-edged: simultaneously submissive and critical.

Van Dijk-Hemmes scrutinized the entire Hebrew Bible for such passages and, like Goitein[9], classified her findings by genre and life situation.[10] We can safely substitut 'women's traditions' for 'women's texts', especially since the concept of 'texts' or female authorship/composition was later abandoned in favour of 'voice', that is, the gender signature of a text, in our book.[11]

Van Dijk-Hemmes' work is extremely valuable. It gives us a glimpse, albeit a limited one, into Israelite women's lives and traditions. Methodologically, though, let us not forget that her work, her investigation, is a reflexive re-construction many times removed from the assumed originals. Problematizing the criteria used in this scholarly construct, I feel, will not detract from its significance; rather, it might enhance it.[12] Chronologically, some of my remarks actually belong to the gestation period, so to speak, when we were working on "On Gendering Texts" separately and together.

The Narrative Centrality of Female Characters
When do narrated traditions--stories, parables, poetry, customs--which focus on women qualify as F traditions? Such texts indeed make females highly

---

Faculty of Theology, 1992); and in: *On Gendering Texts*.

[8] Following E. Showalter, "Feminist Criticism in the Wilderness", in: E. Showalter (ed.), *The New Feminist Criticism Essays on Women, Literature and Theory*, London 1986, 243-70, after Ardener.

[9] Goitein, "Women as Creators of Biblical Genres".

[10] *On Gendering Texts*, 17-109.

[11] Brenner, Introduction, in: *On Gendering Texts,* 5-8.

[12] The ensuing criticisms are of course applicable also to my own work on both F and M voices: *On Gendering Texts*, 113-63, 178-195.

visible. But what does this visibility consist of? What does it signify in each and every case? In androcentric cultures, women are always on view as objects.[13] Not every woman's story allows the narrated woman a subject position. Furthermore, functioning as a subject does not automatically entail being an approved-of subject. The narrator's location--sympathetic, neutral or condemning--is often of not much help on its own. We may fondly imagine that a thoroughly 'positive' female figuration reflects a female tradition; and that a 'negative' -- that is, sexually and independently active -- woman figuration, like a Delilah (Judges 16) or a Potiphar's wife (Genesis 39), seems more likely a figment of male imagination, fantasy, desire, needs, than of women's fantasy. But is that necessarily so? Like other disadvantaged segments of society, women internalize the predominant norms so that they become ingrained, to the extent that F judgement may become indistinguishable from M judgement. The cultural otherness of certain narrated females--or, for instance, the class- or ethnic concerns imputed to them -- might overcome the gender oneness. Women might then warn their sons and daughters of 'strange' female sexuality[14]; their traditions may be so securely rooted in their M interests so as to be indistinguishable from the latter, especially as reported within the enveloping (literary) framework. Moreover, why should men not be interested in female subjects and even like and appreciate them? Let us assume, for the sake of argument, that [at least] some men like [some] women within the seldom contested framework of

---

[13]   L. Mulvey, "Visual Pleasure and Narrative Cinema", in: *Screen* 16/3 (1975), 6-18, shows how films--a most visual art--construct the spectators as males and women as the object of male gaze. The principle is valid for reading too: the reader is constructed by the (M?) narrative as a male reader. Recently, this approach has been applied to biblical literature in: A. Bach, "Mirror, Mirror in the Text. Reflections on Reading and Rereading", forthcoming, in: A. Brenner (ed.), *A Feminist Companion to Esther, Judith and Susanna*, Sheffield 1995, 81-6 on Esther; S. Durber, "The Female Reader of the Parables of the Lost", in: G.J. Brooke (ed.), *Women in the Biblical Tradition*, Studies in Women and Religion, 31, Lewiston/Queenston/Lampeter 1992, 187-207; J.A. Glancy, "The Accused. Susanna and her Readers", in: *Journal for the Study of the Old Testament* 58 (1993), 103-116, reprinted in: Brenner (ed.), *A Feminist Companion to Esther, Judith and Susanna*, 288-302.

[14]   Cf. my analysis of Proverbs 7 as a possible F text, in: *On Gendering Texts*, 113-130; and A. Brenner, "Some Observations on the Figurations of Woman in Wisdom Literature", in: H.A. McKay and D.J.A. Clines (eds.), *Of Prophets' Visions and the Wisdom of Sages: Essays in Honour of R. Norman Whybray on his Seventieth Birthday*, Sheffield 1993, 192-208, and especially 192-8.

women's social subordination and male dominance; and that male dominance is commonly upheld by female complicity.

Texts/Traditions Attributed to Women in/by the Biblical Text

The attribution of a biblical text to a woman figure as 'her' composition and/or performance is by itself not decisive. It is a fiction. Citing a Deborah (Judges 4-5), or a Miriam (Exodus 15.22), or a Huldah (2 Kings 22.15-20) as an author is an act of fictional a-scription, an appropriation of female voice by a male-edited and transmitted text, a co-option of imaged female interests by the dominant system for its own needs. The recognition of this factor should supercede any other consideration. Whether such appropriation incorporates genuine womanly concerns is another issue altogether. There is a possibility that traditions ascribed to women contain a kernel of authentic, oral or written, material. But the act of ascription--even in the Song of Songs, so outspokenly female and feminine--does not signify much beyond itself.[15] It remains an act of ascription. That women composed and created is self-evident; whether a genuine F voice motivates biblical texts attributed to an F voice is a different question altogether.

The 'Women's Experience' Concept

In recent years this concept has become almost a slogan, perhaps as reaction formation to some previously held views. In the past, Bible scholars insisted that 'the ancients' held worldviews different from ours, and that cultural difference should be privileged while assessing ancient cultures. This perspective, while cautious, could be used as an excuse for everything and nothing, for generalizations and constructs, including a justification of women's social position in the ancient world without further thought. Ancient male sensibilities are depicted by past and present interpreters as human or universal sensibilities, to the exclusion of conjectured female interests. Recently, a feminist recognition arose that in societies which measure women by their biological/anatomical potential, then and now, the differences between ancient and modern female experience could not be too great. Finally, contemporary reader response methods permit and encourage

---

[15]   For instance, while many feminist scholars view the Song of Songs as a predominantly female text, D.J.A. Clines, in: *Why is There a Song of Songs and what Does it Do to You If You Read It?*, a paper read at the [British] Society for Old Testament Study in 1993, re-introduces the possibility that it is a male text preoccupied with women and female desire.

projections of ideas and perceptions onto ancient texts. So, once again, how can we use our womanly experience in critiquing the Bible?

Looking at the biblical concept of motherhood might be illuminating. The most prominent figuration of 'woman' in the Bible is the [married] mother. What happens if we adopt most or all of the narratives about mothers as 'women's traditions' expressing 'women's experience' and genuine interest? Should we assume that domestic/biological interests, everything to do with motherhood and wifehood, are the stereotypic hallmarks of an ancient woman's being in her own eyes[16] and, consequently, a distinctive component of timeless women's traditions? If we do that, we comply with the gender position generally advocated for (to distinguish from by) women by M, androcentric societal norms, ancient and modern. Do we actually want to do that, in complicity with the conservative scholarly dictum that the ancients perforce had values dissimilar to ours? Do we want to confine female traditions in the Bible mainly to 'traditional'--in the sense of conventional, common, typical, established, customary, socially acceptable--roles? Do we benefit from pointing out that public female figurations of women are still depicted as 'mothers' or metaphoric mothers (like Deborah, Sisear's mother and even Jael in Judges 5) even when they act as public figures, even in female poetry? This may indeed reflect [some, most] women's world. But constructing such passages as female traditions may be experienced as delimiting by some modern readers of both genders. It may also be, once more, an expression of male concerns.

And to another instructive example. The paradigm of the hero's mother-to-be recurs in the Hebrew Bible and is carried over into the New Testament. Sarah, Hagar, Lot's daughters, Rebekah, Leah, Rachel, Tamar, Moses' mother, Samson's mother, Hannah, Ruth, Mary and Elizabeth experience problems with regard to giving birth to a son. The problem is either infertility (not ascribed to males, logic and modern science notwithstanding)

---

[16]   Cf. K. van der Toorn, *From the Cradle to Her Grave. The Role of Religion in the Life of the Israelite and the Babylonian Woman*, Sheffield 1994. Van der Toorn emphasizes often enough (for instance, see his "Concluding Remarks" on 141-45, esp. 144-45) that the materials he draws on do not, for the most part, furnish women's points of view and are not to be considered women's texts. And yet, he attempts to supply a comprehensive account of ancient (Israelite and Mesopotamian) women's life cycle, with the claim that women's life experience -- including maturation and motherhood -- was governed by their religiosity.

and/or social (lack of a spouse, hostile environment). All the women are configured as desperate for sons. On the face of it, what could be more 'natural' than this? We are taught that women are instinctively maternal; it has always been like this; we are proud of it; pregnancy and giving birth is women's unique, quintessential experience. It would be foolish to argue with this perspective; it would be equally foolish to accept its exclusivity for now as well as for the past. From the ancient perspective, as Carol Meyers shows us, motherhood carried a deadly price.[17] Harsh terrain, lack of proper nutrition, a high rate of infant mortality, hard work, lack of birth control[18] and many pregnancies must have meant fast ageing and early death for fertile women. And yet the dominant biblical ideology is "Be fruitful and multiply" (Genesis 1:26), an ideology with which biblical women apparently complied with enthusiasm -- at any rate, they are presented as if they did, against their own physical survival. The fertility commandment, essential for the survival of society at large, was inscribed on women's bodies. This internalization of societal norms makes sense only if women understood that a sonless female is of no social consequence, but also that the quest for fertility has its dangers. However, no opposition to this female-endangering matrix is recorded. Should we accept the female pining for a son, therefore, as authentic 'women's experience'? Or, rather, should we view it as male propaganda designated to instruct women about their proper biological, equated with social, role? Moreover, if these written traditions of maternal preoccupation are indeed female (which, in my opinion, they are not), are they useful to contemporary female or womanly readers? In our world the ideal of marital state for women is losing ground; personal choice is becoming more acceptable. Population explosion, especially in the so-called Third World, dictates a modicum of birth control.[19] From our modern

---

[17]   A brief and instructive summary is to be found in C.L. Meyers, "Everyday Life. Women in the Period of the Hebrew Bible", in: C.A. Newsom and S.H. Ringe (eds.), *The Women's Bible Commentary*, London 1992, 244-251.

[18]   According to the Bible, female birth control is non-existent. Male birth control in the form of *coitus interruptus* is mentioned, i.e. in the case of Onan, Genesis 38.

[19]   On the problematics of advocating ideology and praxis of birth-control for women in the so-called Third World, which is underlined (once more) by the notion that 'we', the advocates, occupy a privileged position of knowledge and power, see: M. Mies, "New Reproductive Technologies. Sexist and Racist implications" and "From the Individual to the Dividual. The Supermarket of 'Reproductive Alternatives'", in: M. Mies and V. Shiva, *Ecofeminism*, Halifax/London and New Jersey 1993, 174-216. While I find some of Mies's

perspective, the paradigm of the aspiring mother is suitable for some women but not for all. When we accept such texts as products of women's traditions according to the criteria of female centrality and experience, our lives are problematized by our [male] ancestors' or ancestresses' views.

Female Mutedness
Silence, relative silence and mutedness are women's lot--in history, religion, narrative, art and many more fields. Silence is a gap to be filled in. But the filling-in process is a matter of gendered approach and readerly interest. And so is the finding of a critical, double-edged voice in texts ascribed to biblical women. As a reading strategy, the quest is a sound quest. But it may also turn out to be so heavily biased by the reader's gender position as to minimize its usefulness. While each text incorporates many subtexts, ambiguities and dualities many have other sources than a duality of voice.

So What?
I have pointed out the difficulties rather than the merits of gendering biblical traditions as F or, for that matter, as M in order to problematize them once more. This problematization has a purpose. Feminist and womanly readers, especially those who wish to remain within their religious community and its institutions (be they Jewish, Christian, Moslem or otherwise), often resort to the seemingly most obvious tactics of salvaging 'women's traditions' from the scriptures they share with their male and manly colleagues. On the surface, this looks like an bright critical move for re-establishing self-esteem and woman power through the most efficient agent: knowledge, the obtaining of information out of a gaping system of disinformation. We are stuck with the Bible: it is part of our common heritage. We live by it, even when our lifestyle is secular. It permeates our civilization and informs our culture. We must search it so as to be equal partners in the culture. The search is therefore experienced as an act of appropriation, a contribution to the revival of woman

---

claims overstated, her analysis foregrounds the ethical and practical issues involved, among which the claim of knowing the truth for the Other, as classified by gender, race, location, social structure, education, etc. The analogy to 'knowing' or 'knowing better' about biblical woman figures--by the text, in the text, by the readers--is striking. In both cases the women, instead of functioning as objects/subjects in turn (which is the usual state of affairs), are denied subjectivity in the name of a higher intelligence/power.

spirit and a prerequisite for women's theology. The quest varies from fanciful fabrications to more balanced views of: matriarchal states[20], goddess worship[21], female traits of the divine being[22], traces of women's texts[23], combinations of old-new canons.[24] All these inquiries, impressive and laudatory and weighty contribution to female knowledge (hence power) as they are, are motivated by the wishful equation: our mothers = our sisters = ourselves. But our mothers and sisters were re-cast and re-imaged by male-written, male-transmitted historiography- or, at the very least, processed to the point of no easy recall.

Male impoundment of Scripture has resulted in a claim of truth: indivisive, absolute, monomaniac, incontestable, orthodox, canonical, divine truth. Is this what we want to achieve by labeling certain handed-down scriptural texts as 'women's traditions'? If so, we are no better than our M colleagues: we imitate their techniques of exclusion. Will this strategy of Ersatz imitation serve us in the long run?

Conclusions: On Reading 'As If'

Given the androcentric bent of scriptures, no probable traces of women's texts, traditions and even voices can be salvaged from it; even when we do

---

[20] E. Reed, *Woman's Evolution. From Matriarchal Clan to Patriarchal Family,* New York/Toronto 1975. A more balanced view is advanced by G. Lerner, *The Creation of Patriarchy,* New York/Oxford 1986.

[21] A misleading example of goddess pursuit is, in my opinion, G. Weiler, *Das Matriarchat im Alten Israel,* Stuttgart/Berlin/Köln 1989. However, balanced views are advanced by some feminist scholars. Cf., for instance, by M.-Th. Wacker, especially in her most recent work: "Spuren der Göttin im Hoseabuch", ... See also Wacker's many other works, including: "Die Göttin kehrt zurück: Kritische Sichtung neuerer Entwürfe", in: M.-Th. Wacker (ed.), *Der Gott der Männer und die Frauen,* Düsseldorf 1987, 11-37; "Matriarchale Bibelkritik: ein antijudaistisches Konzept?", in: L. Siegele-Wenschkowitz (ed.), *Verdrängte Vergangenheit, die uns bedrängt: Feministische Theologie in der Verantwortung für die Geschichte,* München 1988, 181-242. See also U. Winter, *Frau und Göttin,* OBO, 53, Freiburg/Göttingen 1983.

[22] For example: H. Schüngel-Straumann, "Gott als Mutter in Hos 11", *ThQ* 166 (1986), 119-134, reprinted in English translation in: A. Brenner (ed.), *A Feminist Companion to the Latter Prophets,* Sheffield 1995; M. Gruber, "The Motherhood of God in Second Isaiah", in: *The Motherhood of God And Other Studies,* Atlanta 1992, 3-15.

[23] Van Dijk-Hemmes in: *Sporen* and *On Gendering Texts.*

[24] J. Bekkenkamp, *Canon en Keuze. Het bijbelse Hooglied en de Twenty-One Love Poems van Adrienne Rich als bronnen van theologie,* Ph.D. Dissertation, Kampen 1993.

manage to unearth them, there is no denying the general framework.[25] And nothing can be rescued with any modicum of certainty. The process of eradication, obliteration, muting, muffling, stifling, suppressing, oppressing, silencing, writing-out, blotting of women's tradition in the Bible was so effective in most cases as to render the quest impracticable. Which is perhaps fortunate: otherwise, we would have found ourselves trapped in the same epistemological space our male colleagues are ensnared by. Imputing to imaginable traces of women's traditions in the Bible a decisive status will be way beyond the credible. Moreover and besides, such passages are quantitatively insignificant.

Should we continue to attempt the gendering of texts and of written traditions, then? Yes, of course. Re-defining male texts as M and not simply and unproblematically as 'universal' is valuable, although the pitfalls resemble those of defining F traditions and voices. Re-defining texts as traces of F traditions remains empowering--providing we remember that, in most cases, this is one possibility out of two.

Ascribing a dual-voice option to written traditions perhaps furnishes a good interim strategy. If we look for the submerged F voices in a text, we thus undermine the older view of dogmatic M exclusivity. However, this gendering process depends heavily on the reader's position and gender.[26] Moreover, looking for possiblities to ascribe dual F/M voices, to read a passage as if it might be configured as an M or an F text simultaneously, may be the best option for the time being. Whenever this can be done, like with certain passages of the Song of Songs, a bi-gender balance is restored -- to the text, to our reading of it, to the implied world of authors and societies behind the text, to our culture. This is perhaps what we should do: until we know more, until we find sharper means for gendering texts and

---

[25] P. J. Milne, "The Patriarchal Stamp of Scripture. The Implications of Structural Analysis for Feminist Hemeneutics", in: A. Brenner (ed.), *A Feminist Companion to Genesis*, Sheffield 1993, 146-172. To quote (p. 172): "... to claim the Bible as a text which authoritatively enunciates the divine-human relationship is, inevitably, to tie that relationship to patriarchal values. To be a 'Christian Feminist' or a 'Jewish Feminist' is to subordinate feminist ideology to the patriarchal ideology of Christianity and Judaism, an ideology founded upon and sustained through their 'sacred scriptures'".

[26] A. Brenner, *On Gendering Texts*, Introduction, 8-10; A. Brenner, "'Come Back, Come Back the Shulammite' (Song of Songs 7.1-10). A Parody of the *wasf* Genre", in: A. Brenner (ed.), *A Feminist Companion to the Song of Songs*, Sheffield 1993, 234-257, esp. 256-257.

voices as F, we should focus on ways and means for collecting those HB passages that can serve readers of both genders. I am sure that these are not as numerous as decidedly M-voice texts; I'm also fairly confident that they are more numerous than biblical F-voice texts, be those 'muted' or 'double' or both or neither.

It seems to me that, for the time being, it would be beneficial to emphasize that our feminist approaches (in the plural!) are subjective, motivated by reader response or reader perception and by our different life situations. We can make no claim for exclusivity. If we want to live and let live, we have to go about our work in the best humanist, pre-science and also post-modernist manner -- a wedding of apparent contradictions. We can insist, perhaps, that some biblical [and other canonical, scriptural, cultural] texts can be read and used as if they contained implied women's voices, many times removed. The what if, as if qualifiers promote knowledge, power, survival and recognition of the Other--in our case, the recognition of the androcentric male tradition we are stuck with and enveloped by. It is my deepest conviction that women's traditions have to be created, not re-created. They must be created from the here and now; looking to the past, in most cases, will result mainly in frustration and well-meant falsification. Or -- perish the thought -- it might lead to the adoption of conventional, heavily-substantiated and impeccably-argued M attitudes. In other words, the concept of 'tradition', generally and as in 'women's traditions', should be discussed and re-negotiated. We have a problem: we are excluded -- still -- from the symbolic order which is not only M but largely, by definition, male. Whether we want to join this psycho-social order[27], to bring it down, or to [re]create a new order depends to a great extent upon the tools we choose for shaping our ideologies and identities. 'Tradition' is one of these ideological tools. The quest for women's traditions (or voices, or texts) is as political as it is exegetical/hermeneutical. Fortunately, more than one choice can be made: there is no single, 'correct' answer.

So how can we defend ourselves? By recalling, for instance, Habermas' words that, ultimately,

> ... we all can learn the basic hermeneutic wisdom that it is an illusion to suppose one could retain the last word.[28]

---

[27] And if so, do we not want to join on our own terms? And is this at all possible?
[28] J. Habermas, *Philosophical Political Profiles* (trans. from the German by F.G. Lawrence,

Being women and feminists, we might decide to retain our hold on hermeneutics rather than embrace so-called science uncritically or without humble restraint.[29] We might choose to search for possibilities rather than go for imagined certainties.

Athalya Brenner is associate Professor at the Department of General Studies, The Technion, Haifa, Israel, and currently holds the chair of Feminism and Christianity at the Catholic University of Nijmegen, The Netherlands. Her main research interests are Semitic philology and feminist critism of the Bible, about which she has published extensively. She is the compiler and editor of *A Feminist Companion to the Bible*, Sheffield Academic Press: Sheffield, England; 10 volumes.

Cambridge, MASS 1983), 197. This statement is originally about Gadamer and his work.

[29] Cf. H.-G. Gadamer, *Hermeneutics versus Science?*, 1988.

I. BIBLIOGRAPHIE - BIBLIOGRAPHY - BIBLIOGRAPHIE[1]

I.1. Frauenkirche und feministische Theologie - Womenchurch and Feminist Ecclesiology - Femmes/église et ecclésiologie féministe

(Veröffentlichungen seit 1990 - Publications since 1990 - Publications depuis 1990)

Eine Bibliographie zum Thema "Frauenkirche" bis zum Jahr 1990 ist erschienen in: Schlangenbrut, Heft 32/1991, S. 20 (zusammengestellt von Gunhild Buse).

Karen Armstrong, **The End of Silence. Women and Priesthood**, Fourth Estate: London 1993, ISBN 1-85702-145-2.

*Martine Bakema & Lies Sluis (ed.), **Een ander ambt. 25 jaar vrouwen in het ambt in de Gereformeerde Kerken in Nederland**, Kok: Kampen 1994, ISBN 90-242-8464-3.

Andrea Bieler u.a., **"Darum wagt es, Schwestern..." Zur Geschichte evangelischer Theologinnen in Deutschland**, (Historisch-Theologische Studien zum 19. und 20. Jahrhundert 7), Neukirchener Verlag: Neukirchen-Vluyn 1994, ISBN 3-7887-1477-8.

E.A. de Boer/ D.J.J. Dijk/ T. Hibma/ M. Jansen, **Vrouw, Taal en Liturgie**, Narratio: Gorinchem (2nd print) 1993, ISBN 90-5263-0682.

Riet Bons-Storm / Corrie Dijkstershuis / Martha Kroes / Eva Ouwehand, **Ruimte en richting. Vrouwen op zoek naar veelbetekenend geloof**, Boekencentrum: Den Haag 1990, ISBN 90-239-0183-5.

---

[1] Zu Büchern mit * siehe unter "II. Rezensionen" - For books with a * look under "II. Book Reviews" - Pour les livres avec un * voire sous "II. Critiques"

Riet Bons-Storm / Diana Vernooij (ed.), **Beweging in Macht. Vrouwenkerk in Nederland?**, Kok: Kampen 1991, ISBN 90-212-3389-5.

Riet Bons-Storm, **Pastoraat als bondgenootschap**. **Aanzet tot vernieuwing van de kerkelijke praktijk van het vrouwenpastoraat**, Kok: Kampen 1992, ISBN 90-242-6701-3.

Anne Brotherton (ed.), **The Voice of the Turtledove**. **New Catholic Women in Europe**, Paulist Press: New York 1992, ISBN 0-8091-3307-5.

Foka Brouwer, **Een bééld van een beweging**. **Onderzoek naar de organisatie van de vrouw-en-geloofbeweging in Nederland**, Leusden, 1992 *(te bestellen bij: Dienstencentrum Gereformeerde Kerken, tel. +31-33-960360)*.

Marianne Bühler, **Frauen im Ehrenamt**. **Entwicklungen und Perspektiven der pastoralen Mitarbeit von Frauen in einer veränderten Kirche** (Diss. Trier 1992/3).

Martine Buitink / Ineke Hekman / Jessica Prager-Stein / Anita van Steyn, **En de Godin schudde de wateren. Geschiedenis van een beweging, Vrouw en Geloof Zeeland**, Zeeland 1992.

Lavinia Byrne, **Woman at the Altar. The Ordination of Women in the Roman Catholic Church**, Mowbray: London, ISBN 0-264-67335-2.

Young-Sook Chun, **Das Problem der Frauenordination aus ökumenischer Perspektive. Ein Vergleich zwischen den evangelischen Kirchen in Südkorea und denen der Bundesrepublik**, Universitätsverlag Dr. N. Brockmeyer: Bochum 1993, ISBN 3-8196-0106-6.

Paula van Cuilenburg / Jeannette Deenik-Moolhuizen / Paul Oskamp, **Dochters en zonen van God. Inclusief taalgebruik in de kerk**, Driebergen 1991, ISBN 90 239 9502 3 *(te bestellen bij: Centrum voor Educatie NHK, Postbus 1100, NL-3970 BC Driebergen)*.

Sally Cunneen, **Mother Church. What the Experience of Women is Teaching Her**, Paulist Press: New Jersey 1991.

Regina Degen Ballmer u.a. (Hg.), **Neuer Wein in alten Schläuchen - Frauen in kirchlichen Ämtern**, Basel 1993 *(te bestellen bij: Projekt Frauen Theologie Basel, c/o H. Jetzer, St. Johanns-Ring 26, CH-4056 Basel)*.

Margret Dekker / Catie te Dorsthorst e.a., **Perspectief op vieringen. Practische suggesties voor vrouwvriendelijke liturgie**, Informatiecentrum Vrouwen en liturgie: Vught 1991.

Sieth Delhaas, **Vrouwen heb 't lef. Vrouw-en-geloof in wereldwijd perspectief**, Narratio: Gorinchem 1992, ISBN 90-5263-984-4.

Marjet Derks / Catharina Halkes / Annelies van Heijst (Red.), **"Roomse dochters". Katholieke vrouwen en hun beweging**, Arbor: Baarn 1992, ISBN 90-8158-047-9.

Bert van Dijk / Liesbeth Huijts / Trees Versteegen (Red.), **Katholieke vrouwen en het feminisme. Een onderzoek door de Acht Mei Beweging**, De Horstink: Amersfoort 1990, ISBN 90-6184-360-X.

Verna J. Dozier / James R. Adams, **Sisters and Brothers: Reclaiming a Biblical Idea of Community**, Cowley Publications: Cambridge MA 1993, ISBN 1-56101-076-6.

Susan Dowell & Jane Williams, **Bread, Wine and Women. The Ordination Debate in the Church of England**, Virago Press: London 1994.

Brigitte Enzner-Probst, **Pfarrerin. Als Frau in einem Männerberuf**, Kohlhammer: Stuttgart 1995, ISBN 3-17-013226-1.

Jacqueline Field-Bibb, **Women Towards Priesthood. Ministerial Politics and Feminist Praxis**, Cambridge University Press: Cambridge 1991, ISBN 0-521-392-83-7.

Frauen und Macht. Dokumentation der Ersten Österreichischen Frauensynode. 2.-4. Oktober 1992, Puchberg/Wels, hg. von der Initiativgruppe Frauensynode, Wien 1993 *(Eigenverlag Wien, Johannesgasse 10/1, A-1010 Wien)*.

Frauenräume, Themanummer von: *Schritte ins Offene* 22 (1992) 4 *(zu beziehen über: Badenerstr. 69, Postfach, CH-8026 Zürich)*.

Ivy Frith, **Daughters of Jerusalem. The Influence of the Old Testament on Attitudes towards Women in Christian Ministry**, Avon Books: 1994, ISBN 1-897960.

Monica Furlong, **A Dangerous Delight. Women and Power in the Church**, SPCK: London 1991, ISBN 0-281-04551-8.

Gillespie, Joanna Bowen, **Women Speak. On God, Congregations and Change**, Trinity Press International: Valley Forge 1994, ISBN 1-56338-104-4.

Ineke de Kam, **Ik denk dat het door mijn geloof komt. Over vrouwen, religie en hulpverlening**, Kok: Kampen 1994, ISBN 90-242-8249-7.

Christine Globig, **Frauenordination im Kontext lutherischer Ekklesiologie. Ein Beitrag zum ökumenischen Gespräch**, (Kirche und Konfession 36), Vandenhoeck & Ruprecht: Göttingen 1994, ISBN 3-525-56640-2.

Christine Hojenski / Birgit Hübner / Reinhild Hundrup / Martina Meyer (Hg.), **Meine Seele sieht das Land der Freiheit. Feministische Liturgien - Modelle für die Praxis**, (Mit einem Vorwort von Hedwig Meyer-Wilmes), Edition Exodus: Münster 1990, ISBN 3-923792-35-2.

Ada Maria Isasi-Diaz / Yolanda Tarango, **Hispanic Women. Prophetic Voice in the Church**, Fortress: Minneapolis 1992, ISBN 0-8006-2611-7.

F. Kamphaus, **Mutter Kirche und ihre Töchter. Frauen im Gespräch**, Herder Verlag: Freibug/Basel/Wien (2nd print) 1990.

Melanie A. May (ed.), **Women and Church. The Challenge of Ecumenical Solidarity in an Age of Alienation**, W. Eerdmans/Friendship Press: Grand Rapids/New York 1991, ISBN 0-8028-0552-3.

*Jean Mercier, **Des femmes pour le Royaume de Dieu**, Ed. Albin Michel: Paris 1994, ISBN 2-226-06800-7.

R. Mercsanitz, **Die Europäische Frauensynode**, Wien 1993.

Diemut Meyer, **Ekklesiologische Konsequenzen aus dem Beispiel der ökumenischen Frauenbewegung in den Niederlanden**, Driebergen 1994 *(zu bestellen bei: Kerk en Wereld, Postbus 19, NL-3970 AA Driebergen)*.

B. Morel, H.H. Muns, H.J.M. Vossen, **Vrouweninitiatieven en een andere kerk**, Themanummer van *Praktische Theologie* 16 (1992) 2, Waanders: Zwolle 1992, ISBN 90-6630-358-1.

Hedwig Meyer-Wilmes / Lieve Troch (ed.), **Over hoeren, taarten en vrouwen die voorbijgaan. Macht en verschil in de vrouwenkerk**, Kok: Kampen 1992, ISBN 90-242-6573-8.

Rosie Miles, **Not in Our Name. Voices of Women Who Have Left the Church**, Southwell Diocesan Social Responsibility Group, 1994, ISBN 0-9522809-1-4 *(order with: St.Catharine's House, St. Ann's Well Road, GB-Nottingham NG3 1EJ)*.

Nyambura Njoroge, **Reformed Women in the Life and Work of World Alliance of Reformed Churches**, WARC: Geneva 1993.

Mercy Amba Oduyoye, **Who Will Roll the Stone Away? The Ecumenical Decade of the Churches in Solidarity with Women**, (Risk Book Series 47), WCC Publications: Geneva 1990.

Catherine M. Prelinger (ed.), **Episcopal Women. Gender, Spirituality and Commitment in an American Mainline Denomination**, Oxford University Press: New York/Oxford 1992, ISBN 0-19-507433-5.

Marjorie Procter-Smith, **In Her Own Rite. Constructing Feminist Liturgical Tradition**, Abingdon Press: Nashville 1990, ISBN 0-687-18787-7.

Veronika Prüller, **Wir Frauen sind Kirche - Worauf warten wir noch? Feministische Kirchenträume. Anregungen für das Leben in christlichen Gemeinden**, Herder Verlag: Freiburg/Basel/Wien 1992, ISBN 3-210-25123-1.

Rosemary Radford Ruether, **Women-Church. Theology and Practice**, Harper and Row: San Francisco 1988, ISBN 0-06-066834-2.
(dt.Übersetzung: **Unsere Wunden heilen, unsere Befreiung feiern: Rituale in der Frauenkirche**, Kreuz Verlag: Stuttgart 1988, ISBN 3-7831-0931-0).

Marie-Eloise Rosenblatt (ed.), **Where Can We Find Her? Searching for Women's Identity in the New Church**, Paulist Press: New Jersey 1991, ISBN 0-8091-3227-3.

Ursel Rosenhäger / Sarah Stephens, **"Walk my Sister". The Ordination of Women. Reformed Perspectives**, (Studies from the World Alliance of Reformed Churches), WARC: Geneva 1993.

Letty M. Russell (ed.), **The Church with AIDS. Renewal in the Midst of Crisis**, John Knox Press: Louisville 1990.

*Letty M. Russell, **Church in the Round**. Feminist Interpretation of the Church, John Knox Press: Louisville 1993, ISBN 0-664-25070-X.

Sandra M. Schneiders, **Beyond Patching**. Faith and Feminism in the Catholic **Church**, Paulist Press: New York 1991, ISBN 0-8091-3215-X.

Elisabeth Schüssler-Fiorenza, **Discipleship of Equals**. A Critical Feminist **Ecclesiology/Ekklesia-logy of Liberation**, SCM Press: London 1993, ISBN 334-01986-9.

Veronika Straub (Hg.), **Auch wir sind die Kirche. Frauen in der Kirche zwischen Tradition und Aufbruch**, Pfeiffer Verlag: München 1991, ISBN 3-7904-0573-6.

Solidair halverwege. Over het Oecumenisch Decennium Kerken Solidair met Vrouwen, (Raad van Kerken Nederland), Amersfoort 1994.

Synode der Evangelischen Kirche in Deutschland, Die Gemeinschaft von Frauen und Männern in der Kirche, Gütersloher Verlagshaus: Gütersloh 1990.

Caroline Vander Stichele, **Het zwijgen doorbroken. vrouwen over vrouwen en kerk**, Lannoo: Tielt 1989, ISBN 90-209-1685-8.

Miriam Therese Winter / Adair Lummis / Allison Stokes, **Defecting in Place. Women Claiming Responsibility for Their Own Spiritual Lives**, Crossroad: New York 1994.

Ulrike Wagener, **Die Ordnung des Hauses Gottes. Ekklesiologie und Ethik der Pastoralbriefe**, (Wissenschaftliche Untersuchungen zum NT 65), J.C.B. Mohr: Tübingen 1994.

Sue Walrond-Skinner (ed.), **Crossing the Boundary. What Will Women Priests Mean?**, Mowbray: London 1994.

H. Walton / S. Durber (ed.), **Silence in Heaven. A Book of Women's Preaching**, SCM Press: London 1994, ISBN 0-334-01543-X.

Margaret Webster, **A New Strength, A New Song. The Journey to Women's Priesthood**, Mowbray: London 1994, ISBN 0-264-67320-4.

Lieke Werkman, **Recht doen aan vrouwen in de kerken**. De feministische discussie over rechtvaardigheid en zorgzaamheid als bijdrage aan een visie op kerk-zijn, Kok: Kampen 1993 (diss.), ISBN 90-242-6839-7.

Joke Westerhof-Goedvolk, **Mij niet gezien! Aktieve vrouwen verdwijnen uit de kerk**, Boekencentrum: Zoetermeer 1994, ISBN 90-239-1815-0.

Constantine Yokarinis, **The Priesthood of Women as a Problem in the Context of WCC**, Katerini 1993 (unpublished dissertation, in Greek).

I.2. Dissertationen und andere Veröffentlichungen im Bereich Frauenforschung - Dissertations and Other Publications on Women's Studies - Dissertations et autres publications sur 'Women's Studies'

(Erschienen seit 1993 - published since 1993 - paru depuis 1993)

Beatrice Acklin Zimmermann, **Gott im Denken berühren. Die theologischen Implikationen der Nonnenviten**, (Reihe Dokimon 14), Universitätsverlag Freiburg/CH: Fribourg 1993, ISBN 3-7278-0904-3.

Beatrice Acklin Zimmermann (Hg.), **Denkmodelle von Frauen im Mittelalter**, (Reihe Dokimon 15), Universitätsverlag Fribourg/CH: Fribourg 1994, ISBN 3-7278-0942-6.

Elzbieta Adamiak, **Maria in der feministischen Theologie von Catharina Halkes**, Lublin 1994, (masch. geschrieben, Diss., in polnischer Sprache).

Christa Anbeek, **Denken over de dood. De boeddhist K. Nishitana en de christen W. Pannenberg vergeleken**, Kok: Kampen 1994.

*Martina Appich u.a. (Hg.), **Eine andere Tradition. Dissidente Positionen von Frauen in Philosophie und Theologie**, Iudicium Verlag, München 1993.

Jenneke Johanna Bekkenkamp, **Canon en Keuze. Het bijbelse hooglied en de twenty-one love poems van Adrienne Rich als bronnen van theologie,** (Diss. Amsterdam), Kok: Kampen 1993, ISBN 90-391-0558-8.

Teresa Berger, **Liturgie und Frauenseele. Die Liturgische Bewegung aus der Sicht der Frauenforschung**, (Praktische Theologie heute 10), Kohlhammer: Stuttgart 1993, ISBN 3-17-012197-9.

Andrea Bieler, **Konstruktionen des Weiblichen. Die Theologin Anna Paulsen im Spannungsfeld bürgerlicher Frauenbewegungen der Weimarer Republik und nationalsozialistischer Weiblichkeitsmythen**, Chr. Kaiser/Gütersloher Verlagshaus: Gütersloh 1994, ISBN 3-579-00139-6.

Andrea Blome, **Frau und Alter. "Alter" - eine Kategorie feministischer Befreiungstheologie**, Chr. Kaiser/Gütersloher Verlagshaus: Gütersloh 1994, ISBN 3-579-00297-X.

Kari Elisabeth Børresen / Kati Vogt, **Women's Studies of the Christian and Islamic Traditions. Ancient, Medieval and Renaissance Foremothers**, Kluwer Academic Publishers: Dordrecht 1993, ISBN 0-7923-2206-1.

Kari Elisabeth Børresen, **Le Madri della Chiesa. Il medioevo**, Napoli 1993.

Athalya Brenner / Fokkelien van Dijk-Hemmes, **On Gendering Texts. Female and Male Voices in the Hebrew Bible**, (Biblical Interpretation Series Vol. 1), Brill: Leiden/New York/Köln 1993, ISBN 90 04 09642 6.

Athalya Brenner / Fokkelien van Dijk-Hemmes (ed.), **Reflections on Theology and Gender**, Kok Pharos: Kampen 1994, ISBN 90 390 01111.

Athalya Brenner (ed.), **The Feminist Companion to the Bible**, Sheffield Academic Press: Sheffield,
1. A Feminist Companion to the Song of Songs, 1993.
2. A Feminist Companion to Genesis, 1993.
3. A Feminist Companion to Ruth, 1993.
 4. *A Feminist Companion to Judges*, 1993.
 5. *A Feminist Companion to Samuel and Kings*, 1994.
6. A Feminist Companion to Exodus and Deuteronomy, 1994.
 7. *A Feminist Companion to Esther, Judith and Susanna*, 1995.
 8. *A Feminist Companion to the Later Prophets*, 1995.

Gunhild Buse, **Macht - Moral - Weiblichkeit. Eine feministisch-theologische Auseinandersetzung mit Carol Gilligan und Frigga Haug**, Matthias Grünewald Verlag: Mainz 1993, ISBN 3-7867-1723-0.

Klara Butting, **Die Buchstaben werden sich noch wundern. Innerbiblische Kritik als Wegweisung feministischer Hermeneutik**, (Diss. Amsterdam 1993), Alektor-- Verlag: Berlin 1993.

Anne Conrad, **Mit Klugheit, Mut und Zuversicht. Angela Merici und die Ursulinen**, (Topos-Taschenbücher 239), Matthias-Grünewald-Verlag: Mainz 1994, ISBN 3-78671760-5.

Catherine Cornille, **Vrouwen in de wereldgodsdiensten. Teksten, tradities en recente ontwikkelingen**, Lemniscaat: Rotterdam 1994, ISBN 90-6069-933-5.

Jutta Dick/ Marina Sassenberg (ed.), **Jüdische Frauen im 19. und 20. Jahrhundert. Lexikon zu Leben und Werk**, Rowohlt Verlag: Hamburg 1993.

[Fokkelien van Dijk-Hemmes], **De dubbele stem van haar verlangen. Teksten van Fokkelien van Dijk-Hemmes**, verz. en ingeleid door Jonneke Bekkenkamp en Freda Dröes, Meinema: Zoetermeer 1995, ISBN 90 211 3619 8.

Peter Dinzelbacher, **Mittelalterliche Frauenmystik**, Schöningh-Verlag: Paderborn 1993.

Gabriele Disselkamp, **Christiani senatus lumina. Die Religionszugehörigkeit römischer Frauen der Oberschicht im Rom des 4. und 5. Jahrhunderts und ihr Anteil an der Christianisierung der stadtrömischen Senatsaristokratien** (Diss.), Univ. Bochum 1992/3.

Veerle Draulans, **Christelijk geïnspireerd sociaal engagement tussen wenselijkheid en werkelijkheid. Theologisch-ethische reflectie, documentenanalyse en empirisch onderzoek over de Christelijke Arbeidersbeweging vandaag**, Leuven 1994 (unpublished Diss.).

Freda Dröes / Anne-Marie Korte / Marian Papavoine / Jonneke Bekkenkamp (ed.), **Proeven van Vrouwenstudies Theologie**, Bd. 3, Meinema: Zoetermeer 1993 *(te bestellen bij: Meinema, Antwoordnr. 10291, NL-2700 VB Zoetermeer).*

Claudia Eliass, **Frauenmystik im Mittelalter. Weibliches Selbstverständnis in der Frauenmystik des 12. und 13. Jahrhunderts**, (Frauen in Geschichte u. Gesellschaft 28), Centaurus: Pfaffenweiler 1995, ISBN 3-89085-956-9.

*Anneliese Felber, **Harmonie durch Hierarchie? Das Denken der Geschlechter-Ordnung im frühen Christentum**, Wiener Frauenverlag: Wien 1994, ISBN 3-900399-94-8.

*Heidi Bernhard Filli u.a., **Weiberwirtschaft. Frauen - Ökonomie - Ethik**, Edition Exodus: Luzern 1994, ISBN 3-905575-90-6.

Irmtraud Fischer, **Die Erzeltern Israels. Feministisch-theologische Studien zu Genesis 12-36**, (Beih. BZAW 222), De Gruyter: Berlin 1994.

Hanna-Barbara Gerl, **Freundinnen. Christliche Frauen aus zwei Jahrtausenden**. Erich Wewel Verlag: München 1994, ISBN 3-7904-0623-6.

Aruna Gnanadason, **Die Zeit des Schweigens ist vorbei. Kirchen und Gewalt gegen Frauen**, Edition Exodus: Luzern 1993.

Elisabeth Gössmann (Hg.), **Mulier papa, der Skandal eines weiblichen Papstes. Zur Rezeptionsgeschichte der Gestalt der Päpstin Johanna**, (= Archiv für philosophie- und
theologiegeschichtliche Frauenforschung 5), Iudicium Verlag: München 1994, ISBN 3-89129-005-5.

*Elaine Graham & Margaret Halsey (ed.), **Life Cycles. Women and Pastoral Care**, SPCK: London 1993.

Mary Grey, **The Wisdom of Fools? Seeking Revelation for Today**, SPCK: London 1993, ISBN 0-281-04659-X.

Maaike de Haardt, **Dichter bij de dood. Feministisch-theologische aanzetten tot een theologie van de dood**, Boekencentrum: Zoetermeer 1993, ISBN 90-2390443-5.

Maria Häusl, **Abischag und Batscheba. Frauen am Königshof und die Thronfolge Davids im Zeugnis der Texte 1 Kön 1 und 2**, (ATS 41), St. Ottilien 1993.

*Margaret Hebblethwaite, **Six New Gospels. New Testament Women Tell Their Stories**, Geoffrey Chapman: London 1994, ISBN 0-225-66711-8.

Annelies van Heijst, **Leesbaar lichaam - Verhalen van lijden bij Blaman en Dorrestein**, Kok Agora: Kampen 1993, ISBN 90-391-0557-X.

Julie Hopkins, **Towards a Feminist Christology. Jesus of Nazareth, European Women and the Christological Crisis**, Kok/SPCK: Kampen/London 1994, ISBN 90 390 00492.

Britta Hübener, Hartmut Meesmann (Hg.), **Streitfall feministische Theologie**, (mit Beiträgen von u.a. E. Schüssler Fiorenza, L. Schottroff, E. Moltmann-Wendel, U. King, H. Pissarek-Hudelist, M. Käßmann, A. Jensen), Düsseldorf 1993, ISBN 3-491-77941-3.

Annie Imbens-Fransen, **God in de beleving van vrouwen**, Kok: Kampen 1995.

Hedwig-Jahnow-Forschungsprojekt (Hg.), **Feministische Hermeneutik und Erstes Testament. Analysen und Interpretationen**, Kohlhammer: Stuttgart 1994, ISBN 3-17- 013047-1.

Monika Jakobs, **Frauen auf der Suche nach dem Göttlichen. Die Gottesfrage in der feministischen Theologie**, (FrauenForschung 1), Morgana Frauenbuchverlag: Münster 1993, ISBN 3-925592-12-1.

Monika Jakobs, Irene Löfler Mayer, Annette Rembold (Hg.), **Vater Gott und Mutter Kirche. Bausteine für den Religionsunterricht**, Münster 1995.

Elizabeth A. Johnson, **She Who is. The Mystery of God in a Feminist Theological Perspective**, Crossroad: New York 1992, ISBN 0-8245-1162-X.
(dt. Übersetzung: **Ich bin die ich bin**, Patmos: Düsseldorf 1994, ISBN 3-491-77962-6).

Renate Jost, **Frauen, Männer und die Himmelskönigin. Studien zu Jeremia 7: 17 und 18 und Jeremia 44: 15-25**, Gütersloh 1995.

*Katharina von Kellenbach, **Anti-Judaism in Feminist Religious Writings**, Scholars Press: Atlanta/Georgia 1994, ISBN 0-7885-0044-9 (pbk).

Hildegund Keul, **Menschwerdung durch Berührung. Bettina Brentano-Arnim als Wegbereiterin für eine Feministische Theologie**, (Würzburger Studien zur Fundamentaltheologie 16), Frankfurt 1993, ISBN 3-631-4648-1.

Ursula King (ed.), **Religion and Gender**, Blackwell: Cambridge 1994, ISBN 0-631-19377-4.

*Ursula King (ed.), **Feminist Theology from the Third World**, Maryknoll/Orbis: New York 1994, ISBN 0-281-04736-7.

Renate Kirchhoff, **Die Sünde gegen den eigenen Leib. Studien zu porne und porneia in 1 Kor 6, 12-20 und dem soziokulturellen Kontext der paulinischen Adressaten,** (Diss. Heidelberg), (Studien zur Umwelt des Neuen Testaments 18), Vandenhoeck & Ruprecht: Göttingen 1994.

Stephanie Klein, **Theologie und empirische Biographieforschung. Methodische Zugänge zur Lebens- und Glaubensgeschichte und ihre Bedeutung für eine erfahrungsbezogene Theologie,** (Praktische Theologie heute 19), Verlag W. Kohlhammer: Stuttgart/Berlin/ Köln 1994, ISBN 3-17-013176-1.

*Marion Kobelt-Groch, **Aufsässige Töchter Gottes. Frauen im Bauernkrieg und in der Täuferbewegung,** Campus-Verlag: Frankfurt a.M. 1993, ISBN 3-5933-4879-9.

Mathilde Köhler, **Amalie von Gallitzin. Ein Leben zwischen Skandal und Legende,** Schöningh-Verlag, Paderborn 1993.

Tulikki Koivunnen Bylund, **Fear Not. Believe Only. Ebba Boström and the Samaritan House 1882-1902** (in Swedish), *(Distributed by: Almquist and Wiksell, Stockholm).*

Mary Phil Korsak, **At the Start. Genesis Made New,** Doubleday: New York 1993, ISBN 0-385-47180-7.

Monika Maassen, **Biographie und Erfahrung von Frauen. Ein feministisch-theologischer Beitrag zur Relevanz der Biographieforschung für die Wiedergewinnung der Kategorie der Erfahrung,** (Frauenforschung 2), Morgana Frauenbuchverlag: Münster 1993, ISBN 3-925592-13-X.

*Valerie M. De Marinis, **Critical Caring. A Feminist Model for Pastoral Psychology,** Westminster/John Knox Press: Louisville 1993.

Hedwig Meyer-Wilmes, **Rebellion on the Borders. Feminist Theology between Theory and Praxis,** Kok Pharos: Kampen 1995, ISBN 90-390-0046-8.

Hedwig Meyer-Wilmes, **Zwischen lila und lavendel. Schritte feministischer Theologie,** F. Pustet: Regensburg 1995, ISBN 3-7917-1442-2.

Elisabeth Moltmann-Wendel, **Mein Körper bin ich. Neue Wege zur Leiblichkeit,** Gütersloher Verlagshaus: Gütersloh 1994, ISBN 3-579-00543-X.

Gisela Muschiol, **Famula Dei. Zur Liturgie in merowingischen Frauenklöstern,** (Beiträge zur Geschichte des alten Mönchtums und des Benediktinertums 41), Aschendorff-Verlag: Münster 1994.

Pnina Navè Levinson, **Esther erhebt ihre Stimme. Jüdische Frauen beten,** Gütersloher Verlagshaus: Gütersloh 1993, ISBN 3-579-005 38-3.

*Carol A. Newsom and Sharon H. Ringe (ed.), **The Women's Bible Commentary,** SPCK/Westminster-John Knox Press: London/Louisville (Kentucky) 1992, ISBN 0-664-21922-5.
(Nederlandse vertaling: **Met eigen ogen. Commentaar op de bijbel vanuit het perspectief van vrouwen,** Meinema: Zoetermeer 1995).

Claudia Opitz u.a. (Hg.), **Maria in der Welt. Marienverehrung im Kontext der Sozialgeschichte. 10.-18. Jahrhundert,** Chronos-Verlag: Zürich 1993, ISBN 3-905311-12-7.

Dorothée van Paassen & Anke Passenier (ed.), **Op zoek naar vrouwen in ketterij en secte. Een bronnenonderzoek,** Kok: Kampen 1993.

Donate Pahnke (Hg.), **Blickwechsel. Frauen in Religion und Wissenschaft,** (Religionswissenschaftliche Reihe 6), Marburg 1993, ISBN 3-927165-20-4.

Gail Paterson Corrington, **Her Image of Salvation. Female Saviors and Formative Christianity,** Westminster/John Knox Press: Louisville 1993.

*Annemarie Pieper, **Aufstand des stillgelegten Geschlechts. Einführung in die feministische Ethik,** Herder Verlag: Freiburg/Basel/Wien 1993.

Carolyn Pressler, **The View of Women Found in the Deuteronomic Family Laws,** Walter de Gruyter: Berlin/New York 1993, ISBN 0934-2575.

Rosemary Radford Ruether, **Gaia & Gott. Eine ökofeministische Theologie der Heilung der Erde,** Edition Exodus: Luzern 1994, ISBN 3-905575-91-4.

Carla Ricci, **Mary Magdalene and the Many Others,** Burns & Oates/Scholars Press: Wellwood/ Minneapolis 1994.

Ingrid Riedel, **Hildegard von Bingen. Prophetin der kosmischen Weisheit. Hildegards weibliches Gottesbild**, Kreuz Verlag: Stuttgart 1995, ISBN 3-7831-1306-7.

Susan Roll, **"The Point of Intersection of the Timeloss with Time". The Origins of Christmas from a Contemporary Pastoral Perspective**, Kok Pharos: Kampen 1995.

Ursula Rudnick, **Past-Shoa Religious Metaphors: the Image of God in the Poetry of Nelly Sachs**, (unpublished diss. JTS: New York 1994).

*Luise Schottroff, **Lydias ungeduldige Schwestern. Feministische Sozialgeschichte des frühen Christentums**, Chr. Kaiser/Gütersloher Verlagshaus: Gütersloh 1994, ISBN 3-579-1837-X.

Alice Sandblom, **La Tradition de la Bible chez La Fem de la CEZ. Influence de l'ancienne culture et de la pensée biblique d'une certaine conception de la femme au sein de la Communauté evangelique du Zaire** *(distributed by: Almquist & Wiksell International, P.O. Box 4627, S-11691 Stockholm)* (about impurity).

*Theodor Schneider & Helen Schüngel-Straumann (Hg.), **Theologie zwischen Zeiten und Kontinenten. Festschrift für Elisabeth Gössmann**, Herder Verlag: Freiburg etc. 1993.

Silvia Schroer, **Book of Wisdom (ascribed to Salomon)**, Cross Road: New York, 1994.

Elisabeth Schüssler Fiorenza, **Jesus. Miriam's Child, Sophia's Prophet. Issues in Feminist Christology**, SCM Press: London 1995, ISBN 0 334 02585 0.

*Elisabeth Schüssler Fiorenza (ed.), **Searching the Scriptures**,
*Volume 1: **A Feminist Introduction**, SCM/Crossroad: London/New York 1993, ISBN 0-334-02556-7/ISBN 0-8245-1381-9.
*Volume 2: **A Feminist Commentary**, SCM/Crossroad: London/New York 1994, ISBN 0-334-02557-5.

*Petra Schulz, **Versuche dialogischen Denkens in einer feministisch orientierten religionspädagogischen Praxis**, Peter Lang Verlag: Frankfurt/M. /Bern etc. 1994, ISBN 3-631-47319-2.

Thurid Karlsen Seim, **The Double Message**. Patterns of Gender in Luke-Acts, (Studies of the New Testament and its World), T & T Clark: Edinburgh 1994.

Sybil Sheridan (ed.), **Hear Our Voice**. **Women Rabbis Tell Their Stories**, SCM Press: London 1994, ISBN 0 334 02583 4.

Jopie Siebert-Hommes, **Laat de dochters léven! De literaire architectuur van Exodus 1 en 2 als toegang tot de interpretatie**, Kok: Kampen 1993.

Dorothee Sölle (Hg.), **Für Gerechtigkeit streiten**. **Theologie im Alltag einer bedrohten Welt**. **Festschrift für Luise Schottroff**, Chr.Kaiser/ Gütersloher Verlagshaus: Gütersloh 1994, ISBN 3-579 02 0005.

Silvia Soennecken, **Misogynie oder Philogynie?** **Philologisch-theologische Untersuchungen zum Wortfeld Frau bei Augustinus**, Peter Lang Verlag: Frankfurt a.M. etc. 1993, ISBN. 3-631-46069-4.

Angela Standhartinger, **Der Beitrag von "Joseph und Aseneth" zur Diskussion um das Frauenbild in jüdisch-hellenistischer Zeit**, (unveröffentl. Diss., Frankfurt FB Ev. Theologie 1994).

Ulrike Suhr, **Poesie als Sprache des Glaubens**. **Eine theologische Untersuchung des literarischen Werkes von Marie Luise Kaschnitz**, (Praktische Theologie heute), Stuttgart 1992.

Elsa Tamez, **Gegen die Verurteilung zum Tod**. **Paulus oder die Rechtfertigung durch den Glauben aus der Perspektive der Unterdrückten und Ausgeschlossenen**, Edition Exodus: Luzern 1994.

Lieve Teugels, **Midrasj in de bijbel of midrasj op de bijbel?** **Een exemplarische studie van de verloving van Rebekka (Gen 24) in de bijbel en in de rabbijnse midrasj**, 2 vol., (unpublished diss., Leuven 1994).

Eva-Sybille Vogel-Mfato, **Die ökumenische Studie über "Strukturen missionarischer Gemeinden" und ihre Vorgeschichte im Lichte feministisch- und befreiungstheologischer Kritik** (unveröffentl. Diss., Uni Bochum 1992/3).

Thea Vogt, **Angst und Identität im Markusevangelium. ein textpsychologischer und sozialgeschichtlicher Beitrag**, (Novum testamentum et orbs antiquitas 26), Universitasverlag Vandenhoeck & Ruprecht: Fribourg/Göttingen 1993.

Anneke de Vries, **Zuiver en onvervalscht? Een beschrijvingsmodel voor bijbelvertalingen, ontwikkeld en gedemonstreerd aan de Petrus Canisius Vertaling**, VU Uitgeverij: Amsterdam 1994.

Ulrike Witt, **"Wie soll ich aber zu solch' einem herrlichen Durchbruch kommen?" Frauen im Umkreis des Halleschen Pietismus**, (unveröffentl. Diss., Göttingen 1993).

Verena Wodtke-Werner, **Der Heilige Geist als weibliche Gestalt im christlichen Altertum und Mittelalter. Eine Untersuchung von Texten und Bildern**, Centaurus Verlag: Pfaffenweiler 1994.

II. REZENSIONEN - BOOK REVIEWS - CRITIQUE DES LIVRES

II.1. Biblische Theologie - Biblical Studies - Etudes bibliques

Athalya Brenner (ed.)
The Feminist Companion to the Bible, Sheffield Academic Press: Sheffield
1. *A Feminist Companion to the Song of Songs*, 1993.
2. *A Feminist Companion to Genesis*, 1993.
3. *A Feminist Companion to Ruth*, 1993.
6. *A Feminist Companion to Exodus and Deuteronomy*, 1994.

The volumes in this series are already a valuable resource for scholars working in the field of biblical scholarship (whether self-designated as 'feminists' or not) and are destined to become standard inclusions in booklists. And with good reason. They provide a comprehensive survey of both the content and methods of feminist biblical scholarship. The editor has rightly included significant reprinted essays in the collection as well as new and commissioned pieces, and those new to the field will find extremely useful her general introduction to the series and to feminist biblical interpretation generally (in the Song of Songs volume). As might be expected, the Genesis volume is the most substantial of the four being reviewed here, and a large part of it is taken up with examination of that vitally important text, Genesis 2-3. The Exodus to Deuteronomy volume emphasizes Miriam, legal texts (Pressler, Brenner) and the status of women. The Ruth and Song of Songs volumes approach these texts in a variety of ways, illustrating the breadth of feminist approaches and conclusions. (For example, in the Ruth volume, Brenner seeks two oral sources beside Rashkow, who uses the methods of discourse analysis to discuss the dynamics of power within the book. In the Genesis volume, van Dijk-Hemmes' Sarai as victim and 'the object of men's manipulation' appears alongside Teubal's assessment of Sarah as a powerful matriarch.) The long history of feminist biblical interpretation is also acknowledged in many ways, such as the inclusion of extracts from Stanton's nineteenthcentury *The Woman's Bible*, and Goitein's 1957 study suggesting female authorship of the Song of Songs.

For those well acquainted with the field, we find in these volumes much that is familiar in terms of content, style and method. However, there are also interesting new perspectives, such as Korsak's discussion of the translator's task, illustrated from some Genesis texts and Bal's use of other disciplines to enable interpretation of the biblical text (as illustrated in the Genesis and Ruth volumes). Consideration of rabbinic and other interpretations of biblical stories are an important feature of the series. (See, for example, Bach's consideration of the *Testament of Joseph* in the Genesis volume, Jensen's discussion of Ephrem on Ruth, and Graetz on Miriam.)

The overall standard of the contributions to the volumes is high, but, as is to be expected, the type and quality of the various papers vary. There are solid contributions from many (such as those from Brenner, Exum, Meyers and Trible). Others become more speculative (such as Bledstein's imagining of Tamar as narrator of the book of Ruth and the Court Narrative of Samuel-Kings). Further, some contributions will be more accessible than others to interested non-specialists. One frustration is the occasional index lapse. (Some works cited in the article by Davies in the Genesis volume appear in full neither in the notes nor in the bibliography.)

The series discusses explicitly and implicitly important questions of method, and includes consideration of the dilemma facing feminists within faith communities of whether (and how) the Bible is to be treated as authoritative (Milne in the Genesis volume and Bekkenkamp en van Dijk in the Song of Songs one). In addition, the very quality and comprehensiveness of the series raise fundamental questions about possible future directions for

feminist biblical scholars, and even about the very nature of feminist biblical interpretation. The volumes focus, rightly, on narrative and legal texts about women. Should we continue to work on these same texts, either in more detail, or by broadening still further our range of methods of interpretation? Or should we be turning our attention to texts not previously considered (including those not mentioning women) using the new insights we have gained as we have broken new ground? We look forward to future volumes in this much-needed series.
Carol Smith, Oxon

Carol A. Newsom and Sharon H. Ringe (ed.)
The Women's Bible Commentary, SPCK/Westminster-John Knox Press: London/Louisville (Kentucky) 1992.
Elisabeth Schüssler Fiorenza (ed.)
Searching the Scriptures I. A Feminist Introduction, SCM/Crossroad: London/New York 1993.

Zum hundertjährigen Jubiläum der *Woman's Bible* von Elisabeth Cady Stanton (1895ff) sind in den USA zwei feministische Kommentarwerke erschienen, die ihrem Gedächtnis gewidmet sind. Der *Women's Bible Commentary* greift Stantons Konzept erneut auf, während *Searching the Scriptures* den politisierenden Anspruch der Woman's Bible in den Mittelpunkt stellt.

Im *Women's Bible Commentary* kommentieren 41 Bibelwissenschaftlerinnen die Bücher des protestantischen Bibelkanons. Ergänzt werden die Artikel durch kurze Beiträge zur sozialen und literarischen Umwelt der Bibel. Getreu ihrem Vorbild nehmen die Autorinnen nach einem Überblick über Inhalt und Ergebnisse der historisch-kritischen Erforschung der jeweiligen Schrift vor allem solche Abschnitte in den Blick, die eine besondere Relevanz für Frauen haben. Ausgewählt wurden Passagen, die von Frauencharakteren und weiblichen Symbolen handeln oder die das Leben von Frauen prägten beziehungsweise prägen sollten. Entstanden ist so ein interessantes Kommentarwerk, das zum einen Früchte feministischer Bibelkritik einsammelt, zum andern neue Aspekte und neue methodische Zugänge aufzeigt.

Der *Women's Bible Commentary* ist nicht nur für die Bibelwissenschaft, sondern gerade auch für die Predigt- und Unterrichtspraxis konzipiert. Geschmälert wird der Nutzen allerdings dadurch, daß auf Anmerkungen verzichtet wurde, die knappen Literaturhinweise fast ausschließlich amerikanische Titel enthalten und eine Vorstellung der Autorinnen fehlt. Die Beschränkung auf den protestantischen Kanon birgt die Gefahr einer Unterwerfung unter dessen historisch gewordene Autorität. Sie hat aber auch den Vorteil, daß hier einmal 'alle' biblischen Bücher, auch bisher kaum beachtete, einer feministischen Analyse unterzogen werden.

Ganz anders geht *Searching the Scriptures* vor. Gerade in Abgrenzung zum Kanonbegriff soll hier die Pluralität der heiligen Schriften religiöser Gemeinschaften in den Mittelpunkt gerückt werden. 'Searching' bezeichnet dabei nicht nur das Aufspüren des patriarchalen Verschweigens von Frauen, sondern vor allem das Forschen nach Visionen, die Kämpfe für Befreiung und Veränderung nähren können.

In kritischer Abgrenzung zu dem von Stanton vor hundert Jahren noch zugrunde gelegten einheitlichen Konstrukt von Frau und Weiblichkeit bringen hier renommierte feministische Wissenschaftlerinnen ihre unterschiedlichen historischen und sozialpolitischen Erfahrungen ein.

Die 25 Aufsätze des ersten Bandes von *Searching the Scriptures* bereiten das Feld für die Analysen der Schriften im zweiten Band (siehe dazu die Rezension von C. Vander Stichele, Anm. d.Red.) vor. Das feministische 'Grundstück' wird kartiert und ein neues Bauwerk vielfältiger Interpretationen aus afrikanischer, Native- Asian-, Afro-, Latin- und Euro-American, west- und osteuropäischer feministischer Perspektive geschaffen.

Dem 'Vermessen des Grundstückes' kommt der erste Teil mit Beiträgen über die Praxis der Bibelinterpretation in verschiedenen soziohistorischen Kontexten gleich, angefangen bei Theologinnen des europäischen Mittelalters bis hin zu zeitgenössischen asiatisch-amerikanischen, afrikanischen und Mujerista-Theologinnen.

Der spannende zweite Teil erstellt ein programmatisches 'Baugerüst' für feministische Interpretationen, zum Beispiel in Form von zehn Thesen zur Vermeidung von Rassismus und Ethnozentrismus. Drei Beiträge entwickeln unterschiedliche Modelle zum Umgang mit biblischer Autorität in der feministischen Hermeneutik.

Der dritte Teil des Buches unterzieht die herkömmlichen exegetischen Werkzeuge - die historisch-kritische, die materialistische, die soziologische Methode sowie die 'literary criticism' - einer feministischen Kritik, entwirft Konzepte feministischer Übersetzungspraxis und stellt Ansätze einer ökumenischen antiken Frauengeschichte zusammen.

Den eigenen Raum leuchtet schließlich der vierte Teil aus, in dem der Predigtgottesdienst in weißen und schwarzen Gemeinden, Bibelarbeit mit Frauen in den USA und den Niederlanden sowie wissenschaftlicher Unterricht als Praxisfelder feministischer Arbeit reflektiert werden.

Nicht nur wegen der Prominenz der hier versammelten Autorinnen markiert bereits der erste Band von *Searching the Scriptures* einen Meilenstein in feministischer Theologie. Zum ersten Mal wird hier die Pluralität der Perspektiven von Frauen nicht nur behauptet, sondern zum grundlegenden Instrument der Analyse gemacht. Es gelingt so, die wichtige Frage nach dem Umgang mit Schrift(en) und ihrer Autorität umfassend und kontrovers zur Diskussion zu stellen. Daher ist der erste Band von *Searching the Scriptures* keine Einleitung im herkömmlichen Sinn, sondern beinhaltet die vielfältigen Prolegomena feministischer Hermeneutik. Ein packendes und mitreißendes Werk.

Angela Standhartinger, Frankfurt a.M.

Luise Schottroff
Lydias ungeduldige Schwestern. Feministische Sozialgeschichte des frühen Christentums, Chr. Kaiser/Gütersloher Verlagshaus: Gütersloh 1994.

Vier große, etwa gleich umfangreiche Abschnitte gliedern das Werk, wobei die ersten hundert Seiten Theorie (zur historischen Methode und Hermeneutik) die wissenschaftliche Einordnung und eine Auseinandersetzung mit bisherigen Entwürfen bringen. Die Verfasserin schildert ihr Modell als eine Kombination aus den Modellen von Dorothee Sölle, Elisabeth Schüssler Fiorenza und ihres eigenen einer feministischen Sozialgeschichte, die von der Option für die Armen zur Option für die Frauen fortschreitet.

Der zweite große Abschnitt über den Frauenalltag beginnt mit dem frauenfeindlichen Text aus dem ersten Timotheusbrief (2, 9-15), der nicht nur frauenunterdrückend ist, sondern in dem eigentlicher Frauen*haß* an der Wende vom ersten zum zweiten Jahrhundert zum Ausdruck kommt. Dieser Text, der auch schon andernorts besprochen wurde (Küchler, Schüngel-Straumann), gehört unterdessen zum Repertoire aller Kritikerinnen und Kritiker, die zum Thema Frauen und Bibel arbeiten. Es genügt aber nicht, nur den Text kritisch unter die Lupe zu nehmen. Denn er hat - bis heute - eine Unzahl von negativen Wirkungen hervorgebracht. Deswegen wird auch der Kanon 'neu begriffen werden müssen'.

Es folgen detaillierte Ausführungen über Frauenarbeit und Frauenalltag. Diese Beschreibungen, wie Frauen arbeiten und was sie verdienen, sind mit großer Akribie erforscht und zusammengestellt und in Kommentaren nirgendwo zu finden. Beispielsweise wird das, was ein männlicher Taglöhner in der Landwirtschaft verdient, in Beziehung gesetzt zu den Einkünften einer Frau. Solche und viele andere genauen Angaben machen das Buch außergewöhnlich konkret.

Jedoch: Nicht nur der Alltag und die Arbeit der Frauen werden in diesem Kapitel dargestellt, sondern auch ihr *Widerstand*, so besonders an der Geschichte von der hartnäckigen Witwe im Lukasevangelium (18). Diese Frau, die weder als geduldig noch als friedfertig geschildert wird, wie Frauen aus männlichem Blickwinkel gern gezeichnet werden, ist als Vorbild hingestellt und steht in markantem Gegensatz zum Androzentrismus der Bergpredigt, wo - offensichtlich für Männer - ein Verzicht auf Widerstand und Gewalt gefordert wird.

Am Beispiel der Thekla aus den Schriften der frühen Christenheit wird nochmals deutlich gemacht, worum es geht; Nicht um *die* Frauen gegen *die* Männer, sondern gegen bestimmte patriarchale Muster, gegen Frauenrollen, die zum Beispiel Frauen dazu zwingen zu heiraten. Gegen diese Rolle wehrt sich mit Erfolg die Paulusschülerin Thekla.

Mit der Patriarchatskritik beschäftigt sich der ganze dritte Abschnitt, wobei hier überwiegend paulinische und eschatologische Texte zu Wort kommen. Die Ambivalenz des Paulus - er kann weder als extrem frauenfeindlich noch als halber 'Feminist' bezeichnet werden, so weit geht das Spektrum - wird durch das "gespaltene Bewußtsein" (195ff.) erläutert. Auch Paulus, der viel von Unterdrückung und von Sklavinnen und Sklaven weiß, sieht doch die Welt aus der Perspektive des Mannes. So werden die Frauen und die Armen, die immer den Hauptteil der Christen ausmachen, an vielen Stellen doch wieder unsichtbar. Auch in der eschatologischen Diskussion wird dann nicht verständlich, daß das *Ende* von denen, die in absoluter Armut und Not leben, nur als etwas Positives herbeigesehnt werden kann, weil das Elend dann vorbei ist. So kritisiert die Verfasserin das lineare Zeitverständnis der meisten Exegeten, so wie sie lange im ganzen Buch immer auf die Texte selbst *und* auf eine Auslegungsgeschichte eingeht.

Die Kritik und das Negative haben aber nicht das letzte Wort. Das vierte Kapitel beschäftigt sich mit der befreienden Praxis von Frauen und Männern.

Zuerst werden die Geschichte von der Ehebrecherin, die gesteinigt werden soll (Joh 7, 53- 8,1), und die Kindheitsgeschichten (Maria und Elisabeth nach Lukas) nebeneinandergestellt. Diese zunächst befremdliche Zusammenstellung hat eine tiefere Verbindung: In einem Schema (259-261) wird anschaulich die Erniedrigung von Frauen und ihre darauffolgende Befreiung zusammengestellt. Dabei kann auch ein ganz neues Licht fallen auf die Geburt Jesu durch die jungfräuliche Maria. Nicht ihre Demut oder Unterwürfigkeit wird gepriesen, sondern *Gott,* der so Unfaßbares bewirkt wie die Schwangerschaft einer Greisin (Elisabeth) und die Geburt Jesu ohne einen Mann. Erst bei Matthäus werden diese Vorgänge wieder stark aus männlicher Sicht verändert.

Es gibt zahlreiche hoffnungsvolle Ansätze im Neuen Testament, die zeigen, daß in der christlichen Praxis eine andere Rollenverteilung *maß*gebend war als in den überkommenen Strukturen, nämlich im Sinn von Gegenseitigkeit und Geschwisterlichkeit, ohne daß man diese frühe Zeit idealisieren darf. Denn es gab viel Streit; aber es war "fruchtbarer Streit" (312).
Helen Schüngel-Straumann, Kassel

Margaret Hebblethwaite
Six New Gospels. New Testament Women Tell Their Stories, Geoffrey Chapman: London 1994.

In her book Margaret Hebblethwaite retells the story of six prominent women in the New Testament: Elisabeth, the mother of John the Baptist; Mary, Jesus' mother; the Samaritan woman she names Photina; Martha and Mary of Bethany and Mary of Magdala. The subtitle of the book is, however, somewhat misleading. Rather than that the women considered tell *their* stories, they tell *Jesus'* story, or: how Jesus changed their lives. The title is more accurate: they are indeed six new *Gospels.*

It is not Hebblethwaite's intention to make an exegetical study of the texts where these women occur, in an effort to reconstruct history. She rather prefers to make an imaginative reconstruction. This she does first of all by retelling these women's stories from their own viewpoint. She uses the first person to do so. The story of Elisabeth begins as follows: "My name is Elisabeth, and I am a descendant of Aaron, the first great priest of our people..."

Margaret Hebblethwaite's interest is not in what the evangelist wants to say. She does not stick to one Gospel or one story, but uses them to complement each other. Nor does she limit herself to the information she can deduct from the gospel stories, but she sketches in the blank spaces. Starting from John 4:18, for example, where the Samaritan woman is said to have had five husbands, she lets the woman tell what happened. Another option of the author is to use modern language. In avoiding terminology that is culturally alien for women today, she wants "to enable these figures from the past to speak to their modern sisters and brothers with maximum immediacy and relevance." (p.2)

Together these six stories form a mosaic of Jesus' life, told from different perspectives. They are complemented by footnotes, which provide the reader with relevant theological background information. It makes this book, for instance, a useful tool for discussion groups. It gives a sometimes surprising new perspective on the Bible texts under discussion. It offers readers a new entry to the texts as well as to their own experience.

Margaret Hebblethwaite is well aware of the methodological and herme-neutical problems involved in her enterprise. She does not pretend to have written the only possible and correct version of these stories, but indeed, six *new* gospels.
Caroline Vander Stichele, Amsterdam

Elisabeth Schüssler Fiorenza (ed.)
Searching the Scriptures, Volume 2, A Feminist Commentary, SCM/ Crossroad: London/New York 1994.

With its almost 900 pages, the second volume of *Searching the Scriptures* cannot be overlooked. The same goes for its content. The reader who expects a conventional commentary will be disappointed, but might change her mind if she takes a closer look at its content.

In her introduction E. Schüssler Fiorenza explains the unusual selection that has been made in order to transgress the canonical boundaries. On the one hand, the canonical Christian books of the New Testament are treated, on the other hand, the perspective is broadened by the inclusion of extra-canonical writings, like the Sibylline Oracles, Judith or the Acts of Thecla. That no books of the Hebrew Bible or the Torah are discussed is due to limitations of space and resources, explains Schüssler Fiorenza. This Christian focus does not go, however, for the perspective from which the articles are written. The contributors come from Christian as well as Jewish backgrounds. Although most of them are American, some European women are included together with a Central-American (Elsa Tamez) and Australian scholar (Elisabeth Wainwright).

The books discussed have been arranged by genre under three headings. Part I includes 'revelatory discourses', Part II 'epistolary discourses:' and Part III 'biographical discourses'. The common theme of all three parts, however, is Sophia. The "open, cosmic house of divine Wisdom" is used as "a positive image for the function of scripture in feminist struggles to transform religion and society." (p.9) Therefore, Part I is also titled 'Manifestations of Sophia'; Part II: 'Submerged Traditions of Sophia'; Part III: 'Essays of Sophia'.

Over against the image of the closed garden surrounded by the canonical walls of exclusion erected by the 'fathers', Fiorenza thus sets the image of Wisdom's dwelling without walls. As Eve climbed over the garden's wall to meet Lilith, feminist interpretation must overcome canonical boundaries, not to erect new ones but to roam in an interpretive open space without boundaries. Searching the Scriptures is a step in this direction. It makes scholarly feminist research on the New Testament visible and a number of extra-canonical sources accessible to a broader public. It takes us one step further.

Caroline Vander Stichele, Amsterdam

II.2. Kirchengeschichte - Church History - Histoire ecclésiastique

Anneliese Felber
Harmonie durch Hierarchie? Das Denken der Geschlechter-Ordnung im frühen Christentum, Wiener Frauenverlag: Wien 1994.

Harmonie durch Hierarchie? ist eine Anfrage an das Denken der Geschlechterordnung im frühen Christentum; eine Studie zum Stellenwert des Weiblichen und der Frau. In sieben Kapiteln geht die Autorin dabei zu Werk: Kapitel 1 beschäftigt sich mit der Thematik des schöpfungsmäßigen Minderwertes der Frau; welcher eine Übertragung von der biologischen auf die intellektuelle Ebene erfahren hat - wie in Kapitel 2 aufgezeigt wird. Die

daraus resultierende sozial-ökonomische Unterordnung der Frau wird in Kapitel 3 beleuchtet. Der Institution Ehe, in der die Geschlechterhierarchie besonders deutlich zum Tragen kommt, widmet sich Kapitel 4. 'In jeder Frau ist Eva' nennt sich das 5. Kapitel, das die Untermauerung der moralischen Inferiorität alles Weiblichen mittels der Sündenfallgeschichte (Gen 3) untersucht. Kapitel 6 beschäftigt sich mit der Frage: 'Die Gottebenbildlichkeit: Privileg des Mannes?'. Mit den all diesen Überlegungen zugrunde liegenden Wertbegriffen 'männlichweiblich' setzt sich abschließend Kapitel 7 auseinander. Die vorliegende Arbeit unternimmt eine Art Systematisierung der Denkstrukturen, die christlichen Autoren in der Zeit von ca. 100 - 500 n. Chr. bestimmen. Dabei wird immer wieder auf den normativen Charakter der Bibel, ihren wesentlichen Einfluß bezüglich der Legitimierung der Unterordnung der Frau hingewiesen, genauso wie auch auf geistiges Erbe und Einflüsse aus der Umwelt, die zu Fixierungen im Geschlechterverhältnis führten. Dadurch, daß die Autorin die christlichen Autoren in zahlreichen Zitaten immer wieder für sich selber sprechen läßt, gelingt es vorliegendem Werk in sehr anschaulicher Weise, die ideengeschichtliche Linie nachzuzeichnen, und zwar derart, daß die enorme Wirkungsgeschichte dieser frühchristlichen Texte bis ins Hier und Jetzt deutlich spürbar wird. Und damit eröffnet die Untersuchung, die primär als eine Studie zum negativen Frauenbild christlicher Tradition konzipiert wurde, auch neue Perspektiven - als eine Art geistiges Sprungbrett hin zu Frauen als denkende, handelnde, selbstbewußte und selbstbestimmte, ganz und gar nicht minderwertige Geschöpfe Gottes.
Elke Fahrner, Innsbruck

Theodor Schneider & Helen Schüngel-Straumann (Hg.)
Theologie zwischen Zeiten und Kontinenten. Festschrift für Elisabeth Gössmann, Herder Verlag: Freiburg/Basel/Wien 1993.
Martina Appich et al. (Hg.)
Eine andere Tradition. Dissidente Positionen von Frauen in Philosophie und Theologie, Iudicium Verlag: München 1993.

Deux ouvrages, qui paraisssent simultanément, rendent hommage au docteur Elisabeth Gössmann à l'occasion de ses soixante-cinq ans. Les éditions Herder présentent le recueil officiel d'articles et papiers rédigés en son honneur. L'autre, moins volumineux, qui paraît chez Iudicium Verlag, reprend et résume les discussions du groupe réuni à Munich, où elle enseigna à partir de l'automne 1986.

La *Festschrift* rassemble une trentaine de textes d'un éclectisme tel que le critique doit se borner à ne commenter que ceux qui se trouvent dans son champ de compétence. Aussi je voudrais signaler mon désaccord avec la théorie avancée ici par le dr. Kari Børresen, et si largement répandue, que la recluse Julienne de Norwich devrait son érudition au fait qu'elle eût été bénédictine. Au quatorzième siècle le niveau de formation intellectuelle des mondiales connaissait déjà une détérioration importante. Par ailleurs, Julienne avait-elle une culture si académique? Ses écrits audacieux et créateurs sur la maternité divine jaillissent-ils de ses intuition profondes de femme (et peut-être de mère), plutôt que des leçons reçus des hommes?

Il est regrettable qu'un papier intéressant, traitant de la vie de Ste. Brigitte de Suède, rédigé en anglais, est gâché par de nombreuses erreurs d'orthographie.

Le dr. Heinrich Dumoulins SJ, dans un papier sur la femme dans le bouddhisme, constate que Gautama Buddha, à la différence de beaucoup de ses disciples mâles, ne dédaigna pas la compagnie des femmes et considéra qu'elles étaient aussi capables de l'éveil et de la libération spirituels que les hommes. Il nous fait remarquer que la misogynie n'investit qu'ultérieurement la tradition bouddhiste. Un air que nous connaissons bien!

Le dr. Otto Hermann Pesch, dans une critique sympathique mais perspicace, fait état du caractère superficiel des propos de certaines théologiennes féministes. Son essai nous apporte quelques charmantes touches d´humour, et il termine avec une hommage élégant à son illustre collège.

Ce livre, à prix élevé et hautement spécialisé, par la nature même de ses diverses contributions, trouvera sa place dans les rayons d´une bibliothèque universitaire plus facilement que chez le particulier.

Eine andere Tradition nous sert d'introduction à l'étude du rôle de la femme dans l'histoire culturelle de l'Europe, et du refus de certaines de s'assujettir à la tradition. Martina Appich décrit le chemin, en effet classique, parcouru par Angela de Foligno, à travers le 'vide' et 'la nuit obscure' pour découvrir sa vraie identité en Dieu. Dans son exposé sur Gertrude la Grande, Elisabeth FischerFeckl tire notre attention sur le fait que Gertrude doit sa grandeur à sa compétence théologique qu'à son abandon du 'soi' et à son 'éveil', qui la rendaient capable d'expérimenter ce qui est inaccessible à l'intelligence rationnelle et qui reste nécessairement théorique dans les livres de théologie. Chose curieuse, la théologie féministe, préoccupée souvent par la quête des images de Dieu et du soi, ignore, jusqu'aujourd'hui, l'élément apophatique dans toute tradition spirituelle qu'elle soit chrétienne ou autre. Ce n'est qu'au niveau 'intégratif' (terme de Jean Gebser), que se trouvent l'identité authentique et la libération totale, autant pour les femmes que pour les hommes.

A la fin de la *Festschrift*, le dr. Helen Schüngel-Straumann évoque brièvement la vocation de théologienne d'Elisabeth Gössmann au sein d'une église patriarcale, vocation fortement marquée par des épreuves et des frustrations, qui ne l'ont jamais détournée du chemin choisi. Celles qui ont l'ambition courageuse de la suivre auront besoin non seulement des mêmes qualifications, mais aussi de la même ténacité, du même refus de baisser les bras. Elisabeth Gössmann mérite, ô combien, l'hommage de ces deux ouvrages qui l'honorent.

Margaret Collier-Bendelow, Remoulins

Marion Kobelt-Groch
Aufsässige Töchter Gottes. Frauen im Bauernkrieg und in der Täuferbewegung, (Geschichte und Geschlechter, Bd. 4), Campus-Verlag: Frankfurt am Main 1993.

Frauen haben in Zeiten des gesellschaftlichen und religiösen Umbruchs "auffallend oft im Rampenlicht" (S. 17) gestanden - dies ist eine der Erkenntnisse der historischen Frauenforschung, die sich auch für die sozial-religiösen Bewegungen im Gefolge der Reformation bestätigt. Auf der Grundlage von Quellen zum Bauernkrieg und zur Täuferbewegung (ca. 1520-45) geht Kobelt-Groch der Frage nach Motivation, Art und Umfang der Beteiligung von Frauen nach. In den Bauernaufständen widersetzten sich Frauen als einzelne, aber auch in organisierten Frauengruppen der Obrigkeit; angesichts der wirtschaftlichen und sozialen Bedrückung war es für sie offenbar selbstverständlich, diese Kämpfe nicht allein den Männern zu überlassen (S. 34-63). In den radikal-reformatorischen Bewegungen der Täufer bildeten Frauen den größten Teil der Anhängerschaft, wenn auch die Führungspositionen von Männern besetzt wurden. Zu den wenigen Frauen, die Aufsehen erregten, gehört die Münsteraner Täuferin Hille Feicken, die in Nachahmung der alttestamentlichen Judith einen Attentatsversuch auf den Erzbischof unternahm und dafür hingerichtet wurde. An ihrem Beispiel

gelingt Kobelt-Groch eine - auch mit Vermutungen und Möglichkeiten spielende - faszinierende Rekonstruktion weiblicher Alltagswelt im Täuferreich (S. 64-132). Welches Selbstbewußtsein und welche Freiräume Frauen gewinnen konnten, wenn sie sich - in Radikalisierung der reformatorischen Theologie - unabhängig von allen irdischen (männlichen) Instanzen auf die unmittelbare Autorität Gottes beriefen, wird ebenfalls deutlich an dem Eheverständnis der TäuferInnen (S. 133-146, am Beispiel Halberstadt) und ihrer Deutung des "Priestertums aller Gläubigen" (S. 147-163): Frauen verließen wegen ihres Glaubens ihren Ehemann und wandten sich neuen gemeinschaftlichen Lebensformen zu, sie 'hielten Messe', 'lasen' und 'predigten'. Auf lange Sicht wurden die Möglichkeiten der Frauen jedoch wieder beschnitten, die Geschlechterhierarchie wiederhergestellt, "Mechanismen der Verdrängung" wurden wirksam (S. 161-163) - eine Verdrängung, die von Männern ausging, der aber die Frauen offenbar keinen nennenswerten Widerstand entgegensetzten. War es Resignation? Erzwungene Anpassung? Oder bewußte Distanz gegenüber männlichen Organisation- und Herrschaftsformen? Nicht zuletzt diese Fragen sind es, die das spannende Buch (eigentlich eine Dissertation) nicht nur für TheologInnen und HistorikerInnen, sondern für 'aufsässige Frauen' überhaupt lesenswert machen.
Anne Conrad, Heppenheim

II.3. Ekklesiologie, Frauen im Amt - Ekklesiology, Women's ordination - Ecclésiologie, ordination des femmes

Letty M. Russell
Church in the Round. Feminist Interpretation of the Church, John Knox Press: Louisville 1993.

Dieses Buch ist der Entwurf einer Lehre von der Kirche aus feministischer Perspektive. Letty Russell möchte, daß christliche Feministinnen nach dem Lesen dieses Buches sagen können: 'Dies ist die Kirche, nach der ich mich sehne und für die ich zu kämpfen bereit bin' (S.14).

In allen drei Teilen des Buches wird der runde Tisch als Bild für die verschiedenen Aspekte einer Ekklesiologie benutzt: Der runde Tisch ist Symbol für Gastfreundschaft, Solidarität und Verbundenheit. Theologisches

Tafelgespräch bedeutet für Russell, sich in eine theologische Spirale von Engagement und Reflexion (S. 30ff.) zu begeben: Ausgehend von einer Grundhaltung der Verbundenheit aller werden am runden Tisch bisher ungehörte Stimmen gehört und Erfahrungen miteinander geteilt; diese Erfahrungen werden dann im Lichte ihres jeweiligen Kontextes kritisch reflektiert. Von einem auf diesem Hintergrund neu bestimmten Standpunkt werden Fragen an Bibel und Tradition gestellt, mit dem Ziel, neue Einsichten in die Bedeutung des Evangeliums als frohmachende Botschaft für alle, insbesondere für bisher an den Rand Gedrängte zu gewinnen. Ein solches, neu gewonnenes Verständnis der Tradition führt zu Aktion, Feier und zu fortgesetzter Reflexion in der theologischen Spirale.

Neben der Darlegung ihres methodologischen Ausgangspunktes befaßt Letty Russell sich im ersten Teil mit der Art der Leitungsdienste im Rahmen einer feministichen Ekklesiologie. Die Frage, ob das Amt sich ändert, wenn Frauen es ausüben - ob Frauen z.B. menschennäher oder beziehungsfreudiger sind - möchte Russell mit Vorsicht behandelt wissen; zu leicht könnten alte Weiblichkeitsstereotype nunmehr in Amts-Kleidung verpackt werden. Russell bevorzugt die Suche nach bereits vorhandenenen Rollenvorbildern, die zeigen, wie Autorität ausgeübt werden kann, die sich als in der Gemeinschaft verwurzelt und solidarisch mit Außenseitern versteht. Ein solches Rollenvorbild findet sie in der Prophetin Miriam, die durch ihr Auftreten patriarchalabsolute Autorität anprangert (Numeri 12,2). Die Ausübung von Leitung bzw. Autorität sollte jedoch gerade Partnerschaft oder Gemeinschaft ermöglichen, indem Menschen dazu befähigt werden, ihre Zungen zu lösen und ihre ureigenste Sprache zu sprechen, ihre eigene Geschichte auszudrükken und dies als von Gott geschenkte Gaben zu betrachten.

Im zweiten Teil steht die konkrete Art und Weise im Blickpunkt, wie eine Gemeinschaft Solidarität teilen kann mit denen, die Unterdrückung und Ausschluß erleiden. Russell nennt dies die "Küchentisch-Solidarität"; wo sie praktiziert wird, verändert sich Kirchesein. Der letzte Teil spezifiziert den Tisch näherhin als Tisch der Gastfreundschaft. Russell geht in diesem Abschnitt auf die Veränderungen ein, die eine Ekklesiologie berücksichtigen muß, wenn sie wirklich davon ausgeht, daß *alle* eingeladen sind, an diesem Tisch Platz zu nehmen und zu essen.

Der runde Tisch als Bild für die Kirche ist eine gelungene Metapher: Althergebrachte Konnotationen wie die Kirchwerdung einer Gemeinschaft durch das gemeinsame eucharistische Mahl werden beibehalten, gleichzeitig

wird der Tisch aber auch mitten ins Leben, mitten in die Küchen und Wohnplätze von Menschen gestellt und gezeigt, wie sehr materielle und geistliche Nahrung zusammengehören.
Angela Berlis, Bonn

Jean Mercier
Des femmes pour le Royaume de Dieu, ed. Albin Michel, Paris 1994.

On lit ce livre avec plaisir: je l'ai trouvé captivant comme un roman. Jean Mercier est journaliste. Laissant à d'autres des études académiques ou proprement théologiques sur l'ordination des femmes-prêtres, il a voulu écrire un livre pragmatique, qui rassemble les témoignages de dix femmes de l'Eglise d'Angleterre avant leur ordination à Cantorbéry au printemps 1994. Il nous donne ainsi l'occasion de rencontrer Joyce Bennet, Susan Cole-King, Juliet Woollcombe, Nerissa Jones, Alison Meere, Clare Nicholson, Katherine Rumens, Faith Claringbull, Dilly Baker and Sally Theakstone, dont le seul point commun est la nationalité anglaise. A partir de situations variées, elles racontent leur foi, leurs difficultés, leurs joies... et leur vocation de prêtrise.

On chercherait en vain dans ce livre des arguments pour ou contre l'ordination des femmes. C'est par la réalité de leur présence et par leur travail (considérable) que ces femmes invitent à la conversion. Jean Mercier raconte, par exemple, comment Hugh Montefiore, évêque de Birmingham, fut gagné à la cause des femmes-prêtres en assistant à une eucharistie célébrée à Hong Kong en 1964: il apprit, après coup, que "le" prêtre était une femme (chinoise). Il s'est ainsi rendu compte de l'absurdité de ses préjugés contre la prêtrise féminine.

En lisant les témoignages de ces femmes, on sent à quel point elles sont à même d'apporter un changement au sein de l'Eglise, aussi simplement et naturellement que le levain qui lève la pâte.

L'enquête auprès des femmes est précédée par une introduction historique, volontairement limitée aux Eglises d'Angleterre et de Hong Kong. On y apprend que la première ordination de femme-prêtre dans la Communion anglicane eut lieu à Hong Kong en 1944 et que deux autres femmes furent ordonnées en 1971, aussi à Hong Kong. Ces femmes n'étaient ni féministes, ni personnellement ambitieuses, elles ne visaient pas nécessairement la prêtrise: les évêques qui les ont ordonnées étaient plutôt de tendance conservatrice. Leur dévouement et leur générosité à l'égard de leurs communautés ecclésiales, les besoins de ces mêmes communautés, la lucidité et le courage des évêques face à leur conscience ont été les éléments décisifs: la prêtrise s'est imposée comme le seul moyen de permettre aux femmes de continuer à remplir la place qu'elles avaient prise au sein de leurs communautés.

En présentant les faits ainsi, Jean Mercier ne cherche nullement à diminuer le rôle du fémininisme dans le combat pour l'ordination des femmes. Bien au contraire. Reste à lui faire une petite reproche: l'utilisation du "franglais" qui s'infiltre dans son texte, fruit sans doute de sa grande plongée dans le monde anglican.

Mary Phil Korsak, Bruxelles

Martine Bakema & Lies Sluis (ed.)
Een ander ambt. Vijfentwintig jaar vrouwen in het ambt van de Gereformeerde Kerken in Nederland, Kok: Kampen 1994.

Im November 1994 waren es 25 Jahre her, daß die Synode der 'Gereformeerden Kerk' in den Niederlanden die Ämter für Frauen zugänglich machte. Die Gereformeerde Kerk entstand im letzten Jahrhundert aus der Trennung von der reformierten Kirche, die lange Zeit niederländische Staatskirche war. Anläßlich des 25jährigen Jubiläums der Einbeziehung von Frauen in die Ämter erschien das Buch "Ein anderes Amt". Darin wird auf gut lesbare Weise auf die Vorgeschichte des Beschlusses eingegangen; im zweiten Teil werden Erfahrungen von Amtsträgerinnen beschrieben und im dritten Teil Perspektiven für die Zukunft entworfen.

Um das Jahr 1930 herum fing die Diskussion um die Einbeziehung von Frauen in die Ämter an. Die Frage, ob Frauen Autorität über Männer ausüben dürften, spielte anfangs eine wichtige Rolle. Nach und nach änderte sich jedoch die Position von Frauen in der Gesellschaft und Kirche. In den sechziger Jahren war auch die inhaltliche Formgebung der Ämter verändert; die Ausübung von Disziplinargewalt trat in den Hintergrund. Dadurch wurde undeutlich, was zum Aufgabenbereich von Amtsträgern gehörte. Die Öffnung der Ämter für Frauen im Jahr 1969 folgte diesen historischen Entwicklungen.

Aus den Erfahrungsberichten ist ersichtlich, daß Frauen den Ämtern gegenüber ambivalente Gefühle hegen. Einerseits erhalten sie dadurch die Möglichkeit, sich zu profilieren; dies geschieht vor allem auf dem Gebiet der sorgenden Aufgaben. Andererseits fühlen Frauen sich im Bereich von

Amtsführung und Liturgie oft unsicher. Diese Unsicherheit wird durch die Undeutlichkeit bezüglich der inhaltlichen Formgebung der Ämter, die seit 25 Jahren besteht, noch verstärkt.

Wer wissen will, welche Mechanismen dabei eine Rolle spielen, der/dem möchte ich die Lektüre dieses Buch herzlich empfehlen. Die Zusammenstellung der verschiedenen Artikel bietet gute Ansätze für eine Besinnung auf eine Neudefinition der Ämter. Es erscheint mir wichtig, daß Frauen sich auf der Ebene von Amtsführung und Organisation in die Diskussion über die Ämter einmischen, die im Augenblick in der Gereformeerde Kirche geführt wird. Der Anlaß dieser Diskussion ist die fortschreitende Zusammenarbeit der Gereformeerde Kerk, der reformierten Kirche und der lutherischen Kirche in den Niederlanden.

Annie Hasker, Zwolle

II.4. Praktische Theologie - Pastoral Theology - Théologie pastorale

Elaine Graham & Margaret Halsey (ed.)
Life Cycles. Women and Pastoral Care, SPCK: London 1993.
Valerie M. De Marinis
Critical Caring. A Feminist Model for Pastoral Psychology, Westminster/John Knox Press: Louisville 1993.

Women always played an important role in pastoral theological literature: they were the counselees, examples of incompetent human beings, unable to organize their lives as 'normally' adjusted persons. In a research about the sex of counselees in the books of Heye Faber and Charles V.Gerkin, both widely read pastoral theologians, I found that significantly more counselees were of the female sex. (See my forthcoming book The Incredible Woman, Abingdon Press, Nashville 1996).

Since about five years ago women play different roles in pastoral literature: as theory-makers and as counselors in a different voice. It took a rather long time before Womenstudies in practical/pastoral theology emerged. One reason could be that pastoral practice takes place in the realm of the churches, a place considered by many feminist theologians as risky and better to be avoided. But many women still long to find direction for their lives in the

Christian tradition - as in other religious traditions. When the anger of negation and hurt developed their rightful place in women's consciousness, room was made to think about a pastoral care that really helps women in their daily lives, longing not to lose their foothold in God/dess.

I will mention here some books, which are typical for the emerging feminist pastoral theological literature. One is a collection of essays: Life Cycles. Women and Pastoral Care, edited by Elaine Graham and Margaret Halsey, the other is a monograph: Critical Caring. A Feminist Model for Pastoral Psychology by Valerie M. De Marinis.

The collection of essays - an often chosen means of forming a choir of different voices - explores how women give and receive pastoral care. A definite theological methodology is chosen: the concrete and particular changes and developments in women's lives provide the starting point for theological reflections, the assumption being that the specific may be of relevance in a more general context. Reflections on the way women in their particular circumstances try to give meaning to their lives may contribute to a new understanding of Christian faith and the practice of the churches. The touchstone for Christian truth-claims is found in the faith-communities, where human beings, including the culturally and socially marginalized, experience care, support, and a glimpse of life abundant. Pastoral practice is supposed to embody these truth-claims (page 222). Pastoral counseling is understood as being broader than one-to-one conversation: it can be understood as reflection on, and practice of, care and support that members of a church can give each other in a Christian community (page 1). In this book 'women' are looked upon as human beings, socialized by cultural and religious contexts to become dependent, without much opportunity to find their strengths. 'The womb' is not celebrated in this book. Although we hear the voices of single women (of various cultures), lesbian women, mothers, and daughters of aged and senile mothers - positions that involve pain and struggle in a culture and church that looks upon women as dutiful daughters, charming wives and self-sacrificing mothers - the book is written in a matter-offactly and sometimes even a very, very slightly humorous pitch.

Valerie DeMarinis looks for a feminist model for pastoral psychology. Her book is divided in two parts. In part one she constructs her model of Critical Caring. In part two she gives four elaborate case studies, illustrating her model. A cornerstone of the book is found on page 27: "Critical Caring understands human nature as instinctual". Instinct denotes "natural or spontaneous inclinations or tendencies in human beings, that which is innate and basic to human nature" (page 28). According to DeMarinis the fundamental human instincts are the relational instinct and the religious instinct. These two instincts are both understood by the author as fundamentally positive: the one to experience love, to give and receive care and to perceive a connection within the self (body and spirit); the other to nurture the ability to hope, question, embrace chaos and doubt, to trust the universe and to experience a sense of connection between God, others and self. Assuming these (positive) instincts, the author asks the question: "Can a hermeneutical foundation create a worldview that understands and nurtures the relational and religious instincts?" The answer is: "a feminist hermeneutic can create such a worldview" (page 34). In her model of Critical Caring the feminist hermeneutic renders a strategy to nurture the basic instincts and to remove blockades.

I look forward to the opportunity to discuss this with DeMarinis. Is her understanding of the human being not too essentialist and too optimistic? Can we ever discern 'naked instincts' in human beings, or do we meet only culturally constructed inclinations? How about the theological concept of (original) sin? I admire DeMarinis' aims at a critical pastoral psychology that opens a way to healthy functioning, both as a relational and a religious human being, in both men and women. Feminism is supposed to be not only good for women, but for men and women, being a critique on the culture as a whole, as Catharina Halkes frequently argued. But doesn't DeMarinis look upon feminism as too unison? Isn't feminism in itself a choir of different voices?

Riet Bons-Storm, Groningen

II.5.   Ethik - Ethics and Moral Theology - Ethique et théologie morale

Annemarie Pieper
Aufstand des stillgelegten Geschlechts. Einführung in die feministische Ethik, Herder Verlag: Freiburg/Basel/Wien 1993.

Schon von Annemarie Piepers vielgelesener 'Einführung in die praktische Philosophie' (München 1985) wissen wir, daß sie komplexe Sachverhalte verständlich darzustellen weiß. Ich finde es verdienstvoll, daß die Basler Philosophieprofessorin jetzt eine 'Einführung in die feministische Ethik' vorlegt hat. Dieses kleine Buch macht es möglich, sich in kurzer Zeit über die wesentlichen Fragestellungen der feministischen Ethik zu informieren.

Pieper setzt als Ausgangspunkt der feministischen Ethik das Problem der Geschlechterdifferenz, das von Denkerinnen wie Simone de Beauvoir, Luce Irigaray, Judith Butler u.a. - auf durchaus unterschiedliche Weise - zum Angelpunkt eines anderen, herkömmliche Denkweisen grundsätzlich in Frage stellenden Diskurses gemacht wird. In einem zweiten Kapitel befaßt sie sich in einem kompetenten Durchgang durch die europäische Philosophiegeschichte mit dem hartnäckig in den verschiedensten Denksystemen sich haltenden Androzentrismus, weist aber auch auf mögliche Anknüpfungspunkte für feministische Theoriebildung, z.B. im postmodernen Denken, hin.

Schließlich stellt sie die Ansätze einiger profilierter feministischer Ethikerinnen vor. Wegweisend scheint mir dabei zu sein, daß sie die feministische Ethik *nicht* auf die von Carol Gilligan angestoßenen Diskussion über eine 'weibliche Moral' reduziert, sondern drei Modelle - das theologische, das entwicklungspsychologische und das philosophische - unterscheidet und so die Denkbewegung feministischer Ethik auf eine breite Basis stellt. Zwar wird sie der Komplexität des Denkens etwa einer Mary Daly nicht gerecht - die neueren Bücher werden lediglich am Rande erwähnt. Der Sinn einer Einführung liegt aber auch weniger in der Detailgenauigkeit als vielmehr darin, ein Gebiet vollständig zu erfassen, plausibel zu systematisieren und Querverbindungen zwischen den einzelnen Denkrichtungen herzustellen. All dies scheint mir in Annemarie Piepers Einführung bestens gelungen zu sein.

Ina Praetorius, Krinau/CH

Heidi Bernhard Filli, Andrea Günter, Maren Jochimsen, Ulrike Knobloch, Ina Praetorius, Lisa Schmuckli, Ursula Vock
Weiberwirtschaft. Frauen - Ökonomie - Ethik, Edition Exodus: Luzern 1994.

"Weiberwirtschaft" heißt die jetzt bei Edition Exodus in Luzern erschienene zweite Buchpublikation der 'Projektgruppe Ethik im Feminismus'. Die Auseinandersetzung der Theologinnen, Philosophinnen und Ökonominnen mit Wirtschaft geht aus von der Beobachtung der Fremdheit, die Frauen dem

Wirtschaftsbereich gegenüber empfinden. Diese Distanz wird von den Autorinnen entschlüsselt als Konsequenz einer androzentrischen symbolischen Ordnung, die Frauen aus dem Bereich des Ökonomischen ausschließt. Demgegenüber ist es Zielsetzung der Gruppe, "unerzähltes Frauenleben zur Sprache zu bringen" und zu "enttrivialisieren". Es geht also um feministische Dekonstruktionsarbeit an der androzentrischen symbolischen Ordnung und damit an der Sprache, wie schon im Titel deutlich wird: "Weiberwirtschaft", üblicherweise "ein pejorativer Begriff, wird zur programmatischen "Bezeichnung für die ökonomischen Tätigkeiten der Frauen, die in der offiziellen Theorie nicht vorkommen" (26). Er soll das ökonomische Handeln beschreiben, das aus der Beziehung unter Frauen entsteht, Frau/en repräsentiert und Frau/en dient (19).

Um das bisher vernachlässigte ökonomische Handeln von Frauen zu beschreiben, plädieren Maren Jochimsen und Ulrike Knobloch in ihrem Beitrag "Auf dem Weg zu einer vorsorgenden Wirtschaftsweise" für eine doppelte ethische Erweiterung der zweckrationalen Perspektive um die von der Ökonomie in Anspruch genommenen nicht-zweckrationalen Grundlagen (Respektierung des Gegenübers als KommunikationspartnerIn sowie Funktionieren ökologischer Kreisläufe) als auch um den Gegenstandsbereich der von Frauen getätigten Haushaltsökonomie des Erhaltens/Unterhaltens. Im vorsorgenden Wirtschaften der Frauen sind ökonomische Prinzipien zu finden, die sich von denen der Marktwirtschaft unterscheiden und einen Ausweg aus der derzeitigen globalen Krisensituation aufzeigen können; es sind dies die Orientierung am Lebensnotwendigen, das Vorsorgeprinzip und Kooperation statt Konkurrenz. Diese Prinzipien der vorsorgenden Ökonomie thematisiert auch die in den Band aufgenommene Predigt von Ursula Vock zu 1. Könige 17,8-16.

Ein weiterer Aufsatz von Lisa Schmuckli befaßt sich mit der Ökonomisierung von Zeit und Zeitstrukturen von Frauen. Am Beispiel eines konkreten Falles analysiert Andrea Günter Kriterien zur Verteilung öffentlicher Gelder und das Verhältnis von Frauen und Geld. Heidi Bernhard Filli legt in ihrem Beitrag das für Frauen nutzbare kritische Potential des radikalen Konstruktivismus dar. Der Aufsatz von Ina Praetorius "Kandinsky im Badezimmer" macht eine von einer Studentin geschriebene Alltagsgeschichte zur Grundlage von Überlegungen zur Enttrivialisierung von Frauenleben. Ein Beitrag über die Geschichte der Projektgruppe 'Ethik im Feminismus' rundet den Band ab.

Was diese feministische Auseinandersetzung mit Wirtschaft besonders spannend macht, ist der Mut, gegen die ökonomischen Theorietraditionen Frauenerfahrung konsequent zum Ausgangspunkt zu machen - bei gleichzeitiger Identifizierung von Berührungspunkten mit anderen neuen Theorieansätzen wie etwa einer grundlagenkritischen Wirtschaftsethik.
Ulrike Wagener, Münster

II.6. Religionswissenschaften - Religious Studies - Etudes religieuses

Ursula King (ed.)
Feminist Theology from the Third World, Maryknoll/Orbis: New York 1994.

In this volume, Ursula King presents us with a reader on third world theologies. One of the characteristics of feminist theology in general and of third world feminist theology in particular is its rootedness in the concrete experience and the existential context of women. Although there may be some similarities in the dynamics of oppression and suffering, that context differs radically for women from Latin America, Asia, and Africa. King has nevertheless attempted to classify the different articles, poems and excerpts which appear in this volume around certain topics.

Part one deals with "Doing Theology from a Third World Women's Perspective". The texts selected for this part deal mainly with general theological and methodological issues. Kwok Pui-Lan offers here an interesting Asian feminist critique of the existing paradigms in the theology of religions. While the exclusivist paradigm is associated with religious imperialism and sexism, the inclusivist model is also found wanting because it tends to overlook real differences. She thus argues for a pluralist model and within this for a rediscovery of the language of the erotic. In this part, terms such as "womanist" and "mujerista" theology are also explained. The latter refers to a "Hispanic woman who struggles to liberate herself not as an individual but as a member of the Hispanic community.

Part two of the volume is entitled "Women's Oppression and Cries of Pain" and deals with such concrete forms of oppression of women in the third world countries as prostitution and rape, the difficulties for women to acquire a decent education, and the triple subjugation of women through sex, race and class. Here, it is pointed out that increases in prostitution and violence against women may be directly related to the materialism, development and militarism of the first world.

Part three deals with the Bible as a source of the empowerment of women. It points not only to inspiring female figures of the Bible, but also to ways of reinterpretation of well-known biblical texts, and to possible exegeses and sermons which may be derived from the texts. Elsa Tamez points here to the problem of the revealed authority of the scripture, on the one hand, and the sexist ideas in it, on the other. The hermeneutical key which is generally proposed is based on the idea that God is on the side of the poor and the oppressed.

In the fourth part, entitled "Challenging Traditional Theological Thinking", articles have been collected which represent a more direct attack upon or challenge to traditional theological methods and theories. New theological ideas developed here include the Spirit as female, God as mother, as an immanent and creative reality, or God as community rather than as an individual. New life is also given to Mariology. The last part, on "Liberating Spirituality", mainly emphasizes Asian women and their approach to God as womb, as creative, nurturing and caring. As in the theological part, the accent here is on community and creation. Inspiration is also drawn from such traditional religious symbols and figures as the shamaness, the African indigenous healer, and the goddess Kwan Yin.

An anthology such as the one presented in this volume seems particularly suited to represent feminist theology of the third world. It reflects the great diversity of situations and voices which feminist theology seeks to preserve and celebrate. While only a sample of the available material could be included, Ursula King begins every chapter with suggestions for further reading on the topic. However, the general structure of the book in five parts seems rather artificial and arbitrary. Most of the articles could have been classified under at least two or three of the headings. In might have been more interesting to classify the articles according to their lived contexts so that the diversity of concrete starting points for doing theology and the variety of responses to these situations would have come more to the fore. As it is, however, the volume offers a very helpful and appropriate companion to Ann Loads' Reader on *Feminist Theology*, as it set out to be.
Catherine Cornille, Leuven

II.7. Religionspädagogik - Religious Education - Pédagogie religieuse

Petra Schulz
Versuche dialogischen Denkens in einer feministisch orientierten
religionspädagogischen Praxis, Peter Lang Verlag: Frankfurt/M./-
Bern/New York 1994.

Ausgangspunkt dieser Untersuchung ist die Frage, wie es möglich ist,
"feministisches Selbstverständnis" in den Religionsunterricht einzubringen.
"Feministisches Selbstverständnis" meint zum einen die feministische Identität
der Lehrerin, zum anderen pädagogische Inhalte, wie das Aufdecken
sexistischer Strukturen im Alltag. Dieses Anliegen bettet die Autorin in
Martin Bubers pädagogisch-philosophisches Konzept des dialogischen
Denkens ein.

Bubers Ansatz eignet sich aus verschiedenen Gründen. Sein Konzept ist
keine Technik, sondern eine "grundsätzliche Möglichkeit mit der Welt in
Beziehung zu treten" (S. 16). Auch geht es in Bubers Konzept nicht primär
um Wissensvermittlung, sondern um eine Beziehung zwischen Lehrenden und
Lernenden. "Zwischen dialogischem Denken und Feministischer Theologie
lassen sich zum einen Parallelen entdecken, die ihre partielle Nähe ausweisen.
Zum andern trägt ihre Verbindung zu einer äußerst fruchtbaren Weiterfüh-
rung des jeweiligen Ansatzes dergestalt bei, daß dialogisches Denken von
(unbewußter) patriarchaler Ausdeutung, Feministische Theologie vor
ideologischer Enge und damit verbundener Beziehungslosigkeit bewahrt wird"
(S. 53).

Schulz' Forschungsansatz ist ein feministischer, d.h. es geht der Autorin
nicht um eine scheinbar objektive Analyse des schulischen Religionsunterrichtes, sondern sie bringt sich bewußt als Subjekt in diesen Prozeß ein,
indem sie von ihren eigenen Erfahrungen als Lehrerin ausgeht und diese
kritisch im Licht Buber'scher Philosophie reflektiert. Petra Schulz ist
parteilich, insofern als es ihr darum geht, ganz als Frau mit feministischen
Interessen im Religionsunterricht vorzukommen: "... Analyse geschieht um
der befreienden Aktion willen" (S. 22). Die Praxis wird hier nicht nur
reflektiert, um zu einer Theorie zu gelangen, sondern auch um zu einer
besseren Praxis zu kommen.

Daher ist der letzte Teil ihrer Dissertation: "Möglichkeiten schulpraktischer Konkretion", in dem es um die Umsetzung der gewonnenen Erkenntnisse geht, der spannendste. Da dialogisches Denken situativ und personal geprägt ist, stellt Schulz in diesem Abschnitt keine Unterrichtseinheit vor, sondern beschreibt Situationen, in denen sie dialogisches Denken in ihrer Praxis erlebte, bzw. wo sie als Lehrende auf Probleme stieß. "Dialogisches Denken ist nicht planbar. Es ereignet sich in der Situation in einem Zusammenspiel von Wille und Gnade" (S. 84). Auch wenn es nicht planbar ist, so gibt es dennoch bestimmte Voraussetzungen, die ein dialogisches Geschehen möglich machen. Hierzu gehören: Selbstwerdung, Beziehungsfähigkeit und Gestaltung. Selbstwerdung heißt, daß die Lehrende als ganze Person im Unterricht vorkommt und nicht nur eine Rolle spielt - sei es die der Supermutter oder die der professionellen emanzipierten Frau - bzw. daß sie versucht, sich auf die Vermittlung von Wissen zu beschränken. Wichtig ist hierbei, daß es nicht darum geht, vollkommen zu sein, sondern einen Weg zu gehen, der der eigenen Persönlichkeit angemessen ist. Beziehungsfähigkeit bedeutet, Stärke in Auseinandersetzungen zu entwickeln, sowie Nähe und Distanz zuzulassen.

Der Autorin ist es gelungen, deutlich zu machen, daß Martin Bubers dialogisches Prinzip sich gerade für einen Religionsunterricht mit feministischen Intentionen eignet. Die Stärke dieser Arbeit besteht darin, daß die Autorin als Lehrerin über ihre Ziele, einen feministischen Religionsunterricht zu gestalten, nachdenkt und ihre eigene Praxis kritisch reflektiert. Dadurch kommen konkrete und reale Probleme des schulischen Alltags in den Blick.
Ursula Rudnick, Hannover

II.8. Anti-Judaismus - Anti-Judaism - Anti-judaïsme

Katharina von Kellenbach
Anti-Judaism in Feminist Religious Writings, Scholars Press: Atlanta/ Georgia 1994.

Katharina von Kellenbach ist eine der ersten Theologinnen gewesen, die auf das Problem des Antijudaismus in feministisch-theologischen Entwürfen aufmerksam gemacht hat. Ihr Buch, das eine Überarbeitung ihrer Dissertation darstellt, bietet einen klaren, systematisch aufgearbeiteten Einblick in antijudaistische Grundstrukturen und Argumentationsmuster, versucht deren Herkunft und Ursachen zu ergründen und zeigt Wege zu ihrer Überwindung auf.

Das Anliegen der Autorin ist es, deutlich zu machen, daß es sich bei der Frage nach dem christlichen Antijudaismus nicht lediglich um ein Randproblem oder Mißverständnis einzelner WissenschaftlerInnen handelt, sondern daß er die Grundstruktur christlicher Identität betrifft. Theologischer Antijudaismus sei eine der Wurzeln des rassistischen Antisemitismus und damit nicht zu verharmlosen. Sie beschreibt Anti-Judaismus als internationales Problem, das christliche Theologie insgesamt betrifft. Dennoch unterscheiden sich laut von Kellenbach die deutschen feministisch-theologischen Entwürfe durch eine stärker anti-jüdische Sprache und Symbolik von denen nordamerikanischer Feministinnen. Von Kellenbach führt dies auf den dort möglichen Austausch mit einem lebendigen Judentum zurück. Sehr eindrücklich beschreibt sie ihre ersten Berührungen mit Jüdinnen als deutsche Theologin in den USA: "As a critical person I had believed myself exempt from racial and religious bias. I had not been aware of any prejudgment until I met my first Jew. My views of Judaism had not revealed themselves as warped and distorted because they had never been measured by and compared with reality."(3). Die Stärke dieses Buches liegt für mich in der Eindringlichkeit und Aufrichtigkeit, mit der Katharina von Kellenbach sich dem Problem des Antijudaismus stellt. Es wird deutlich, daß es sich um einen schmerzhaften Prozeß handelt, der die eigene christliche Identität berührt. Sie möchte Strukturen aufdecken, die feministische Theologinnen aus der herrschenden Theologie 'geerbt' haben und weitertragen. Auch wenn sie diese Kritik an einzelnen Entwürfen festmacht, bedeutet dies nicht, daß damit der Anti-Judaismus einzelner angeprangert werden soll.

Den Hauptteil ihrer Arbeit bildet die Analyse der Aussagen, die das Judentum geringschätzen bzw. abwerten, die sie unter der Rubrik "Teaching of Contempt" behandelt. Hier sind drei grundsätzliche Argumentationsmuster festzustellen: Erstens, das Judentum wird als Antithese zum Christentum gesehen; zweitens, das Judentum wird zum Sündenbock gemacht; drittens, das Judentum bzw. das 'Alte' Testament wird lediglich als Prolog für das Christentum wahrgenommen. Die Möglichkeit einer Überwindung des Antijudaismus in der christlichen Theologie sieht von Kellenbach im Konzept des "Teaching of Respect". Dazu gehört nach ihr in erster Linie Kenntnis des Judentums, Wahrnehmung seiner Vielfältigkeit in der Periode des zweiten

Tempels sowie seiner geschichtlichen und religiösen Entwicklung bis in die Gegenwart. Das bedeutet auch, die jüdische Partikularität und eigenständige Identität zu akzeptieren und die Behauptung der Überlegenheit des christlichen Glaubens zurückzunehmen. Ein oberflächliches Bekenntnis reicht hier nicht aus, es müssen grundlegende Veränderungen in der Definition christlicher Identität vorgenommen werden. Ein unkritischer Philosemitismus oder eine unreflektierte Romantisierung werden dieser Aufgabe ebensowenig gerecht.

Dieses Buch stellt eine Herausforderung an alle theologisch Arbeitenden dar, sich in ihren Arbeitsbereichen die Frage nach antijudaistischen Denkschemata zu stellen. Für die häufig sehr emotional geführte Dabatte bietet es Hilfestellungen, ohne polemisch zu werden. Für die weitere Diskussion um den Antijudaismus in der (feministischen) Theologie ist es nun nötig, erarbeitete Ergebnisse und sich daraus ergebende neue Fragestellungen zusammenzutragen. Viele feministische Theologinnen haben bereits Schritte in diese Richtung getan. Der Weg in eine vollständig nicht-antijudaistische christliche Theologie - sollte es eine solche je geben - ist jedoch noch weit, wie die Arbeit von von Kellenbach deutlich macht. Sich dieser Aufgabe mit allen aus ihr erwachsenden Frustrationen, der Konfrontation mit Schuld, mit Scham und Zorn zu stellen, ermöglicht aber auch einen neuen Zugang zu den eigenen Traditionen und eröffnet die Perspektive eines Christentums, das sich nicht auf Kosten anderer und mittels ihrer Unterdrückung und Vernichtung definieren muß.

Claudia Janssen, Marburg

Epilog

Wir, eine Gruppe von Ausländerinnen in den Niederlanden machen ein Jahrbuch der Europäischen Gesellschaft für theologische Forschung von Frauen in Europa. Ist dieser Umstand überhaupt erwähnenswert, denn was unsere Arbeit betrifft, sind wir den Niederländerinnen gleich, arbeiten hier, weil die meisten von uns in ihren Vaterländern keine Arbeit in den theologischen Wissenschaften bekommen. Teils willig, teils freiwillig sind wir hier. Sind die Niederlanden deswegen unsere Heimat? Für manche ja, für manche nein. Europa, ist das ein Ausweg für Frauen, die nicht in ihrer Sprache und Kultur arbeiten und leben. Europa als ein Forum für 'ansässige Ausländerinnen', wie Elisabeth Schüssler Fiorenza sich als Deutsche in Amerika bezeichnet. Doch was in Europa schafft unseren gemeinsamen Kontext? Die Gesellschaft, die Frauenkirchebewegung, die 1996 ihre erste europäische Synode veranstaltet, die internationale Frauenbewegung? Die 'science community' feministischer Theologinnen?

Die Europäische Gesellschaft für theologische Forschung von Frauen stellt für uns ein Forum für Wissenschaftlerinnen und gewitzten Frauen in der Theologie aus verschiedenen Nationalitäten, Hierarchien, Traditionen und 'herstories'dar.Europa ist der gemeinsame geographische Kontext, Forschungs- und Bewegungspraxis unsere Passion, Theologie unser Rahmen. Es ist ein Forum, das sich durch unterschiedliche Erfahrungen, Einsichten und Machtgefälle auszeichnet. Es gibt ein West-Ost-Gefälle, ein ökonomisches Gefälle, ein Säkularisierungsgefälle und ein Professionalisierungsgefälle. Es gibt bestimmte historische Gegebenheiten, an denen wir als Europäerinnen nicht vorbei können (Kolonialismus, Antisemitismus, Fundamentalismus und Rassismus). Es gibt auch Kooperation, Patenschaften, Austausch, Freundschaften, gemeinsame Treffen zwischendurch, Lernen voneinander und Publizieren miteinander. Das Eigentliche geschieht zwischen den großen Konferenzen. Das Jahrbuch ist ein kleiner Schritt in diese Richtung, miteinander über nationale Grenzen hinweg zu kommunizieren, nicht mehr und nicht weniger.

Wir sind eine Gesellschaft jenseits dieser großen Prozessionen. Das Jahrbuch ist für uns ein Mittel, um in der großen Prozession ein bißchen anwesend zu sein, mit Themen, die in der großen Prozession keine Chance hätten. Wir haben von dieser Chance Gebrauch gemacht.

Angela Berlis

Wohnen in den Niederlanden, weilen in Deutschland, wo ich an einem theologichen Seminar arbeite, das ist meine Situation.

Der Zug in dem ich wöchentlich von A nach B fahre, verbindet zwei Welten, zwei Sprachen, zwei Kontexte. Ich bin keine "ansäßige Ausländerin", ich bin eine reisende Fremdgängerin.

Der Zug, in dem ich sitze, führt mir immer wieder meine Wurzeln und Visionen - besonders die über Kirchesein - vor Augen.

Ich engagiere mich in der Kirche, der ich angehöre und in der ich ein geistliches Amt bekleide und ich beteilige mich am feministischen Diskurs - beides tue ich in zwei Ländern. In beiden Ländern, beiden kirchlichen, theologischen und kulturellen Sprachspielen fühle ich mich zuhause und fremd zugleich.

Irgendwann ist mir bewußt geworden, daß viele feministische Frauen, die sich in ihrer Kirche zuhause fühlen (wollen), in ähnlchen Zügen sitzen wie ich.

Viele Frauen fühlen sich zuhause und fremd zugleich, sind vom alten Zuhause abgereist, aber noch nicht wieder angekommen. Das Dasein einer reisenden Fremdgängerin schärft den Blick und ölt die Stimme. Die Gabe der Unterscheidung wächst im reisenden Bewußtsein. Ich kann sehen und sagen, was mich befremdet und wo ich heimisch werde.

Übrigens verstehe ich jetzt auch immer besser, warum es in der Geschichte so viele Seherinnen und profetische Künderinnen gegeben hat...! Ihre Heimatlosigkeit schuf ihnen wohl den Raum für ihre u-topischen Visionen. Sie sind mir Weggenossinnen, der Chor ihrer Stimmen gibt meiner Stimme Heimat und ihre "prophetische Sukzession" (A. Jensen) läßt mich Wurzeln schlagen, die über mich selbst hinausreichen.

Fremdsein gehört zur Gabe des Unterscheidens, fremdeln schmerzt.

Es tut mir zum Beispiel weh, wenn manche in meiner Kirche meinen, die Frauenfrage sei mit der Einführung der Frauenordination "erledigt". Dann möchte ich rufen: "Werft nicht den Frauen eure Gewänder über, die euch auf den Leib geschnitten sind! Die Prozession wird ihre Form nicht ändern, wenn Frauen einfach eingefügt werden. ändert eure Gangart, ändert eure Blickrichtung. Laßt euch und eure Prozessionsordnung von der heiligen ruach zerzausen!"

Es tut mir aber auch weh, zu sehen, wie negativ manchmal feministische Theologinnen 'Kirche' erfahren und wie wenig Heil sie darin sehen, sich für eine Änderung der Strukturen einzusetzen. Auch ihnen möchte ich etwas zurufen, nämlich: "Deine Erfahrungen mit dieser Kirche sind erschreckend und entmutigend. Aber: Ist das nicht ein Zerrbild von Kirche, das auf deinen Körper geätzt wurde? Male ein neues Bild, klinke dich nicht aus, überlasse doch nicht einfach den schwarzgekleideten Schwarzmalern die Pinsel und die Farbtöpfe! Benutze deine Tünche und den Regenbogen deiner prophetischen Kraft, Frau, Schwester!" Fremdeln schmerzt. Eine der größten Herausforderungen an die feministische Theologie ist es meines Erachtens, unser Fremdeln aneinander miteinander auszuhalten und im Fremdsein einander Heimat zu werden.

Hedwig Meyer-Wilmes

Arbeiten in den Niederlanden, wohnen auf der deutschen Seite der Grenze. Lehraufträge an deutschen Universitäten, um den Kontakt nicht zu verlieren. Schreiben in zwei Sprachen, leben in zwei Sprachen, das ist meine Situation. 'Zweisprachigkeit' im breiten Sinne ist etwas, was meinen Weg kennzeichnet: als Bauerntochter in die Wissenschaft gehen, als christliche Feministin in die Politik, als Deutsche nach Nijmegen. 'Auf der Grenze' wohnen, denken, leben und rebellieren. Rebellion tut Not: in Deutschland kriegen Frauen beinahe keine Stellen an theologischen Fakultäten. In den Niederlanden wird feministische Theologie an den Fakultäten abgebaut. Gleichzeitig wächst die Zahl feministisch interessierter und religiös engagierter Frauen (-gruppen). Diese Frauen sind meistens zwischen 45 und 75. Ich fühle mich zuhause und ich fühle den Abstand. Meine Kollegen sind an feministischer Theologie interessiert, doch das reicht noch nicht für einen Austausch. Ich kenne ihren Diskussionszusammenhang, doch sie nicht den meinen.

Manchmal träume ich von einer Universität in der 'Stadt der Frauen'. Es ist eine Stadt auf der Grenze. Eine Stadt, die Frauen öffentlich Raum gibt, sie aus der Intimität der Gruppen herausführt. Mit Streit-, Gebets- und Gemeindehaus, Tanzpalast, Ruhewiesen, Theater, Museum, geräumigen Häusern, engen Höhlen und dem Duft von Kastanienbäumen.

Julie Hopkins

The question with which I have been confronted during the editing of this yearbook is the following: are we feminist theologians, by virtue of our collective work and goals, participants in 'Womenchurch'?

Inspite of the many articles I have read about 'Womenchurch', 'the ekklesia of women' and 'Christa community' I am still not convinced that it exists as anything more than a utopian goal or a mythic construct. Perhaps 'Womenchurch' is best understood very loosely as the collectivity of messianic, charismatic and liberational impulses and movements which resist the patriarchal tendency to institutionalise Christianity. But if this is the case, why use the term church/ekklesia to describe a critical impulse or movement? In my opinion the word 'ekklesia' cannot be deconstructed from two thousand years of ecclesiology simply by appealing to its ancient socio-political role in the Greek polis. What we found in Europe when we went in search of 'Womenchurch' was in practice a great diversity of women involved in disparate schools of theology and Christian tradition who are connecting with other feminists in networks and alliances of solidarity, spirituality and scholarship in order to resist different oppressive structures in religion and society. The Ruach blows where she will.

Caroline Vander Stichele

I'm on the move. Travelling from a small village in Flanders to big city Amsterdam. Different worlds, different lives. I want to have both.

I'm on the move. Making this spiritual voyage from a local Roman Catholic parish to an unlocated community of soulmates. Refusing to choose. I want to have it all.

I have it all. Living in rich Europe. I can travel, I don't have to flee for war or hunger. Torn apart by guilt and compassion. What can I do? What should I do? My roots in the 'First World', dreaming from just one world with justice for all: A green world.

I'm on the move. Wandering around. Staying and leaving, coming back to find the lost coin. Wisdom has build me a home, I share it with wonderful women.

I'm on the move. Leaving behind me the securities from the past. My old skin has grown too tight. I left it behind in the Garden and I move on.

EUROPEAN SOCIETY OF WOMEN IN THEOLOGICAL RESEARCH

EUROPÄISCHE GESELLSCHAFT FÜR THEOLOGISCHE FORSCHUNG VON FRAUEN

L'ASSOCIATION EUROPÉENNE DES FEMMES POUR LA RECHERCHE THÉOLOGIQUE

President - Präsident - Président:
Professor Ursula King, University of Bristol, Great Britain

Vice-President - Vizepräsidentin - Vice-Président:
Professor Lone Fatum, University of Copenhagen, Denmark

Secretary - Sekretärin - Secrétaire:
Monika Jakobs, Saarbrücken, Germany

Vice-Secretary - Vizesekretärin - Vice-Secrétaire:
Magda Misset - van de Weg, The Netherlands

Treasurer - Schatzmeisterin - Trésorière:
Irene Löffler-Mayer, Friedberg, Germany

Vice-Treasurer - Vizeschatzmeisterin - Vice-Trésorière:
Maaike de Haardt, Tilburg, The Netherlands

Revisor - Revisorin - Reviseur:
Regula Ströbel, Fribourg, Switzerland

Contact for Bulletin of the ESWTR:
Magda Misset - van de Weg, The Netherlands